COLLEGE CLASSICS IN ENGLISH

General Editor

NORTHROP FRYE

GEOFFREY CHAUCER

A SELECTION OF HIS WORKS

Edited by

KENNETH KEE

Victoria College

University of Toronto

MACMILLAN OF CANADA – TORONTO

© The Macmillan Company of Canada Limited 1966

All rights reserved — no part of this book may be reproduced in
any form without permission in writing from the publisher, except
by a reviewer who wishes to quote brief passages in connection
with a review written for inclusion in a magazine or newspaper.

Library of Congress Catalogue Card Number 66-13408

First Printing 1966
Fourth Printing 1975

ISBN: 0-7705-0370-5

Printed in Canada

Contents

A Brief Biography

Those facts concerning Geoffrey Chaucer's life that have come down to us from the fourteenth century suggest the career of an astute and frequently successful social climber rather than that of a poet. He was born probably between 1340 and 1345, probably in London, and certainly into a family that was successful in the wine trade and that had some connection with the court of Edward III. The father, John Chaucer, was a vintner, and had served the government in the capacity of Collector of Customs in the Port of Southampton and other ports. Surviving records also indicate that a John Chaucer – probably to be identified with the poet's father – accompanied Edward III and his queen to Flanders in 1338. A court connection such as this explains many of the events in the career of the son Geoffrey.

Some remnants of the household accounts of Elizabeth, Countess of Ulster and wife to Lionel, Duke of Clarence and third son of Edward III, tell us that minor sums were granted to a Geoffrey Chaucer in April and at Christmas in 1357. From this it has been inferred that the poet-to-be was serving in the household of the countess at this time, probably as a page. Other records indicate that she spent part of her time at her estates at Hatfield in Yorkshire. The records indicate also that one of the young visitors to the countess during this period was John of Gaunt, another of the sons of Edward III, who was later to become the Duke of Lancaster and a patron of the poet. It is highly likely that Chaucer, serving in the household of the countess, made the acquaintance of the future duke at this time.

We can be fairly certain that during the winter of 1359-60 Chaucer was serving in the army of Edward III in northern France; at any rate, the king contributed £16 to the ransom of one Geoffrey Chaucer who had been made prisoner by the enemy. It is difficult to say with any certainty what the corresponding sum would be in modern money since the conditions of life have changed so completely since the fourteenth century, but the sum was possibly in the neighbourhood of two thousand dollars. Such a donation from the royal treasury might be interpreted to mean that the king placed a high value on his young servant, until one remembers that the king also donated £16 13s. 4d. to the ransom of one Robert de Clynton's horse. One can only conclude that medieval monarchs seemed to have a good eye for livestock, whether two-legged or four-legged.

For the period 1360-66 there are no records to indicate where the poet was or what he was doing, and it is perhaps idle to speculate on his activities during these years. We do know that during part of this period Lionel was serving as Lord Lieutenant in Ireland; possibly Chaucer was with him at this time, though if such is the case, the experience has left no mark on his poetry. In February of 1366, however, we find that Chaucer was given a safe conduct by the King of Navarre to pass through his kingdom. At this time Edward III and his son the Black Prince were trying to restore Don Pedro to his throne in Castile in Spain, and Chaucer was probably on some sort of diplomatic mission. In September of this year also we find a grant made from the king's treasury to a Philippa Chaucer as a *domicella* or lady-in-waiting to the queen. She is undoubtedly to be identified as the poet's wife, and she had probably been married for only a short time when this grant was made. She is also probably to be identified with one Philippa Paon, daughter of Paon de Roet, a Flemish knight who had accompanied Edward III's queen Philippa from Hainault in Flanders at the time of her marriage to the English king. And it is equally likely that she was the sister of Katherine, wife to Hugh de Swynford until his death in 1372 and then the mistress of John of Gaunt, now Duke of Lancaster. She bore the duke four children who were named Beaufort after the castle in Anjou where they were born, and these were legitimized when he married her in 1396. Providing these speculations on these family relationships are all correct, Chaucer ultimately became brother-in-law to the father of the future Henry IV. Family interest at court, a fortunate marriage, and good luck, then, combined to elevate the poet to a position of eminence his social origins would seem to belie.

In June of 1367 Chaucer is listed among those receiving an annuity from the king for service as a *valettus* or yeoman, and in 1368 and 1370 we find him travelling abroad on the king's service. These missions abroad were probably of a diplomatic nature, and they suggest that Chaucer must have attracted the king's notice as an able and discreet person. This royal attention resulted in Chaucer's being sent to Italy from December 1372 to May 1373 on the king's business. It is conjectured that this was Chaucer's first journey to Italy, and the Italian journeys were to have a profound influence on the development of Chaucer's poetry.

In May of 1374 Chaucer leased a house over Aldgate, one of the city gates of London, which at that time was still a walled town. The reason for Chaucer's taking up residence in London on a permanent basis becomes clear when we discover that in June of that year he was appointed Controller of the Custom and Subsidy of Wools, Hides, and Woolfells in the Port of London, and also of the Petty Customs on Wines. The appointment explicitly states that he was to keep the accounts in his own hand, and thus permanent residence in London was required. In this year also Chaucer received from John of Gaunt a grant of £10 annually for his own and for his wife Philippa's services. We find that he and his wife also were receiving an annuity from the king, Edward III, during these years, an annuity that was continued until the king's death in 1377. It can justifiably be concluded that this period was the height of Chaucer's material prosperity, and his average annual income during these years may have been as high as $20,000. The records indicate that the sums paid to him in this period were for his services as a customs official and as an ambassador; the records make no mention of his activity as a poet. Chaucer was engaged in secret negotiations for the king in 1376 and 1377; in the latter year the poet was abroad in France.

On the accession in 1377 of Richard II, grandson of Edward III and son of the Black Prince who had died in 1376, Chaucer's position as Controller of the Customs was confirmed once more. Since the young king was only ten years old at this time, it is safe to assume that his advisers were content with Chaucer's services. In March of 1378 the old king's annuity to Chaucer was confirmed by Richard, and in this year the poet was sent abroad once more on royal business, this time to Italy. Here he conferred with Bernabo Visconti, the powerful and wealthy ruler of Milan, and with Sir John Hawkwood, the extraordinary English adventurer who had risen to a position of eminence in Italian politics through his ability as a military commander. It is presumed also that manuscripts of the *Teseide* and *Il Filostrato*, poems by the famous Italian poet Boccaccio, came into the English poet's hands, though probably without the Italian's name on the manuscripts, since Chaucer never mentions the name in his own work. In all likelihood Chaucer never did know the identity of the author of these works.

In 1379 and 1380 Chaucer seems to have been in some kind of legal difficulties, for in the former year he appointed an attorney to represent him in an action brought for contempt and trespass, and in the latter year, one Cecilia Chaumpaigne released to Chaucer all her rights of action against him in a suit involving rape – *de raptu meo* is the Latin legal phrase of the period, and it could mean anything from assault and battery to actual rape. In 1381 we find him disposing of certain real estate in London which had been in the family's possession since his father's time. In the early years of this decade also we find that he was re-appointed Controller of the Petty Customs on Wines and other merchandises, and at that time he was given permission to appoint a permanent deputy to perform his duties in this position. Similar permission to appoint a permanent deputy to carry out his duties as Collector of Customs on Wools was granted in 1385. Thus freed from the necessity of a permanent residence in London, he was sent abroad during this period on occasional missions of a diplomatic nature for the king. In these years also we find Chaucer collecting the annuity granted to himself and his wife by the king. Philippa was, in addition, honoured at this time by New Year's gifts from John of Gaunt, a fact that has occasioned some unseemly scholarly speculations on the relationship between the duke and the poet's wife.

In October of 1385 Chaucer was appointed one of the Justices of the Peace for Kent; apparently he had to reside in that county in order to hold this position. It would seem, then, that he had retired at least temporarily from residence in

London. In the following year we find him elected to parliament as one of the Knights of the Shire of Kent. This election would again support the notion that he had retired from London, since residence in the shire was required of the parliamentary representatives. At any rate he was back in London during October of 1386 when parliament was convened. During this period also was held one of the most celebrated trials of the fourteenth century, the Scropes-Grosvenor trial. The two families were disputing each other's right to the same coat-of-arms, and Chaucer gave evidence at the trial. His evidence is both interesting and exasperating for the biographer, for he gave his age as "forty years and upwards". It is just possible that he meant that he was forty years and a few months. If so, he would have been twelve years old as page in the household of the Countess of Ulster in 1357, and fourteen when serving in France in 1359.

The parliament to which Chaucer had been elected was for the most part hostile to Richard II, and was used as a tool by the king's uncle, Thomas, the Duke of Gloucester. Parliament refused to conduct any business until the king had appointed a committee of inquiry into the affairs of the country, and when Richard was forced into appointing such a committee by Gloucester, parliament was dissolved. Chaucer left his post in the Customs in December of that year, 1386. Whether he was forced to resign or whether he resigned on principle as a member of the king's party we do not know. Nor do we know how Chaucer managed to escape the fate that overtook his friend and associate in the Customs, Sir Nicholas Brembre, who was brought to trial and executed in the following year at the instigation of Gloucester and those opposed to the king. Chaucer continued to collect his annuity from Richard for both himself and his wife, though after June 1387 the records indicate that the annuity was paid to Chaucer alone. It is assumed that Philippa Chaucer died some time between June and November of 1387. Just what Chaucer's feelings for his wife were we have no indication. Except for a few conventional expressions in minor poems poking fun at the married state, Chaucer never in his own person remarks on marriage.

Chaucer did not resume public office until 1389 when Richard asserted himself against his political enemies and regained control of his own affairs. We find the poet appointed Clerk of the King's Works in this year, a position he filled for almost the whole of the next two years. His duties were to supervise repairs to the Tower, the palace of Westminster, St. George's Chapel at Windsor, and sundry other public buildings. The position must have entailed a great deal of travelling, and we find on one occasion in September of 1390 that he was robbed twice in four days of public moneys. It is gratifying to discover that he was forgiven the repayment of these losses. In June of 1391 he gave up his position as Clerk of the King's Works and in the same year was appointed a deputy forester of the royal forest at Petherton in Somerset in the west of England. Presumably he was able to carry out the duties of this position by a substitute, and it is possible to regard the appointment as a sinecure. The records reveal that the appointment was renewed in 1398, and they indicate also that he continued to enjoy the favour of the king. In January of 1393, for example, he received a grant of £10 from Richard for unspecified services, and in 1397 he received the grant of a butt of wine yearly.

After the deposition of Richard in 1399 by Henry Bolingbroke, the son of John of Gaunt, Chaucer continued to enjoy royal favour even though a new king was on the throne. Henry IV reconfirmed the grants made to Chaucer by Richard and added an additional annuity of forty marks. Thus the poet continued to benefit from the friendly attentions of the house of Lancaster even after the death of his brother-in-law. But he did not live much longer to claim new benefits from Henry, for in the following year his name disappears from the records of those receiving their annuities from the king. The date of his death as recorded on his tomb in Westminster Abbey is October 25, 1400. Though this tomb was not erected to the poet's memory until the sixteenth century, there is no reason to question the accuracy of the date.

This brief review of the principal facts in Geoffrey Chaucer's life reveals a man who, though of comparatively modest origins, played an active part in the events of his time and rose to such eminence that he gained the notice and friendship of the royal court. His career as a customs official, an office involving the laborious and tedious task of keeping the accounts in his own handwriting, and his frequent diplomatic missions abroad in an age when travel was time-consuming and dangerous, leave one wondering how he managed to find the leisure and the energy for his enormous poetic output. And perhaps even more remarkable for this poet, whose name and fame as the celebrated raconteur of the *Canterbury Tales* have been a by-word for centuries, is the fact that the documents recording the events of his life give not one hint of this poetic activity.

General Introduction

Literature as we understand it was not a conception familiar to the Middle Ages. In the medieval period the poet was regarded as a craftsman, or to use Chaucer's word a "maker", a man whose skill with words enabled him to construct a poetic artifact just as the skill of the carpenter enabled him to construct a table or chair. Words alone, however, were not enough for the medieval maker. He employed also a set of traditional and conventional ideas and literary forms that were an accepted part of his literary heritage. These conventional ideas and forms were so much a part of the intellectual climate of the poet's age that it is doubtful if any writer of the period ever gave them much thought. But since the intellectual climate has changed in the six hundred years separating us from Chaucer, these conventional ideas and forms have to be isolated and identified for the modern reader. Their identification is necessary so that the modern reader will get some idea of the basic premises accepted by the medieval writer and his public, and so that he will also understand in what ways Chaucer transcended the conventions of his time. Every age has its own set of conventional literary types and forms, our own included. Our remote descendants will face the same problem concerning literature written now that we face concerning Chaucer's poetry. Even the simplest conventional figures of our era, such as the secret agent of modern spy fiction or the super-sleuth of detective stories, will have to be identified and explained for future generations. And just as the literary historian of the future will never be certain that he has attached the right interpretation to these conventional figures, so an aura of uncertainty hangs over our explanations of the conventions of the past.

The perspective of history does, however, simplify our task. Our explanations of past literary modes may be simplifications, but the simplification itself enables us to identify and explicate the conventions of the past. One such convention that has been explored is the phenomenon known as Courtly Love. Though the phrase lacks a precise definition, for our purposes here we can identify it as a revolution in the attitude to woman which took place in the south of France at the end of the eleventh century and which spread across the cultures of western Europe almost without exception in the century that followed. In this new attitude to woman the female was elevated to a position of eminence above the male. Thus Courtly Love established a relationship between the sexes that ran counter to and rivalled the conventionally accepted relationship implied by marriage. In the medieval conception of marriage the male played the dominant role, an idea reflected in the woman's marital promise to "obey" her husband. In the new relationship established by Courtly Love, however, the roles of the sexes were reversed. Woman was given the dominant role, and the male was reduced to the status of her unworthy suitor.

Medieval society in western Europe was predominantly a feudal society, and this new conception of the relationship between the sexes was adapted to the framework of feudalism. Woman was given the part of the feudal overlord, while the man was thought of as her vassal. And just as the feudal overlord expected obedience and service from his vassal in return for the lord's favour, so the Courtly Love mistress could and did impose tasks on those who sought her favour, as the Franklin's Tale indicates. Very often the woman courted by the male was another man's wife, and when this courtship was successful in its aim, an adulterous union was established between the lady and her suitor. When the lady was not a married woman the object of the courtship might be marriage itself, or the establishment of a non-marital sexual union between the couple.

In this new tradition, which developed and spread very rapidly, a code of conduct appropriate for the courting of the lady's favour was evolved. According to this code of conduct, which is outlined in perhaps humorous fashion by a twelfth-century writer, Andreas Capellanus,[1] the male was always regarded as

1 See Andreas Capellanus, *The Art of Courtly Love*, trans. J. J. Parry (New York, 1941).

the inferior in spiritual worth of the near-divine lady. His suit to win her favour was generally long and arduous, and lucky was the lover on the day when his lady granted him her grace. The constant yearning by the lover after his beloved constituted a sort of purgatorial penance that cleansed his character of its defects. Thus his love became the source of inspiration for his high ambitions and noble aspirations.

The foregoing might be called the theory behind Courtly Love; the practice involved a ritualistic pattern of behaviour on the part of both the lover and his lady. The role of the lady was primarily one of unapproachably aloof disdain. She might or might not be aware of the existence of the suitor; more likely not. And even if by chance it came to her attention that she was being courted, her public response would assuredly be one of rejection, though her private response to the suitor might give him some encouragement. The suitor, on the other hand, was committed to a much more elaborate pattern of behaviour. According to Andreas,[2] there were thirty-one rules of conduct that the lover had to follow. These involved loss of appetite, sleeplessness, tears, confinement to bed, making songs in praise of the lady, pallor and speechlessness in her presence, and a number of other peculiarities that set the lover off from the rest of humanity. Some of these observances merely record the behaviour of the human male at the mating age; others were derived from the Latin poet Ovid's *Ars Amatoria* and may or may not have been taken seriously by the first writers on Courtly Love. Whether or not this elaborate code of love with its attendant ritual had any existence outside a literary framework, whether Courtly Love existed as a social phenomenon as well as a literary phenomenon, we really do not know. As we have seen, adultery and therefore secrecy were accepted parts of the ritual, and unlike our own age, with its published lists of Judgments Absolute Granted in jurisdictions where adultery is the main ground for divorce, the Middle Ages did not publish its adulteries. But despite our lack of knowledge concerning the practice of Courtly Love in medieval society, it is abundantly clear from the literature composed for a courtly audience that the aristocratic

2 *Ibid.*, 184-6.

society enjoyed and expected to see itself portrayed in literature
in the elegant manner prescribed by Courtly Love. Thus the love
relationship between the sexes in literature composed for the
aristocracy was usually depicted in terms of this convention.

The convention of Courtly Love did not die out with the pass-
ing of the Middle Ages. In a somewhat modified form its influence extended into the Renaissance and even beyond. In
Shakespeare's *Romeo and Juliet*, for example, we find Romeo
pining for the love of his unattainable Rosaline in "whining
poetry", to use a phrase of Shakespeare's contemporary John
Donne. And even in our times, the belief that courteous conduct
towards ladies is an essential quality in the make-up of a gentle-
man is an attenuated survival of the code of courtly behaviour
devised by the troubadours almost a thousand years ago.

The convention played a major role in Chaucer's early poetry,
and in *Troilus and Criseyde* it played a dominant role. However, in the *Canterbury Tales*, the product of the poet's maturity,
the convention is subordinated to the poet's larger interests, and
the presuppositions of the convention concerning the relationships between men and women are tacitly assumed rather than
overtly stated. But those presuppositions have to be understood
by the modern reader before he can read the *Canterbury Tales*
properly. Two tales in the present selection incorporate in an
important way aspects of the convention – those told by the
Merchant and the Franklin. In the Merchant's Tale the young
wife May plays a role similar to that of the aristocratic lady of
the Courtly Love convention: she is young, beautiful, amorous,
married to a man much older than herself, and willing to com-
mit adultery. The squire Damian reacts to her beauty in just the
fashion that the suitor of the Courtly Love convention should:
he languishes, takes to his bed in sickness, and finally declares
his love and his adulterous intentions in a letter to the lady. But
here the resemblance to the Courtly Love romance ends, for the
Merchant's Tale is a fabliau, the point of which is to heap scorn
on women, marriage, and any noble idealism concerning love, as
the ironic line "Lo pitee renneth soone in gentil herte!" indicates.[3]
Where the Merchant exhibits in his tale the uncomprehending

3 See below, the Merchant's Tale, 127, note 23.

contempt of the mercantile trader for what he considers aristocratic romantic nonsense surrounding love and marriage, the
Franklin adopts whole-heartedly the ideals implicit in the convention, with the result that his hero and heroine, Arveragus and
Dorigen, attempt to continue in their marriage the relationship
between the suitor and his courtly lady. The efforts of the squire
Aurelius to seduce Dorigen fail because he wants to engage her
in an adulterous Courtly Love union when she is already psycho-
logically in just such a relationship with her own husband. We
have already remarked that the aristocracy of Chaucer's day
liked to have their opposite numbers in literature depicted through
the rosy haze of a misty idealism. Courtly Love provided just
such an idealized view of love which would appeal to the aristocracy, but Courtly Love also postulated that love could not
exist within the framework of marriage.[4] In the Franklin's Tale
Chaucer works out a compromise in which love and marriage
can co-exist, possibly out of what seems to be a characteristic
English diffidence to accept tales of adultery.[5] But the fact that
Arveragus and Dorigen are married should not obscure the presence of Courtly Love elements in the tale. Another tale that
shows the influence of the convention in a minor way is that told
by the Nun's Priest. Though it is a story of a cock, a fox, and a
hen, these creatures are endowed with human characteristics.
And on one occasion the hen Pertelote, prompted by Chauntecler's apparent cowardice, lists the qualities women look for in
men: the man must be brave, wise, generous, secret in matters of
love, not niggardly nor foolish, not easily frightened, and not
boastful. Though they are here brought down to a barnyard level,
we can still glimpse the idealized sentiments of Courtly Love.

Another aspect of medieval literature that requires attention
is the habit of medieval authors of regarding their works as
vehicles of instruction as well as of entertainment. Since the content of what constitutes knowledge has changed drastically since
medieval times, the modern reader is sometimes put off by long
passages in medieval works which contain an almost virtuoso
display of what some might consider out-of-date learning. Every

4 Andreas Capellanus, *op. cit.*, 250.
5 See A. B. Taylor, *An Introduction to Mediaeval Romance* (London,
1930), 250.

reader of Chaucer comes away from his poetry with the sense that Chaucer was a very widely-read man who was steeped in the traditional learning of his age. It is this learning, this wide-ranging but not superficial grasp of all facets of medieval intellectual activity, which gives the General Prologue its encyclopedic nature.

The curriculum of a medieval university provided instruction in what were called the Seven Liberal Arts: the Trivium (grammar, logic, and rhetoric), and the Quadrivium (music, astronomy, arithmetic, and geometry). The Trivium would introduce the student to what we would consider courses in humane learning involving an extensive acquaintance with the classical and post-classical writers, while the Quadrivium provided what may be regarded as more practical information, though the reader should remember that the concept of "practical science" is a fairly recent development. There is no evidence that Chaucer ever attended either of the two English universities of his day – Oxford and Cambridge – but his poetry and other writings make it clear that he had mastered the intellectual requirements necessary for a university degree, even if extramurally. His poetry makes it clear also that he had mastered what was essentially the requirements for a degree in Modern Languages and Literatures since it demonstrates a thorough acquaintance with French and Italian literature of the fourteenth century. Despite all this heavy intellectual freight Chaucer's poetry never sinks into tediousness, and in the *Canterbury Tales* the poet is even able to derive humour from the display of learning. The Wife of Bath's skilful manipulation of theological opinion to prove her contentions is a case in point, as is the succinct résumé of the discussion of free-will and necessity in the Nun's Priest's Tale, a résumé that is abruptly and amusingly broken off when the Nun's Priest realizes how far he has strayed from his main theme. It should also be noted that though Chaucer puts knowledge to humorous purposes in the tales, his comic treatment of learning in no way involves a debasement of that learning.

Among the subjects Chaucer had mastered was medieval rhetoric. It has already been pointed out that the medieval poet was regarded as a "maker" or craftsman who constructed artifacts out of words. The handbooks on rhetoric available to the medieval writer provided complete instructions on how the poet should go about his task. These instructions are detailed, in the modern reader's view, to the point of lunacy when they itemize under their complicated Latin-derived names the ten difficult ornaments of style, the thirty-eight easy ornaments, the eight methods of amplifications and the seven methods of abbreviation, the hints on how to begin a work and the suggestions on how to conclude. One handbook even provides models for the guidance and edification of prospective poets.[6] These models show how the poet should undertake the description of a garden or the description of a woman, and they provide sufficient detail that the poet under their tutelage cannot help including all the elements required for acceptable descriptions.

Chaucer seems to have absorbed the precepts contained in these rhetorical handbooks, both through imitation of poets who had studied the rhetoricians and through direct contact with the handbooks themselves. Thus it is easy to fit Chaucer's descriptions of gardens and women, for example, into the traditional patterns of these descriptions in medieval literature. The gardens of the Merchant's and Franklin's tales, in which the details have been curtailed in the interests of the continuity of the narrative, are abbreviated versions of the traditional pattern of description, and many of the traditional characteristics of the descriptions of women are found in the portrait of the Prioress in the General Prologue. One of these rhetoricians, Geoffrey of Vinsauf, is mentioned by name in the Nun's Priest's Tale in an amusing passage that constitutes an elaborate spoof of the whole art of rhetoric.[7] But the presence of this passage in the tale should not mislead the modern reader: a close examination of the tale will reveal how much it gains from Chaucer's use of those very rhetorical precepts he is making fun of. The role of rhetoric in Chaucer's poetry is one more illustration of how the poet rose above the conventional and traditional preoccupations of his age. The poetry is not dominated by an over-attention to

6 See Matthew of Vendôme, *Ars Versificatoria*, ed. E. Faral, *Les Arts poétiques du XIIe et du XIIIe siècle* (Paris, 1924), 109-93.
7 See below, the Nun's Priest's Tale, lines 540-7 and note 27.

rhetorical theory and practice; the poet has mastered this aspect of his craft and has incorporated it into a poetry that transcends the conventions of the age in which it was produced.

Chaucer's career as a poet probably began with the composition of short ballades, roundels, and virelays – "many a song and many a leccherous lay", as he refers to them in the Retraction – which were undoubtedly intended to be sung at public entertainments in the household of his employer and probable patroness, the Countess of Ulster. Only a few of these short pieces survive, though Chaucer continued to use these forms for composition throughout his career. These early works indicate that Chaucer's first poetic efforts were not meant to be considered poems in the proper sense of the word, but were in reality intended as songs, and popular songs at that. They also indicate that Chaucer modelled his early pieces on the work of his predecessors and contemporaries across the Channel. This fact should not occasion any surprise. The royal court of England in the fourteenth century was almost completely bilingual, the English monarchy often turned to France when seeking a bride, and English kings still held extensive possessions in France. In fact, of the two languages in use in the English court in Chaucer's lifetime, it is quite possible that French was heard more often than English. In addition, the political ambitions of the English kings during these years were centred in France, and many of the royal children were born on the Continent. The example of John of Gaunt (or Ghent, as it is called in modern English) immediately springs to mind, and the successor of Edward III, Richard II, was born at Bordeaux and spent his childhood years there. It is not surprising, then, to discover that the English aristocracy preferred things French, including French musical and literary entertainment. English commercial interests were also directed to the continent, English wool making its way to Flanders in large shipments and French wines being imported into England in quantity. Much of the royal revenue was derived from import and export duties, and competent customs officials were a necessity.

If Chaucer undertook to imitate the fashions of French poetry in his early career, then, we need not be surprised. What does surprise us, however, is the fact that he should write in English.

The early works that have survived suggest that what Chaucer did at the outset of his career was write French poetry in the English language. The reasons for Chaucer's choice of English as the language of his poetry we shall never really know. In his translations and adaptations from French Chaucer reveals an excellent command of that language, and later in his career, when he worked from Italian models, he indicates a good grasp of that language also. Latin was the language schoolboys were exposed to when they were first introduced to learning, and Latin was also an international language in the Middle Ages. Chaucer seems to have mastered it at an early age. The choice of English as a medium for poetry may have resulted from circumstances obtaining locally in the household of the Countess of Ulster where it is possible that French was not so prominent as in the royal court, and Chaucer, once having begun writing in English, continued to do so throughout his poetical career. The example of Chaucer's contemporary, John Gower, is interesting in this respect, for Gower wrote poetry in English, French, and Latin. More than one language was available for the poet writing in England, then; but Chaucer chose English.

It is a commonplace in Chaucerian criticism to divide the poet's work into three categories. The earliest of these is called the French period because of the heavy indebtedness of the poetry of this period to French literature. It is difficult to assign dates to almost all of Chaucer's poems, or even to arrange them in a definite chronological sequence, but we are fairly safe in assuming that the works of the French period were composed before the poet's first Italian journey in 1372. Probably the bulk of Chaucer's work belonging to this period was made up of short pieces or songs that would have had only an ephemeral interest and life-span. But it is also fairly certain that the *Book of the Duchess*, an elegy probably on the death of Blanche, Duchess of Lancaster, who died in 1369, belongs to this early period. Scholars have demonstrated that the poem is heavily indebted to French models, and indeed many lines seem to be direct translations from poems by Froissart and Deschamps,[8]

---

8 Jean Froissart (1338-1410), better known as an historian because of his celebrated *Chronicles*, nevertheless was an accomplished poet. Eustache

both poets whom Chaucer probably knew personally.

The second period of Chaucer's poetry is the Italian period, and the poetry composed in it, while much of it still reveals a strong French influence, is increasingly indebted to Italian literature, to the writings of Dante, Petrarch, and Boccaccio in particular.[9] To this period, from 1372 to 1386, we may assign such works as the *House of Fame*, the *Parliament of Fowls*, the translation of Boethius' *De Consolatione Philosophiae*, *Troilus and Criseyde*, and the *Legend of Good Women*. The final period, sometimes called the English period to suggest that the poet had freed himself from the tyranny of foreign models and had developed his own highly individualistic style, extends from 1386 to the poet's death in 1400. In this period were composed the *Canterbury Tales* and two of the short poems included in the present selection, "Lenvoy de Chaucer a Bukton" and the "Complaynt of Chaucer to his Purse".

One work that exerted an enormous influence on Chaucer's poetry of all periods, and which Chaucer says he translated, is the *Roman de la Rose*, begun about 1225 by Guillaume de Lorris and left unfinished after 4,000 lines until taken up about forty years later by Jean de Meun, who continued the poem in a very different vein to a total of 19,436 lines. Parts of this poem exist in a Middle English version known as the *Romaunt of the Rose*, and the first part of this Middle English translation is usually attributed to Chaucer. It is not possible to date this translation accurately; we can only set it into the context of Chaucer's other poetry. In the Prologue to the *Legend of Good Women* the God of Love accuses the poet of having sinned against Love

---

Deschamps (1346?-1406?) was a very prolific writer of lyric and narrative poetry. He seems to have been personally acquainted with Chaucer and sent him a copy of his own work prefaced by a ballade, the refrain of which runs "Grant translateur noble geffroy chaucier". This ballade is usually assigned to 1386.

9 Dante (1265-1321), author of the *Divina Commedia*, is the most celebrated of the Italian poets. Petrarch (1304-74) was the author of works in both Italian and Latin; Chaucer refers to him by name in the Clerk's Tale. Boccaccio (1313-75) is nowhere mentioned by name in Chaucer's works, but Chaucer borrowed the plots of *Il Filostrato* and the *Teseida* for *Troilus and Criseyde* and the Knight's Tale respectively. There is no direct evidence that Chaucer knew Boccaccio's *Decameron*.

by writing *Troilus and Criseyde* and by translating the *Romaunt*. All we can say with any certainty, then, is that the translation was made before the composition of the Prologue to the *Legend*, and this last-named work is usually assigned to 1386.

The foregoing survey is a simplification of Chaucer's poetical career, but it suggests one possible method of approaching the poet's development. Most good poets continue to experiment and to develop throughout their entire lifetime – W. B. Yeats is a good modern example – and many poets whose work exhibits these characteristics also reveal in their early work qualities that persist throughout their whole development, and which receive amplification and deepening as the poet progresses. Chaucer possesses this characteristic to a high degree. In his earliest poetry of substantial length (as, for instance, in the *Book of the Duchess*, not included in this selection), even though he is closely adhering to the traditions of French poetry, he reveals qualities that receive expansion and modification as time goes on. The first of these qualities is his depiction of himself as a self-deprecating, modest, slow-witted, and slightly overweight narrator who was singularly unsuccessful in matters of love. It is certainly a mistake to assume that this role the poet adopts for his poetic purposes is an accurate autobiographical portrait, just as it is wrong to assume that the "I" of modern fiction writers is identical with the author. Chaucer's age was one of orally delivered poetry; that is, the poet confronted his audience directly, not through the pages of a book as the modern writer does, and he either read or recited his poetry to that audience. By assigning to the fictitious "I" of a poem the qualities he does, Chaucer sets up a subtly ironic relationship between himself as the audience knows him to be and the semi-comic "I" who appears in such a ludicrous stance in the poem being recited. Chaucer's original audience would both associate this "I" with the poet and dissociate him from the poet, and would also be entertained by the irony of the contrast. But they would not make the mistake of assuming that the poet and the "I" of the poem were identical. In the subsequent poetry Chaucer's use of this mask, or "persona" as some critics would call it, is developed and expanded and put to subtle uses, as in the General Prologue to the *Canterbury Tales*. In this last work the "I" appears to fill several roles simultaneously: on the one hand, he is the awe-struck, simple-minded narrator who is reduced to superlatives when confronted by the elegant Prioress; on the other hand, he is the shrewd observer of human pretensions who is well able to see the poverty-stricken reality behind the Merchant's opulent façade. The reader of the General Prologue would do well, then, to decide which role he should assign to the "I" narrator describing the pilgrims at any given point in the recital.[10]

In addition to Chaucer's adoption of a mask, which becomes a familiar and even traditional element in his poetry, we find another quality in the early poetry that undergoes development and is also a permanent feature. This quality can best be described by the vague and general term "humanity". Chaucer exhibits a compassion for his fellow men that sets him off from his contemporaries. In the *Book of the Duchess*, the poet displays a deep understanding of and a keen sense of sympathy with the sorrowing Black Knight. And even when recounting the infidelity of Criseyde in his tragic love story *Troilus and Criseyde* he cannot bring himself to condemn his heroine for this act. To understand is to forgive, the proverb has it, and it is probably Chaucer's very deep understanding of his fellow creatures that makes his equally deep compassion possible. For this reason, I believe, it is impossible to speak of Chaucer as a satirist in the true sense of the word. Chaucer may be aware of the distance between a man's pretensions and the reality of that man's life, but his compassion seems to dictate amused tolerance for the foibles of human nature rather than condemnation. When the tolerance cannot be extended to include amusement, as is the case in the depiction of the Pardoner and the Summoner, that compassion ensures that the portrayal of these social and religious parasites will be dispassionate. We may not like what is portrayed, but the clarity of the portrayal is not clouded by moral indignation on the part of the poet.

The third quality revealed in the early poetry is Chaucer's mastery of the poetic conventions of his age. An early work, the

10 On this point see E. T. Donaldson, "Chaucer the Pilgrim", *Publications of the Modern Language Association* LXIX (1954), 928-36.

Book of the Duchess referred to above, for example, is cast in the mould of the fashionable dream-vision. The dream-vision was a conventional device used by Chaucer's contemporaries and predecessors to introduce a poem usually concerned with a love adventure. Chaucer makes it clear that he is a master of this highly conventionalized form. But even in this early period Chaucer displayed traces of that originality that was to be developed to such a high degree in his later poetry. For here Chaucer, even though relying heavily on the work of his French predecessors and contemporaries, combined the traditional dream-vision form and its attendant love-vision with the elegy to produce something entirely new. This ability to manipulate traditional and conventional forms, the mark of a major poet, is extended and amplified as he continues to develop, so that even what appear to be completely conventional forms will suddenly reveal a new and unexpected twist. Some of the selections in the present anthology illustrate this facet of Chaucer's poetic artistry. The triple roundel "Merciles Beautee" is one example. The opening two sections of the poem are a perfectly conventional expression of the love complaint so frequently encountered in medieval poetry and represented also by the opening stanzas of "To Rosemounde". The final section of the roundel, however, with its sudden reversal of tone and its jubilant defiance of love, is entirely unexpected.[11] The tales related by the Canterbury pilgrims provide a much more complex illustration of Chaucer's ability to twist new artistic patterns and meanings out of traditional and conventionalized forms.

The *Canterbury Tales* is constructed around a device known as the frame-story. In this device the reader is presented with a narrative framework – in this instance, the Canterbury journey

11 The above argument is not affected by the fact that an exact parallel to the opening line of the third section of the poem is found in "Puiz qu'a Amors suis si gras eschapé", the first line of the Duc de Berry's response to the Cent Ballades (G. Raynaud, ed., *Les Cent Ballades* [Paris, 1905], 213-14). The response is usually dated 1389: Chaucer may have borrowed the line, but Chaucer's fame as a poet was already established by 1386, as Deschamps's testimony indicates (see above note 9), and the line may have been borrowed from Chaucer by the Duc de Berry.

of a group of pilgrims – and within this larger framework are related a number of shorter narratives. The shorter narratives are contained within or "framed" by the larger narrative structure in somewhat the same way that a grouping of pictures is contained by its frame. But in Chaucer's work the outer frame, instead of being a neutral confining structure, is an active element that exerts an influence on what goes on inside it. And Chaucer even provides us with a General Prologue in which are presented all, or nearly all, the story-tellers in the *Canterbury Tales*; he provides us, in other words, with a detailed close-up of the intricate design of the frame itself.

Chaucer's project was an ambitious one. From the Host's remarks at the end of the General Prologue we learn that each pilgrim was to tell two stories on the outward trip from London and two on the return trip from Canterbury, a total of 116 tales if we accept the figure of twenty-nine pilgrims.[12] The poet came nowhere near completing this large design. We have only one tale each from nineteen pilgrims, two tales – one unfinished – from Chaucer himself, one unfinished tale from the Cook, one unfinished or perhaps interrupted tale from the Squire,[13] and one tale told by the Canon's Yeoman, a new character who dramatically joins the cavalcade of pilgrims on their journey: a total of twenty-four tales in all. Our conception of what would constitute the complete design of the *Canterbury Tales* is hampered, then, by the unfinished state of the work itself, but it is hampered also by the fact that the poet changed his plans as he carried out his projected work. As he developed the pilgrims, and as his conception of the characters of the individual pilgrims became more and more complex, Chaucer switched tales from one story-teller to another. Just how much of this mind-changing took place we cannot be certain. Occasional evidences of Chaucer's assigning a tale to a pilgrim different from the original

12 In line 24 of the General Prologue Chaucer tells us that the number of pilgrims was twenty-nine. If we count *three* priests, as line 164 says, then the number of pilgrims is thirty-one. There is reason for doubting that the Prioress would be accompanied by three priests.

13 On the possibility that the Squire's Tale is interrupted, not unfinished, see D. A. Pearsall, "The Squire as Story-Teller", *University of Toronto Quarterly* XXXIV (1964), 82-92.

teller of the tale can be found, as in the remarks in the Merchant's Tale that indicate that the story was designed originally to be told by someone in orders.[14] The result of both the unfinished state of the work and the alterations in plan while the poet was carrying out his design is that we cannot be certain of the order in which we should group the tales. The General Prologue tells us that we must put the Knight's Tale first, and editors are agreed that the Parson's Tale must come last, "To knytte up al this feeste, and make an ende". But the order of the tales in between is not absolutely certain. The tales told by the Wife of Bath, the Merchant, and the Franklin make a consecutive unit and are accordingly grouped in that sequence in the present selection. The Nun's Priest's Tale has been placed after this group because it seems to contain specific references to the discussion of marriage carried on in the three tales mentioned. The Pardoner's Tale is well able to stand by itself.

If Chaucer rearranged tales, and it is certain that he did, his reasons for doing so seem to be based on a growing sense of the complexity of the characters of the pilgrims he had launched on this journey to Canterbury and a growing appreciation of the dramatic effect to be gained by setting off one strong personality against another. It has been attempted to incorporate into the present anthology some of this dramatic interplay between the pilgrims, some of their clashes of personality, by including portions of what are not properly the tales at all, but those sections of poetry that are referred to as the links. It would be a mistake to assume, as many readers who read only individual tales in isolation might be tempted to do, that the framework of the *Canterbury Tales* as a whole was a mere lifeless mechanism designed to permit the recounting of a variety of stories. Chaucer had already experimented with just such a lifeless frame in the *Legend of Good Women*, the work that occupied his time immediately preceding the composition of the *Canterbury Tales*. At his best, Chaucer is a poet who deals with human beings in action and reaction with one another; the links between the tales suggest how he adumbrates dramatic techniques by the exploitation of conflicts between the pilgrims. In addition, these links

14 See below, Merchant's Tale, line 39 and note 2.

add a dimension to our conception of his comic genius as well as to our impression of his keen observation of human nature.

Because of Chaucer's interest in the dramatic interplay of character, then, it is not surprising to find that the tales told are in some way a reflection of the personality of the teller. Thus the Knight begins the recital with a long story of chivalry – derived from the Italian writer Boccaccio – tempered by a worldly wisdom we associate with the Knight as he is described in the General Prologue. The Wife of Bath is depicted as a colourful militant feminist, and the long prologue to her tale vividly recounts her marital adventures. The tale itself is a further comment on and illustration of her character, embodying as it does her central thesis that in marriage the dominant role must be played by woman. The Merchant's Tale sheds new light on the naturally secretive disposition of the Merchant himself, and while the General Prologue gives no hint that the Merchant is unhappily and only two months married, it does specifically inform us that his prosperous exterior conceals a world of debt. Perhaps Chaucer means to suggest by the Merchant's Tale that where there are skeletons in the closet they may be of a surprising variety. The Franklin's Tale, with its emphasis on gentility and its almost middle-class insistence on the proprieties of marriage, is much what we would expect from this prosperous landowner, or what the Middle Ages would call *vavasour*, with his fondness for the finer things of life. No description of the Nun's Priest is provided by the General Prologue, and so we are unable to make the equation between the character sketch in the General Prologue and the tale he tells, as is possible with the other story-tellers. The General Prologue unmasks the Pardoner as a hypocritical scoundrel, but the tales he relates bears out Chaucer's opinion that in preaching he was "a noble ecclesiaste", while the unseemly exchange between the Host and the Pardoner at the conclusion of the tale reminds us once more of his hypocritical rascality.

With an after-wisdom conferred by the passage of six hundred years, modern scholars have been able to classify the medieval narrative structures according to different types. Whether or not medieval authors were aware of these different types of narrative we do not know, and in a sense the question is irrelevant.

The frame-story itself is one type of narrative structure, though its use was not confined to the medieval period. The tale told by the Wife of Bath fits into a pattern of stories typical of the Middle Ages called the Arthurian verse romance. In this type of story the action usually begins in the court of King Arthur, the hero is obliged to set out on a quest, the hero meets a lady with whom he becomes amorously entangled, and finally the action returns to its starting-point, Arthur's court, where there usually occurs a happy resolution of the complications of the plot. The reader will easily see how the plot of the Wife of Bath's Tale fits into this skeletal outline, even while noticing that the narrative type has been accommodated to the exigencies of the drama of the so-called Marriage Debate.[15] The Merchant relates a story that belongs to the category known as the *fabliau*. Various kinds of story belonged to the fabliau type, but essentially the genre contained satire on humans, very frequently satire on women, the tone was of such a nature that it appealed to an uneducated audience, there was usually a strong strain of the bawdy, the setting was realistic, and the action was performed by easily recognizable types of characters. Like the Wife of Bath's Tale, the Merchant's story can stand in isolation on its intrinsic merits, but the type has been adapted to the larger framework of the *Canterbury Tales* as a whole. Seven of the Canterbury pilgrims – the Miller, Reeve, Friar, Summoner, Shipman, and Manciple, in addition to the Merchant – relate stories of the fabliau type, a fact which may be a significant comment on medieval literary taste.

As its opening lines indicate, the Franklin's Tale is a Breton lay. Originally the Breton lay appears to have been a short narrative poem recited or sung in the Breton language to the accompaniment of a musical instrument by wandering minstrels. The earliest recorded Breton lays are in French, however, and belong to the twelfth century, many of them by the poetess Marie de France.[16] The subject-matter of Marie's lays invariably concerned love, and an atmosphere of gentle melancholy per-

15 See below, 54.
16 Marie de France was a twelfth-century poetess probably writing in England, probably at the court of Henry II. Her *Lais* were likely composed before 1189.

vaded the story. The supernatural or the marvellous usually made an appearance, and the main interest was concentrated on the psychology of the characters concerned in the action rather than on the action itself. The Franklin's Tale preserves all of these features: the plot is negligible, supernatural magic appears in the story, though the story has a happy ending there is a pervasive sadness throughout, the plot involves a very real psychological dilemma, and we have the Franklin's word for it that the Bretons "with hir [their] instrumentz" sang lays like this one.

The Nun's Priest's Tale is classified as a beast epic and borrows its main plot from the most famous medieval example of the genre, the Old French *Roman de Renart*, an enormous compilation of stories with animals as principal actors, put together by various writers in the twelfth and thirteenth centuries. In the beast epic the different animals are given set characteristics that become conventional aspects of their character; thus slyness and cunning are traditionally associated with the fox, vanity with the rooster, stupidity with the wolf, and so forth. It should be noted that the attribution of these characteristics to these animals was partly based on observations of the animal habits in their natural state. These observations became incorporated into what were essentially handbooks of zoological information called bestiaries. The bestiaries were extremely popular in the Middle Ages, and in them the information and misinformation concerning animals was allegorized and given a Christian interpretation. The beast epic built upon the traditional information thus provided and used it for its own purposes. Those purposes were, in the main, to satirize human follies by attributing them to animals, and to inculcate some sort of moral. The Nun's Priest seems to be intimately acquainted with the genre, and his tale exhibits all of its characteristics.

The exemplum is represented in the *Canterbury Tales* by the Pardoner's Tale. An exemplum was an anecdote or story illustrating the theme of a sermon. The device is not dead today and many modern preachers employ anecdotes to point their moral and adorn their tale. In Chaucer's day preachers were guilty of neglecting their sermon entirely and merely reciting a series of anecdotes, according to the complaint of Chaucer's contemporary Wyclif. The Pardoner does not fall into that vice; his tale is essentially a sermon on avarice well illustrated by the eerie story of the fate of the three evil revellers.

Thus the five tales in the present anthology represent five different types of medieval narrative structures. Among the tales not represented here we find the variety amplified: the Knight relates a long courtly romance; the Squire, an unfinished tale of wonder; the Second Nun, a saint's legend; and so forth. The reader of the *Canterbury Tales* is impressed by the extensive variety of medieval narrative types that the work represents. And he is even more impressed when he discovers how many of them represent the best medieval example of the type.

The *Canterbury Tales* begins with the Knight's Tale and ends with the Parson's Tale. According to the traditional medieval theory of the social hierarchy, the duty of the knight in society was to protect that society from its earthly enemies. The churchman, on the other hand, was to act as a bulwark against the spiritual enemies of mankind. Between the figures of the Knight and the Parson comes the motley group of Canterbury pilgrims, saints, sinners, and ordinary people – "sondry folk", as Chaucer calls them. These Canterbury pilgrims with their faults, their ambitions, their sorrows, and their aspirations – all expressed in the stories they relate to one another – make their way with adventure and misadventure to pay their respects at the shrine of Thomas à Becket. Embraced, as it were, by the arm of secular power symbolized by the Knight and by the arm of spiritual power symbolized by the Parson, they move on to their destiny. As they continue on their way they become eternal types representing all humanity. And their pilgrimage to Canterbury becomes, in the words of the Parson,

> . . . thilke* parfit, glorious pilgrymage   that
> That highte* Jerusalem celestial.   is called

CHAUCER'S LANGUAGE

Modern historians of the English language refer to the language of Chaucer's poetry as Middle English, and this term is used to designate the language between 1100 and 1500. The language before 1100 is called Old English and after 1500, Modern English. It is axiomatic that all living languages are constantly changing, though these changes are not usually perceptible in the lifetime of the ordinary individual. When a language ceases to change it becomes what is known as a "dead" language. Latin, which still exists as a medium of communication in the Catholic Church but whose restricted use has removed it from the pressures causing linguistic change, is thus a "dead" language. Since English is still a living language and is still constantly changing, it is reasonable to expect that the changes that have taken place in it during the six hundred years separating us from Chaucer's day will be extensive. An intelligent response to Chaucer's poetry requires the modern reader to be aware of the differences between his own language and Chaucer's.

The sounds of the language represent one area in which it changes. Since profound changes in the way English is pronounced have taken place since Chaucer's time, it is essential for the modern reader to grasp some of the basic elements of Chaucer's pronunciation in order to approximate the sound of the poetry. The following description outlines the principal sounds.

Vowels and Diphthongs

The vowels of Middle English were closer in pronunciation to vowels of modern European language than to those of Modern English. The diphthongs in Chaucer's English are what are called falling diphthongs: that is, the stress is on the first element of the diphthong, and the second element, though present, receives much less emphasis. In the table below, the words *short* and *long* refer to the length of the vowels, and the words *close* and *open* indicate tense or relaxed condition of the muscles while these vowels are pronounced.

CHAUCERIAN SPELLING	CHAUCERIAN WORD	APPROXIMATE EQUIVALENT MODERN SOUND
Vowels		
a (short)	that, whan	(German) Mann
a, aa (long)	bathed, maad	calm
e (short)	wende, presse	den, press
e, ee (long, close)	semed, sweete	bake, hate

e (in unstressed position)	soote, londes	china
i, y (short)	swich, hym	which, him
i, y (long)	lif, ryde, I	machine
y (in final position)	redy	pretty
o (short, open)	folk, holpen	got, hot, moth
o, oo (long, open)	hooly, longen	law
o, oo (long, close)	to, roote, goode	go, slow
u, o (short)	lusty, sone, yonge	put, good
ou, ow (long)	hous, licour, gowne	boon, brood

Diphthongs

au, aw	straunge, felawe	now
ai, ay, ei, ey	compaignie, day, curteisie, sovereyn	a of hat and short i
u, eu, ew	vertu, reule, knew	few
eu, ew, eau	lewed, beautee	ai of fairy and short u
oy	coy	boy
ou, ow	soules	aw of law and short u
o, ou, ow	noght, though, unknowe	short, open o and short u; o of got and short u

Note: The endings -ion and -ioun were always disyllabic in pronunciation.

Consonants

The consonants b, d, j, k, l, m, n, p, r, t, v, w, and x were pronounced much the same as in Modern English. It should be remembered, however, that all consonants were pronounced: thus the g of gnawe, the k of knyght, the l of half, and the w of write were all sounded.

The consonants listed below have special values according to their position or origin.

c   1. as in English came when followed by a, o, u; or when followed by a consonant: cattle, corage, curteis, croppes

	2. as in English *pace* when folowed by *i* or *e*: *nacion, perced*
ch, cch	as in English *child,* even in words of French origin: *swich, chivalrie, leccherous*
f	as in English *for, off*: *ferne, of, half*
g, gg	1. as in English *goose*: *game, gesse, gyrdel, dogges* 2. as in English *gender* (usually in words of French origin): *gentil, engyn, jugge*
gh	as in German *ich,* Scottish *loch*: *knyght, thoughte*
gn	1. as in English *sign* (in words of French origin): *compaignie* 2. otherwise the *g* was pronounced: *gnawe*
ng	as in English *single*: *singyng*
h	1. as in English *help*: *holpen* 2. sometimes omitted in pronunciation, primarily in words of French origin: *honour*
qu	as in English *queen*: *quene*
s, ss, z	1. as in English *say, grass*: *songes, was, presse, servantz* 2. as in English *buzz* (usually between vowels): *esed, seson*
sh, ssh	as in English *shall, fresh*: *shal, fresshe*
th	1. as in English *thin* when occurring initially or before consonants: *this, thries* 2. as in English *that* when occurring between vowels: *bathed, natheless*; also *worthy*

The following records indicate how some scholars interpret Chaucer's pronunciation:

J. B. Bessinger, "The *Canterbury Tales* (General Prologue) in Middle English", Caedmon Records TC 1151.

C. W. Dunn, "Early English Poetry", Folkways Records FL 9851.

Helge Kökeritz, "Selections from Chaucer", available from Educational Audio Visual Inc., Pleasantville, New York.

CHAUCER'S GRAMMAR

Chaucer's grammar shows the English language about mid-way in its development towards modern English. Old English was characterized by grammatical gender and by the use of inflexional endings on nouns and adjectives to indicate the different cases. Old English also preserved a system of strong and weak verbs with individual endings for the different persons of the verb in the present and the past tenses. By Chaucer's time grammatical gender had disappeared, and the inflexional endings of nouns and adjectives had been reduced to only a few distinctive forms.

Certain aspects of Chaucer's grammar are of special interest to the modern reader. In Chaucer's day the second person singular pronoun *thou* and the corresponding verbal form ending in *-est* were in common use. The plural forms *ye* and *yow* (reduced simply to *you* in modern English) could be used in a singular meaning when a formal mode of address was intended. The distinction was similar to that in modern French between *tu* and *vous*, or in modern German between *du* and *Sie*. This usage survived until Shakespeare's day at least: in *The Tempest* Shakespeare puts the formal *you* in the speeches of Miranda when she is addressing her father, but Prospero always addresses Miranda as *thou*. This specialized usage seems not to have survived long into the seventeenth century, though the singular forms themselves without the previously recognized distinction were in common use even at the beginning of the eighteenth century, as Congreve's *Way of the World* indicates. Their use seems to have been restricted to dialect speakers in the nineteenth century, and they are found nowadays mainly in prayers addressed to the Deity.

The plural forms of the third person pronoun are also interesting. During the ninth, tenth, and early eleventh centuries England was subjected to repeated invasions by Scandinavian marauders. Many of these Scandinavians eventually settled in the north and east sections of the country, and of course they brought their language with them. The modern pronouns *they*, *their*, and *them* are the descendants of the Scandinavian pronouns. In Chaucer's day, however, only the nominative form *they* had been accepted into common usage in the East Midland dialect, the language of Chaucer's poetry.

Other dialects flourished in Chaucer's England in addition to the East Midland dialect; the Southern, the West Midland, and the Northern dialects were the chief ones. Modern English is descended in the main from the East Midland dialect. Middle English works composed in these other dialects, such as *Piers Plowman* and *Sir Gawain and the Green Knight,* have survived into our times, but their language is relatively difficult for the modern reader to understand.

Nouns

The usual inflexion of nouns is given below, for a noun ending in a consonant (*preest*) and for a noun ending in a vowel (*frere*, friar).

Singular

Nominative	preest	frere
Genitive	preestes	freres
Dative	preest	frere
Accusative	preest	frere

Plural

All cases	preestes	freres

A few nouns have no ending in the genitive singular: *by my fader soule* (by my father's soul); *in his lady grace* (in his lady's grace).

A few nouns preserve an archaic dative singular ending in *e* in set phrases: *to bedde*; *on lyve* (alive).

A few nouns form the plural by adding only *s*: *nacions* (nations).

A few nouns form the plural by adding *n*: *eyen* (eyes); *fon* (foes).

A few nouns have the same form in the singular and plural: *hors* (horses); *swyn* (swine); *sheep.*

Adjectives

Chaucer's language preserves only faint traces of the distinction between strong and weak adjectives common in Old English. The weak form is used after *the, this,* or a possessive, and in vocative phrases; otherwise the strong form is used. Adjectives ending in a consonant (*good*) and a vowel (*swete*, sweet) are given below in their strong and weak forms.

	STRONG		WEAK	
Singular	good	swete	goode	swete
Plural	goode	swete	goode	swete

The Middle English form of an Old English genitive plural *ealra* (of all) is preserved in set phrases: *oure aller cok* (the cock for us all).

Personal Pronouns

The forms of the personal pronouns differ in many respects from those in Modern English. Since these forms are not normally glossed in the selections from Chaucer's poetry, they should be noted carefully here. The second person plural forms are sometimes used with a singular meaning when a formal mode of address is intended.

	FIRST PERSON		SECOND PERSON	
	SINGULAR	PLURAL	SINGULAR	PLURAL
Nom.	I, ich	we	thou	ye
Gen.	myn, my	oure	thyn, thy	youre
Dat.	me	us	the	yow
Acc.	me	us	the	yow

	THIRD PERSON			
	SINGULAR			PLURAL
	MASCULINE	FEMININE	NEUTER	ALL GENDERS
Nom.	he	she	hit	they
Gen.	his	hir, hire	his	hir, hire
Dat.	hym, him	hire	hym, him	hem
Acc.	hym, him	hire	hit	hem

Verbs

Verbs follow two basic patterns, weak and strong. Weak verbs form the past tense by the addition of a suffix with *d* or *t*; strong verbs change the vowel of the stem. Typical verbal patterns are given below.

	WEAK		STRONG	
Infinitive	love(n)	fele(n)	ride(n)	bere(n)
Gerund	to love(n)	to fele(n)	to ride(n)	to bere(n)

Present Indicative

Singular	1	love	fele	ride	bere
	2	lovest	felest	ridest	berest
	3	loveth	feleth	rideth, rit	bereth
Plural	1-3	love(n)	fele(n)	ride(n)	bere(n)

Present Subjunctive

Singular	1-3	love	fele	ride	bere
Plural	1-3	love(n)	fele(n)	ride(n)	bere(n)

Past Indicative

Singular	1	loved(e)	felte	rood	bar
	2	lovedest	feltest	ride, rood	bere, bar
	3	loved(e)	felte	rood	bar
Plural	1-3	lovede(n)	felte(n)	ride(n)	bere(n)

Past Subjunctive

Singular	1-3	lovede	felte	ride	bere
Plural	1-3	lovede(n)	felte(n)	ride(n)	bere(n)

Present Participle

lovyng(e)	felyng(e)	ridyng(e)	beryng(e)

Past Participle

loved	felt, feled	ride(n)	bore(n)

Sometimes the past participle is prefixed by an *i* or *y*, a reduced form of the Old English prefix *ge-*: *ytaught* (taught), *ybore* (carried), *ywroght* (made), *ypurfiled* (trimmed).

The forms of some anomalous verbs are listed below.

	PRESENT TENSE	PAST TENSE
to be	am, art, is; be(n)	was, were, was; were(n)
to want, will	wyl/wol, wylt/wolt, wyl/wol; wylle(n)	wolde, woldest, wolde; wolde(n)
to be able, to know how	can, canst, can; conne(n)	couthe/coude, etc.
to dare	dar, darst, dar; dorre(n)	dorste, etc.

to be able	may, mayst, may; mowe(n)	mighte, etc.
to be permitted, to be under obligation	moot, most, moot; mote(n)/moot	moste, etc.
to be about to, to be under obligation	shal, shalt, shal; shulle(n)	sholde, etc.
to know	wot, wost, wot; wite(n)	wiste, etc.
to do	do, dost, doth; doon	dyde, etc.

Sometimes the negative particle *ne* is combined with a few verbs to produce a composite form: *n'am* (am not), *not* (not know), *nyl* (be unwilling).

Sometimes the personal pronoun is combined with a few verbs to produce a composite form: *icham* (I am), *ichot* (I know), *artow* (are you), *wostow* (do you know).

CHAUCER'S VERSIFICATION

Once the student has learned how to pronounce Chaucer's words he will discover that the poetry is remarkably harmonious. He will also discover that Chaucer avoids monotony in the verse by introducing a surprising variety into the rhythms. The basic rhythmical unit in the selections in this anthology is the five-stress line, though the poet experimented with other verse forms in his long career. The most frequently occurring pattern in these lines is a sequence of five units made up of an unstressed syllable followed by a stressed syllable – in other words, a pattern based on the iambic foot. But the line of poetry very often ends in an unstressed syllable after the fifth stressed syllable. This final unstressed syllable results from the fact that many words in Chaucer's day ended in what is called a final *e,* and before illustrating the scansion of some Chaucerian lines we must first examine the problems posed by this final *e.* In the following discussion, when this *e* is to be pronounced a dot is placed over it (*ė*).

Chaucer's final *e* is the product of several sources; the most important are listed below.

1. It may represent the development of a final unstressed syllable in words of Old English origin: sunu- ► sonė (son); heorte · ► hertė (heart); nama—► namė (name); beforan—► bifo(o)rė (before).
2. It may be the final *e* in words of French origin: facė; largė; langagė.
3. It may be the inflexional ending of an adjective or a noun: fresshė flourės; to beddė; oldė thingės.
4. It may be the adverbial *e* added to adjectives to form adverbs: fairė rydė(ride well).
5. It may represent the development of the final unstressed ending of Old English verbs in the past tense: ridon, rydė; dorston, dorstė.
6. Some Middle English words developed a final *e* that cannot be explained by any of the foregoing reasons: barė (bare).

It is quite possible that the pronunciation of this final *e* died out in ordinary speech within Chaucer's own lifetime. However, it seems to have been preserved in the reading of poetry, though under certain circumstances it was not pronounced. Final *e* is not pronounced when it occurs before words beginning with a vowel, or before words beginning with a silent or a weakened *h*, as in *honour, he, his, hire, hem, hadde*. Final *e* is also simply omitted in some words where the scansion demands the omission. With practice the reader will soon learn when to elide syllables, when to pronounce final *e*, and when to omit it.

In the following examples, note how some syllables are syncopated or contracted; note also how words of French origin are very often pronounced with the stress on the final syllable. The (˘) represents an unstressed syllable, the (′) represents a stressed syllable, and unpronounced final *e* and the vowels of syncopated or contracted syllables are enclosed in parentheses.

Whán thăt Áprĭll(e) wĭth hĭs shóurės sóotĕ (Gen. Prol., 1)

Sŏ príkĕth hém nătúr(e) ĭn hír cŏrágĕs (Gen. Prol., 11)

Tŏ Caúntĕrb(u)rý wĭth fúl dĕvóut cŏrágé (Gen. Prol., 22)

Fŏr hé wăs lát(e) y̆cóm(e) frŏm his vĭágĕ (Gen. Prol., 77)

Thĕ Révĕ wás ă scléndrĕ, cól(e) rĭk mán (Gen. Prol., 587)

Hĭs(e) sévĕn(e) wy̆vĕs wálky̆ng(e) by̆ hĭs sydĕ (Nun's Priest, 385)

Ĭ hóld(e) y̆our(e) ów(e)nĕ cónsĕil ís thĕ béstĕ (Merchant, 278)

Ĭf thát ă pry̆ncĕ úsĕth hásărdry̆ĕ (Pardoner, 137)

Ĭ graúnt(e) ĭt wél, Í hăv(e) nóon ĕnvĭĕ (Wife's Prol., 95)

Selected Bibliography

A. THE SOCIAL BACKGROUND

BREWER, D. S. *Chaucer in His Time*. London, 1963.
CHUTE, M. *Geoffrey Chaucer of England*. New York, 1946.
COULTON, G. G. *Chaucer and His England*. 3rd ed. London, 1921.
HEER, F. *The Medieval World*. Trans. J. Sondheimer. London, 1961.
LOOMIS, R. S. *A Mirror of Chaucer's World*. Princeton, 1965.
RICKERT, E. *Chaucer's World*. New York, 1948.

B. LITERARY HISTORIES

BAUGH, A. C., ed. *A Literary History of England*. New York, 1948.
BENNETT, H. S. *Chaucer and the Fifteenth Century*. New York, 1947.
ZESMER, D. M. *Guide to English Literature, From Beowulf through Chaucer and Medieval Drama*. New York, 1961.

C. EDITIONS

SKEAT, W. W., ed. *Geoffrey Chaucer: Complete Works*. 7 vols. Oxford, 1894-98.
ROBINSON, F. N., ed. *The Works of Geoffrey Chaucer*. 2nd ed. Cambridge, Mass., 1957.
DONALDSON, E. T., ed. *Chaucer's Poetry: An Anthology for the Modern Reader*. New York, 1958.
BAUGH, A. C., ed. *Chaucer's Major Poetry*. New York, 1963.

D. CRITICAL STUDIES

BOWDEN, M. *A Commentary on the General Prologue to the Canterbury Tales*. New York, 1948.
————. *A Reader's Guide to Geoffrey Chaucer*. New York, 1964.
BREWER, D. S. *Chaucer*. London, 1953.
COGHILL, N. *The Poet Chaucer*. London, 1947.
CURRY, W. C. *Chaucer and the Medieval Sciences*. Rev. and enl. ed. New York, 1960.

KITTREDGE, G. L. *Chaucer and His Poetry*. Cambridge, Mass., 1915.

LOWES, J. L. *Geoffrey Chaucer*. Bloomington, Ind., 1934.

MUSCATINE, C. *Chaucer and the French Tradition*. Berkeley, Calif., 1957.

PATCH, H. R. *On Rereading Chaucer*. Cambridge, Mass., 1939.

PRESTON, R. *Chaucer*. London, 1952.

RUGGIERS, P. G. *The Art of the Canterbury Tales*. Madison, Wis., 1965.

SCHOECK, R. J., and J. TAYLOR, eds. *Chaucer Criticism*. Vol I. Notre Dame, Ind., 1960.

WAGENKNECHT, E., ed. *Chaucer: Modern Essays in Criticism*. New York, 1959.

E. CHAUCER'S LANGUAGE

KÖKERITZ, H. *A Guide to Chaucer's Pronunciation*. New York, 1962.

MOORE, S. *Historical Outlines of English Sounds and Inflections*. Rev. A. H. Marckwardt. Ann Arbor, Mich., 1957.

For records of Chaucer's poetry read in Middle English, see xxxv.

Note on the Text

The text of the selections from the *Canterbury Tales* is based on the Ellesmere and Hengwrt manuscripts as published by the Chaucer Society. The reading of line 117 of the Wife of Bath's Prologue is that proposed by E. T. Donaldson, "Chaucer's *Canterbury Tales* D117: A Critical Edition", *Speculum* XL (1965), 626-33, and is used here with his kind permission.

The text of the short poems is also based on the manuscript materials published by the Chaucer Society, with the exception of "To Rosemounde", which is derived from W. W. Skeat, *Twelve Facsimiles of Old English Manuscripts* (Oxford, 1892), 36-7.

Short Poems

INTRODUCTION TO THE
SHORT POEMS

These short poems are included in the present selection to draw attention to one aspect of Chaucer's career as a poet that is habitually neglected. We know that in the Middle Ages a great amount of occasional poetry and music was produced either for special public occasions or for the daily incidental entertainment of patrons and patronesses. Highly specialized verse forms were developed for this type of poetry, and the would-be poet who produced poems such as these before moving on to works larger and different in conception served an arduous apprenticeship. Just such an apprenticeship probably was Chaucer's; if so, we have then an explanation of that facility in verse so characteristic of the poet's later career.

Of these short pieces, the triple roundel "Merciles Beautee" is the one poem whose attribution to Chaucer is not absolutely certain, even though the poem displays a neat Chaucerian upset of conventional expectations in its final section.[1] The roundel, or round as it is now called, is designed to be sung, and as its name implies, it ends where it begins. Such a return to the starting-point naturally involves a repetition of the opening lines. The reader should notice also that the rhyme scheme of the whole poem depends on the rhymes of the first two lines. The ballade, originally a dancing song, exhibits a similar complexity of structure. The little poem "Lakke of Stedfastnesse" is a good example of the type. Traditionally the ballade employs only three or four rhymes which are repeated in the same order in three stanzas of equal length, and the last line of the first stanza is used to conclude the two succeeding stanzas as well. The poem ends with an envoy or address, usually to a prince, urging that person to a course of action suggested by or arising out of the content of the

---

1 See the discussion of this point in the General Introduction, p. xxvi.

preceding stanzas. Both the roundel and the ballade were originally forms of French poetry, but the types, as Chaucer makes clear, are adaptable to English.

In addition to serving as an illustration of the complex verse structures employed by poets of the age, these poems afford us a glimpse of Chaucer in his political and social milieu. "Lakke of Stedfastnesse" seems to have been addressed as a rebuke to Richard II and serves as a reminder that the conduct of monarchs in the Middle Ages was a matter of personal concern to the men who surrounded them. Chaucer's exasperated words to his copyist bring home to us the fact that all books in Chaucer's time had to be produced by hand; they indicate the extent to which the writer was at the mercy of his scribes and also serve to explain textual variants to the modern editor. "Lenvoy . . . a Bukton" shows how Chaucer carried his poetry over into his personal relationships, and the reference to the Wife of Bath suggests that her part in the *Canterbury Tales* must have been well known in 1396.[2] Finally, the very witty "Complaynt . . . to his Purse", while it may or may not indicate a penurious cap-in-hand pensioner, convincingly demonstrates that Chaucer's sense of humour stayed with him even in the final years of his life.

2 See footnote 2, p. 10, for a discussion of the date of this poem.

Merciles Beautee

I

Yowre ÿen* two woll sle* me sodenly;   eyes slay
I may the beautee of them nat sustene*,   endure
So wondeth* hit thorow out* my herte   wounds throughout
    kene*.   keenly

And but your word will helen* hastily   heal
Mi hertis* wound while that hit is grene,   *5* my heart's
   Your ÿen two woll sle me sodenly;
   I may the beautee of them nat sustene.

Upon my trouthe, I sey you feithfully,
That ye ben of my liffe and deth* the quene, death
For with my deth the trouth shal be sene. *10*
   Your ÿen two woll sle me sodenly;
   I may the beautee of them nat sustene,
     So wondeth hit thorow out my herte kene.

II

So hath yowre beaute fro* your herte   from
    chaced*   chased
Pitee, that me n'availleth not to pleyne; *15*
For danger* halt* youre mercy in his cheyne. disdain holds

Giltless* my deth thus han* ye me   innocent have
     purchaced;
I sey yow soth*, me nedeth not to feyne*;   truth   pretend
  So hath yowre beaute fro your herte
      chaced   *19*
  Pitee, that me n'availleth not to pleyne.

Alas! that nature hath in yow compased*   enclosed
So grete beaute, that no man may atteyne
To mercy, though he sterve* for the peyne.   die
  So hath yowre beaute fro your herte
      chaced   *24*
  Pitee, that me n'availleth not to pleyne;
  For danger halt youre mercy in his cheyne.

III

Syn* I fro Love escaped am so fat,   since
I never thenk to ben his prison* lene*;   prisoner lean
Syn I am free, I counte him not a bene*!   bean

He may answere, and sey this and that;   *30*
I do no fors*, I speke ryght as I mene.   I don't care
  Syn I fro Love escaped am so fat,
  I never thenk to ben his prison lene.

Love hath my name i-strike* out of his   struck
     sclat*,   slate
And he is strike out of my bokes* clene   *35* books
For ever mo*; [ther] is non other mene.   more
  Syn I fro Love escaped am so fat,
  I never thenk to ben his prison lene;
  Syn I am free, I counte him not a bene!

To Rosemounde

Madame, ye ben of al beaute shryne
As fer as cercled is* the mapemounde*,   extends   the map of the world
For as the cristall glorious ye shyne,
And lyke the ruby ben your chekys* rounde. cheeks
Therwyth ye ben so mery and so jocounde, *5*
That at a revell* whan that I se you dance,   revelry
It is an oynement unto my wounde,
Thogh ye to me ne do no daliance*.   love-play

For thogh I wepe of teres ful a tyne*,   large tub
Yet may that wo myn herte nat confounde;
Your semly* voys, that ye so small   delicate
  out-twyne*,   *11* force out
Makyth my thoght in joy and blys habounde.
So curtaysly I go, with love bounde,
That to myself I sey, in my penaunce,
"Suffyseth me to love you, Rosemounde, *15*
Thogh ye to me ne do no daliaunce."

Nas never* pyk* walwed* in galauntyne* there was never pike
As I in love am walwed and i-wounde,   immersed spiced sauce
For whych ful ofte I of myself devyne
That I am trewe Tristam[1] the secounde.   *20*
My love may nat refreyde* be nor affounde*; cooled fail
I brenne* ay in amorous plesaunce.   burn
Do what ye lyst*, I wyl your thral* be   please slave
  founde,
Thogh ye to me ne do no daliaunce.
tregentil[2]   chaucer

1 Tristram, lover of King Mark's wife Yseult, and a famous medieval hero in war and love.
2 Possibly the name of the scribe, as the "chaucer" on the opposite side is presumably the name of the author of the poem.

Lakke of stedfastnesse

Some tyme* the worlde was so stedfast and   at one time
    stable
That mannes worde was obligacioun,
And now hyt is so fals and so disceyvable
That worde and dede, as in conclusyoun,
Ys noo thing lyke, for turned up so doun   5
Ys alle this worlde for mede* and   bribery
    wilfulnesse,
That alle is loste for lake of stedfastnesse.

What makith this world to be so variable
But luste* that folk han* in dissensioun?   pleasure have
For amonge us nowe a man is holde unhable*,   incapable
But yf* he kan by somme conclusyoun   11   unless
Do hys neghbour wronge or oppressioun.
What causeth this but wilfulle wreccednesse
That alle is loste for lakke of stedfastnesse?

Trouthe ys put doun, resoun is holden fable;
Vertu hath now noo domynacioun;   16
Pitee exiled, noo man ys merciable.
Thurgh coveityse is blent* discrecioun;   blinded
The worlde hath made a permutacioun
Fro ryght to wrong, fro trouthe to
    fikelnesse,   20
That alle is loste for lakke of stedfastnesse.

L'ENVOY

O prince, desire to be honourable;
Cheryssh thy folke and hate extorsioun;
Suffre no thing that may be reprevable* reprehensible
To thin estaate doon in thy regioun. *25*
Shew forth thy swerde of castigacioun;
Drede God, do law, love trouthe and
  worthynesse,
And wedde thy folke ayeyne* to again
  stedfastnesse.

Lenvoy de Chaucer a Bukton

My maister Bukton,[1] whan of Criste our kyng
Was axed* what is trouthe or sothefastnesse*,   asked   truthfulness
He nat a word answerde to that axinge,
As who saith, "Noo man is al trew," I gesse.
And therfore, though I hight* to expresse 5   promised
The sorwe and woo that is in mariage,
I dar nat writen of hyt noo wikkednesse,
Lest Y* myself falle eft* in swich* dotage*.   I   again   such   foolishness

I wol nat seyn how that hyt is the cheyne
Of Sathanas* on which he gnaweth evere.   Satan
But I dar seyn, were he out of his peyne, 11
As by his wille he wolde be bounde nevere.
But thilke* doted* foole that ofte had levere*   that   stupid   rather
Ycheyned be than out of prison crepe,   14
God lete him never fro his woo dissevere*,   part
Ne noo man him bewayle, though he wepe!

But yet, lest thow doo worse, take a wyfe;
Bet* ys to wedde thanne brenne* in worse   better   burn
  wise.
But thow shal have sorwe on thy flessh thy
  lyfe,   19
And ben thy wifes thral*, as seyn these wise;   slave
And if that Hooly Writte may nat suffyse,
Experience shal the teche, so may happe,

---

1 Bukton is probably Peter Bukton (1350-1414), a friend of Chaucer and
  courtier at the court of Richard II and Henry IV; presumably he was
  contemplating marriage or remarriage.

That the were lever* to be take in Frise[2]   *you would rather*
Than eft* falle of weddynge in the trappe.   *again*

ENVOY

This lytel writte, proverbes, or figure*   *25* *poem*
I sende yow; take kepe of* hyt, I rede*.   *pay attention to advise*
Unwise is he that kan no wele* endure.   *happiness*
Yf thow be siker*, put the nat in drede.   *secure*
The Wyfe of Bathe I pray yow that ye rede
Of this matere that we have on honde.   *30*
God graunte yow your lyfe frely to lede
In fredam, for ful hard it is to be bonde.

---

2 Friesland in the Lowlands. There was an expedition against Friesland by
the English between August 24 and September 30, 1396; so the poem
was probably written in that year.

Chauciers wordes...
unto Adame his owene scryveyne

Adam scryveyne*, if ever it thee byfalle   scribe
Boece[1] or Troylus[2] for to wryten nuwe,
Under thy long lokkes thowe most* have the   may you
   scalle*,   scab
But* after my makyng thowe wryte more   unless
   truwe.
So oft a daye I mot* thy werk renuwe,   must
It to corect, and eke* to rubbe and scrape,   also
And al is thorugh thy necglygence and rape*.   haste

1 Chaucer's translation of *The Consolation of Philosophy* of Boethius (*c.* 475-525).

2 Chaucer's *Troilus and Criseyde*, completed probably in 1385.

The Complaynt of Chaucer to his Purse

To yow, my purse, and to noon other wight*   person
Complayn I, for ye be my lady dere;
I am so sory now that ye been lyght,
For certes, but yf* ye make me hevy chere*,   unless   sad welcome, i.e., a
                                                            pun on heavy
Me were as leef* be layd upon my bere*.   5   I would be glad to   bier
For whiche unto your mercy thus I crye,
Beeth hevy agayne, or elles mote* I dye!   must

Now voucheth-sauf* this day or* hyt be   guarantee   before
    nyght,
That I of yow the blisful soune* may here,   sound
Or see your colour lyke the sonne bryght, *10*
That of yelownesse hadde never pere*;   peer
Ye be my lyfe, ye be myn hertes stere*,   guide
Quene of comfort and of good companye;
Beth hevy ayeyne*, or elles moote I dye!   again

Now purse, that ben to me my lyves* lyght   life's
And saveour, as doun in this worlde here, *16*
Oute of this toune helpe me thurgh your
    myght,
Syn that* ye wole nat bene my tresorere*,   since   treasurer
For I am shave* as nye* as is a frere*!   shaven   close   friar
But yet I pray unto your curtesye,   *20*
Bethe hevy ayen, or elles moote I dye!

L'ENVOY DE CHAUCER

O conquerour* of Brutes* Albyon*,   i.e., Henry IV Brutus's

Whiche that by lygne* and free eleccion[1] lineage   i.e., Britain

Been verray* kynge, this song to yow I   true
  sende,

And ye that mowen* alle myn harme   may
  amende,   *25*

Have mynde upon my supplicacion.

1 Henry IV was received as king by parliament on September 30, 1399.

FROM THE

Canterbury Tales

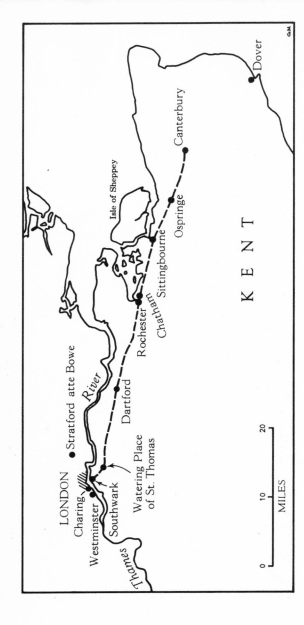

The distance from Southwark to Canterbury on the route generally proposed by scholars for the Canterbury pilgrimage is 56 or 57 miles. The pilgrims made either two or three overnight stops; Dartford, Rochester, and Ospringe seem likely stopping-places. Roads in the Middle Ages were such that rapid travel for ordinary people was virtually impossible; thus it is not unreasonable to assume that 15 miles would constitute a day's travelling.

The small map shows the location of Stratford atte Bowe, the probable site of the convent house to which the Prioress belonged (General Prologue, line 125), and of Charing, in which was situated the Pardoner's religious house of St. Mary Rounceval, (line 670).

The large map shows the location of Oxford, Dartmouth, Bath, and Bawdeswell, the homes of the Oxford Scholar, the Shipman, the Wife of Bath, and the Reeve respectively (lines 285, 389, 445, and 620). Other names mentioned in the selections in this anthology are Orwell and Middleburg (line 277), Ypres and Ghent (line 448), Boulogne (line 465), Dunmow (Wife of Bath's Prologue, line 218), and Hailes (Pardoner's Tale, line 190). A useful reference work for Chaucer's place-names is F. P. Magoun, Jr., *A Chaucer Gazetteer* (Chicago, 1961).

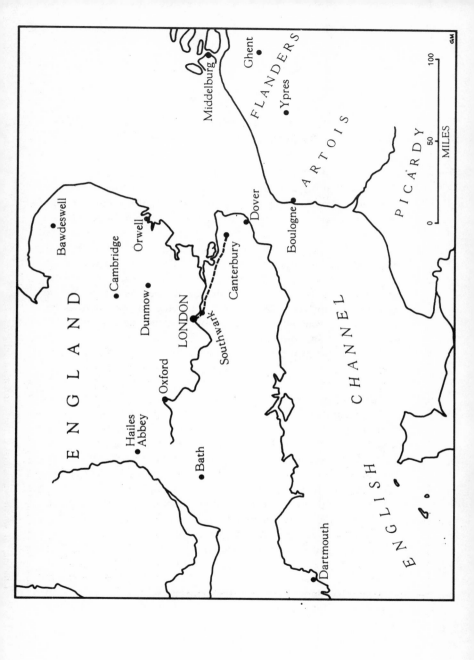

INTRODUCTION TO THE
GENERAL PROLOGUE

In the General Prologue to the *Canterbury Tales* Chaucer presents us with a cross-section of fourteenth-century life. All classes of society, with the exception of the great nobility and the high ecclesiastics, are represented in this collection of pilgrims who take their way to Canterbury on this mid-April journey. Every society is made up of different social ranks and every society contains different types of individuals. The society we meet in the General Prologue is no exception. And it is Chaucer's keen eye for the reality beneath the surface, as well as the reality on the surface, that takes in the details of character as well as the details of physical appearance. Thus we meet here a group of people who stand out vividly in pictorial terms and who also impress us as firmly established psychological identities. And so the Prologue is justly famous as a gallery of portraits of human beings as well as a clear depiction of the different social groups of fourteenth-century society.

The one quality of Chaucer's art in this Prologue that is readily apparent to most readers is irony. Irony can be defined briefly as saying one thing and meaning something quite different, usually just the opposite of the surface meaning of the words. Chaucer is a master of this art. In the Prologue this irony takes several forms. It may take the form of a straight-faced agreement with the Monk's assertion of his own superiority to the stringent demands of monastic discipline, as in the line "And I seyde his opinon was good". Or it may be merely a quiet smile at the Prioress's pretensions to the manners and even the very language of the nobility, as in the sly retailing of the information that "Frenssh of Parys was to hire unknowe". It may be the seemingly simple-minded praise of the unpraiseworthy Friar who was "Unto his ordre . . . a noble post". Or it may take the form of using words from a character's own mouth and thereby emphasizing the pretensions of the character, as in the statement that the unlearned Manciple's wit surpasses "The wisdom of an heep of lerned men". Indeed, it is this pricking the bubble of people's pretensions that constitutes Chaucer's chief preoccupation in the General Prologue. Like all ironists, Chaucer makes capital out of the discrepancies between what people really are and what they pretend to be. The result of this practice differs according to the intellectual climate of the age and, to a lesser degree, the temperament of the writer. Thus in an age that laid strong claims to reason, such as Swift's in the eighteenth century, the practice could lead to violent indignation and ultimately to the wholesale rejection of mankind in favour of the company of horses. In an age such as Chaucer's, when the influence of the Church and a belief in the Divine Providence were very strong, the practice produced a writer who viewed the foibles of his fellow men with a detached and amused tolerance. This fact has put readers who are disconcerted by the ubiquitous application of phrases of approbation to such out-and-out rogues as the Pardoner, the Summoner, and the Shipman to the difficulty of explaining that the phrases meant something quite different from their ordinary meaning when applied to these rogues. It is possible that Chaucerian irony is operating in these instances; it is also possible to take the phrases quite literally and find these rascals "good fellows" in the sense that they were lively, agreeable, and amusing travelling companions. Indeed, Chaucer even put what many readers consider the best of the tales in the whole Canterbury collection in the mouth of one of these rogues. The Pardoner may be an unscrupulous wretch, and in his relations with the Summoner an unsavoury one as well, but Chaucer tells us that he was a "noble ecclesiaste".

The wide representation of characters in the General Prologue implies that the Prologue is a microcosm of the fourteenth-century world in which Chaucer lived. Anyone who lectures on the General Prologue soon discovers the encyclopedic nature of the work. It is for this reason that the Prologue frequently stands by itself in prescriptions for undergraduates. For behind the individual characters in the Prologue rests the whole world of medieval experience and learning. Chaucer begins with the Knight, and we are introduced not only to details of medieval arms and armour, as we should expect, and to medieval ideals of chivalry, as we might not expect, but also to the whole range of military experience available in the fourteenth century to what we nowadays would call the professional soldier. That military experience extended from campaigns undertaken for patriotic motives, such as Edward III's wars against the French, to wars of religion waged against the heathens in the Mediterranean area and in north-eastern Europe as well. A similar situation exists with respect to the "Doctour of Phisik". In capsule form we are presented with the history of medieval medicine and with a vivid picture of the practices of physicians in the fourteenth century. The close connection between medicine and astrology is made clear, as is the excessively heavy reliance on precedent and authority in the treatment of disease. And so it goes with the other pilgrims in this gallery of fourteenth-century portraits: medieval mercantile practices are summed up in the person of the Merchant; the methods and habits of ship captains, their sea routes and their piracy, are presented in the person of the Shipman; and the variety of religious vocations available, plus the many ways those vocations could be abused by the less worthy members of religious institutions, are all neatly summed up for us in the portraits of the Monk, the Prioress, and the Friar. The devices of fourteenth-century lawyers and the different types of land tenure are suggested in the picture of the Sergeant of the Law, and the world of the medieval university is opened up for us in the presentation of the Clerk of Oxford. This partial list could be expanded to include all the characters in the General Prologue, but enough has been said to indicate the vast amount of medieval learning behind this work, and to indicate also why the Prologue is a favourite with the social historian of the fourteenth century.

Another interesting feature of the General Prologue is the way in which the inner psychological reality is suggested by means of the detail describing the outer man. We deduce the Prioress's vanity in her physical appearance by the care she takes with the arrangement of her religious dress, and the running sore on the Cook's shin is a good indication of his general disregard for all the qualities of cleanliness we hope to find in food-handlers. The thick-skinned coarseness of the Miller is graphically suggested by the revelation that he broke down doors with his head, and also by his fondness for that most strident of all musical instruments, the bagpipe. And a neat contrast in natures is implied by the threadbare cloak of the Oxford Clerk side by side with the fur-trimmed garments of the Monk. Details such as these could be multiplied; we need only to draw attention to the different horses the pilgrims ride as an indicator of how much faith they put in that fourteenth-century status symbol.

Where Chaucer got the idea for a pilgrimage as the device to bring together a large group of varied individuals is not known for sure; it may have been suggested to him by the *Novelle* of Sercambi, a fourteenth-century Italian writer whose work Chaucer may or may not have known. But wherever the idea came from, the pilgrimage represents one of the two places where such a group of people would all naturally come together; only in a church or an inn would one find such a widespread collection of individuals. The vividness with which the individual characters in the General Prologue are presented has led some readers to suggest that Chaucer had actual persons of the fourteenth century in mind when drawing these word-portraits. It is true, of course, that literary art, if it is to have any validity, must have some reference to life itself, and we may assume it as axiomatic that Chaucer's observation of the life around him contributed to his presentation of these characters in the General Prologue. But this fact should not divert us from what after all is the most important point – that we are dealing here with art. And the artistry of this art should be our primary concern. If Chaucer's characters have any life at all, their life-likeness is not derived from the existence of similar individuals in fourteenth-century records. What makes these characters live as human beings is the artistry of the poet. And they do live as human beings.

But even here we would be making a mistake if we viewed the characters as detached from the literature of the age in which they were produced. Literature in Chaucer's time, if we may use a term that suggests a dignity the poet himself would lay no claim to, was a highly conventionalized and stylized mode of expression. No premium was put on originality as we know it, and the more writers an author could refer to or borrow from, the more authority his own work possessed. Scholars who have made a close study of some of Chaucer's early poetry have demonstrated that it relies to a very great extent on the poetry of Chaucer's cross-channel contemporaries. Such indebtedness does not mean that Chaucer is to be regarded as a wholesale plagiarist. Rather, it is an indication that our current notions of what constitutes poetic originality are severely restricted by copyright laws. It is also an indication that the poet was steeped in the literature available to his age and did not hesitate to take what he needed when he needed it. Thus, while it is possible to admire the keen observation of the foibles of individual human beings that has gone into the portraits of the General Prologue, that admiration must be tempered by the recognition that behind each of these portraits lies the weight of a long literary tradition. The "eyen greye as glas" of the Prioress can be paralleled by similar eyes of other women in Old French literature (though none of these are prioresses), and the Wife of Bath's knowledge of love – "She koude of that art the olde daunce" – is derived from the Old French *Roman de la Rose* where the identical phrasing is used. And even in that passage where the poet seems to be speaking in his own person and begging his readers' pardon for the scurrility of some of the tales and the crudity of some of the language Chaucer is following an accepted medieval literary device. These few examples will suffice to show that what we often tend to admire as the poet's strong originality may not fit our conception of what is original at all.

What is original in our idea of the word is the strong sense of irony that gives a distinctively Chaucerian flavour and the equally strong sense of compassion for his fellow human beings. Even the most vicious of his characters, such as the Summoner and the Pardoner, are presented with a clear-sightedness unclouded by any intrusion of moral condemnation. Like a camera lens, Chaucer's art allows us to see these people with all their blemishes and with all the detail necessary for us to make a moral judgment. But also like a camera lens, Chaucer's art never passes that judgment itself. In the seventeenth century Dryden remarked about the General Prologue, "Here is God's plenty." We cannot read the work without also having the sense that these are God's creatures. Chaucer's act of creation is an act of redemption as well.

The General Prologue

Whan that Aprille with his shoures soote*   sweet
The droghte* of March hath perced to the   dryness
   roote,
And bathed every veyne in swich* licour*,   such moisture
Of which vertu* engendred is the flour;   power
Whan Zephirus eek* with his sweete breeth 5   also
Inspired hath in every holt* and heeth*   wood heath
The tendre croppes*, and the yonge sonne   shoots
Hath in the Ram[1] his half cours yronne*,   run
And smale foweles* maken melodye,   birds
That slepen al the nyght with open eye, 10
So priketh* hem* nature in hir* corages*,   urges them their hearts
Than longen folk to goon on pilgrimages,
And palmeres* for to seken straunge*   pilgrims foreign
   strondes*,   shores
To ferne* halwes* kowthe* in sondry londes;   distant shrines known
And specially, from every shires ende   15
Of Engelond to Caunterbury they wende,
The hooly, blisful martir[2] for to seke
That hem hath holpen* whan that they were   helped
   seeke*.   ill
   Bifil*, that in that seson on a day,   it happened

1 The "Ram" is Aries, the first sign of the zodiac; thus the sun is "young"
in the zodiacal year. The signs of the zodiac overlap the calendar months,
Aries running from March 12 to April 11. The "half course" is the
second half course; i.e., from March 27 to April 11. The Julian calendar
by which time was reckoned in the Middle Ages did not coincide exactly
with solar time, and thus the date by our reckoning would be about nine
days later.

2 The martyr is Thomas Becket, Archbishop of Canterbury, who was murdered in 1170 and canonized in 1172.

mre specific

In Southwerk* at the Tabard* as I lay,   *20*   Southwark on south bank of
Redy to wenden on my pilgrimage   Thames   name of inn
To Caunterbury with ful devout corage*,   heart
At nyght was come into that hostelrye
Wel nyne and twenty in a compaignye
Of sondry folk, by aventure* yfalle*   *25*   chance   fallen
In felaweshipe, and pilgrimes were they alle,
That toward Caunterbury wolden ryde.
The chambres and the stables weren wyde*,   spacious
And wel we weren esed* atte beste*.   entertained   excellently
And shortly, whan the sonne was to reste, *30*
So hadde I spoken with hem everychon*   every one
That I was of hir felaweshipe anon*   soon
And made forward* erly for to ryse   agreement
To take oure wey ther as I yow devyse*.   relate
   But nathelees*, whil I have tyme and space,   nevertheless
Er that I ferther in this tale pace*,   *36* pass
Me thynketh* it acordaunt to reson   it seems to me
To telle yow al the condicion*   circumstances
Of ech of hem*, so as it semed me,   *39* them
And which they weren and of what degree*, station in life
And eek* in what array* that they were inne, also   mode of dress
And at a knyght than wol I first bigynne.

   A KNYGHT ther was, and that a worthy
     man,
That fro the tyme that he first bigan
To riden out he loved chivalrie,   *45*
Trouthe and honour, fredom* and curteisie.[3] liberality
Ful worthy was he in his lordes werre*,[4]   war

3 The ascription of these four virtues to the Knight, coupled with the mention of chivalry or the knightly code of conduct in the previous line,
  implies that Chaucer intends his audience to attribute to the Knight the
  remaining eight of the twelve chivalric virtues: purity, faith, love, loyalty,
  discretion, perseverance, prowess, and moderation.

4 Probably the French campaigns of Edward III in the Hundred Years
  War are meant here; Chaucer took part himself in the campaign of 1359-
  60 and was captured by the French. The expeditions mentioned in lines

And therto hadde he riden no man ferre*, farther
As wel in cristendom as in hethenesse*, heathendom
And evere honoured for his worthynesse. *50*
At Alisaundre* he was whan it was wonne. Alexandria
Ful ofte tyme he hadde the bord bigonne* sat at the head of the table
Aboven alle nacions in Pruce*. Prussia
In Lettow* hadde he reysed* and in Ruce*, Lithuania campaigned
No cristen man so ofte of his degree.   *55* Russia
In Gernade* at the seege eek hadde he be Granada (Spain)
Of Algezir*, and riden in Belmarye*. Algeciras Benmarin (Morocco)
At Lyeys* was he and at Satalye* Layas (Armenia) Attalia (Asia Minor)
Whan they were wonne, and in the Grete See* Mediterranean
At many a noble armee hadde he be. *60*
At mortal batailles hadde he been fiftene,
And foghten for oure feith at Tramyssene* Tlemçen (Algeria)
In lystes thries*, and ay* slayn his foo. thrice always
This ilke* worthy knyght hadde been also same
Somtyme with the lord of Palatye* *65* Balat (Turkey)
Agayn another hethen in Turkye,
And everemoore he hadde a sovereyn prys*. excellent reputation
And though that he were worthy, he was wys,
And of his port* as meke as is a mayde. bearing
He nevere yet no vileynye* ne sayde *70* coarse speech
In al his lyf unto no maner wight*. any kind of person
He was a verray*, parfit, gentil* knyght. true noble
But for to tellen yow of his array,
His hors* were goode, but he was nat gay. horses
Of fustian* he wered a gypon* *75* type of cloth tunic

51-67 occupied an interval of forty years. The Knight served under Peter of Lusignan, the King of Cyprus, at Alexandria (1361), and Layas in Armenia (1367). The heathen lord of "Palatye" was an ally of Peter in 1365; so this reference would belong to that decade also. The Knight fought the Saracens in the western Mediterranean as well as the eastern, campaigning in Spain at Granada and Algeciras, in Morocco at Benmarin, and in Algeria at Tlemçen. Chaucer's Knight fought also in northeastern Europe against the heathen Lithuanians (converted to Christianity in 1386) and against the Russians, probably serving with the Teutonic Order of Knights where he was honoured above all nations.

Al bismotered* with his harbergeon*,   *made dirty   coat of mail*
For he was late ycome* from his viage*,   *had come   journey*
And wente for to doon his pilgrymage.

  With hym ther was his sone, a yong
  SQUIER,
A lovyere and a lusty* bacheler,[5]   *80* *happy*
With lokkes crulle* as* they were leyd in   *curly locks as if*
  presse*;   *set in curlers*
Of twenty yeer of age he was, I gesse.
Of his stature he was of evene* lengthe,   *average*
And wonderly delyvere* and of greet   *marvellously nimble*
  strengthe.
And he hadde been somtyme in chivachie*   *cavalry expedition*
In Flaundres, in Artois and Picardie,[6]   *86*
And born* hym wel, as of so litel space*   *conducted i.e., considering*
In hope to stonden in his lady grace*.   *his short service*
    favour
Embrouded* he was as it were a meede*   *embroidered meadow*
Al ful of fresshe floures whyte and reede; *90*
Syngynge he was or floytynge* al the day.   *playing the flute*
He was as fressh as is the monthe of May.
Short was his gowne with sleves longe and
  wyde;
Wel koude* he sitte on hors and faire ryde.   *knew how to*
He koude songes make and wel endite*,   *95* *compose tunes and lyrics*
Juste* and eek* daunce, and wel purtreye*   *joust also draw*
  and write.
So hoote he lovede that by nyghtertale*   *night*
He slepte namoore than dooth the
  nyghtyngale.
Curteis he was, lowely and servysable*,   *obedient*
And carf* biforn his fader at the table. *100* *carved*

  A YEMAN* hadde he and servantz namo*   *yeoman no more*

---

5 A "bacheler" was someone who was on the point of, or who had recently acquired, knighthood.

6 There was an English campaign in these regions in northern France in 1383.

At that tyme, for hym liste* ride so,   *it pleased him*
And he was clad in cote and hood of grene.
A sheef of pecok arwes* bright and kene*   *arrows* *sharp*
Under his belt he bar* ful thriftily*.   *105*   *carried* *neatly*
Wel koude he dresse his takel* yemanly*;   *shooting gear* *as a good yeo-*
His arwes drouped* noght with fetheres lowe,   *drooped*   *man*
And in his hand he baar* a myghty bowe.   *carried*
A not* heed* hadde he, with a broun visage;   *close-cropped* *head*
Of woodecraft wel koude* he al the usage*.   *knew* *customs*
Upon his arm he baar a gay bracer*,   *111*   *arm-guard*
And by his syde a swerd* and a bokeler*,   *sword* *small shield*
And on that other syde a gay daggere
Harneised* wel and sharp as point of spere.   *mounted*
A Cristophere* on his brest of silver shene*,   *St. Christopher medal* *bright*
An horn he bar, the bawdryk* was of grene;   *shoulder-strap*
A forster* was he, soothly* as I gesse.   *117*   *forester* *truly*

   Ther was also a nonne, a PRIORESSE,
That of hir smylyng was ful symple* and   *modest*
   coy*;   *quiet*
Hir gretteste ooth was but by Seint Loy.⁷   *120*
And she was cleped* Madame Eglentyne*.   *called* *Sweet-Briar*
Ful weel she soong the service dyvyne
Entuned in hir nose ful semely*,⁸   *fairly*
And Frenssh she spak ful faire and fetisly*–   *elegantly*
After the scole of Stratford atte Bowe,⁹   *125*
For Frenssh of Parys was to hir unknowe.
At mete* wel ytaught* was she with alle;   *meals* *mannered*
She leet* no morsel from hir lippes falle,   *let*

---

7 St. Loy or Eligius of the seventh century. On one occasion he refused to swear upon some saints' relics; Chaucer probably means that the Prioress didn't swear at all.

8 Nasal intonation was a common practice in chanting parts of the service to avoid straining the vocal cords.

9 A Benedictine nunnery was located at St. Leonard's on the outskirts of medieval London near Stratford atte Bowe. Chaucer probably means that she spoke a variety of French appropriate to an English nunnery.

Ne wette hir fyngres in hir sauce depe.
Wel koude she carie a morsel and wel kepe
That no drope ne fille upon hir brest.   *131*
In curteisie* was set ful muchel* hir lest*.   etiquette very greatly delight
Hir over-lippe* wyped she so clene   upper-lip
That in hir coppe* ther was no ferthyng* sene cup trace
Of grece whan she dronken hadde hir
   draughte.   *135*
Ful semely after hir mete* she raughte*.   food reached
And sikerly* she was of greet desport*,   certainly good fun
And ful plesaunt and amyable* of port*,   friendly bearing
And peyned* hire to countrefete* cheere*   took pains imitate be-
Of court, and to been estatlich* of manere,   majestic   haviour
And to been holden digne* of reverence. *141* worthy
But, for to speken of hir conscience*,   moral awareness
She was so charitable* and so pitous*   kind-hearted compassionate
She wolde wepe if that she saugh* a mous   saw
Kaught in a trappe, if it were deed* or   dead
   bledde.   *145*
Of smale houndes* hadde she that she fedde   some small dogs
With rosted flessh or mylk and wastel breed*;   white bread
But soore wepte she if oon of hem* were   one of them
   deed,
Or if men smoot* it with a yerde* smerte*,   struck stick severely
And al was conscience* and tendre herte. *150* solicitude
Ful semely* hir wympul* pynched* was;   fairly head-dress pleated
Hir nose tretys*, hir eyen greye as glas,   straight
Hir mouth ful smal, and therto softe and reed.
But sikerly*, she hadde a fair forheed;   certainly
It was almoost a spanne brood*, I trowe*,   broad believe
For hardily*, she was nat undergrowe.   *156* certainly
Ful fetys* was hir cloke, as I was war*;   neat aware
Of smal coral aboute hir arm she bar
A peire of bedes* gauded al with grene*, *159* rosary adorned with large
And theron heng a brooch of gold ful sheene*   bright   green beads
On which ther was first writen a crowned *A,*
And after, *Amor vincit omnia*.   "Love conquers all"
Another NONNE with hire hadde she

That was hir chapeleyne, and preestes thre.

A MONK ther was, a fair for the maistrie*,   an extremely fine one
An outridere* that lovede venerie*,   *166*   overseer   hunting
A manly man, to been an abbot able.
Ful many a deyntee* hors hadde he in stable,   excellent
And whan he rood*, men myghte his brydel   rode
    heere
Gynglen* in a whistlynge wynd as cleere *170*   jingling
And eek* as loude as dooth the chapel belle   also
Ther as* this lord was kepere of the celle*.   where   small monastic house
The reule of Seint Maure or of Seint Beneit,[10]
By cause that it was old and somdel* streit*,   somewhat   strict
This ilke* monk leet* olde thynges pace*,   same   let   pass
And heeld after the newe world the space*.   meanwhile
He yaf* nat of that text a pulled* hen   *177*   gave   plucked
That seith that hunters been nat hooly men,
Ne that a monk whan he is recchelees*   carefree
Is likned to a fissh that is waterlees –   *180*
This is to seyn* a monk out of his cloystre –   say
But thilke* text heeld he nat worth an oystre;   that
And I seyde his opinion was good.
What sholde he studie and make hym selven
    wood*   mad
Upon a book in cloystre alwey to poure*, *185*   pore
Or swynken* with his handes and laboure   work
As Austyn*[11] bit*? How shal the world be   St. Augustine   bids
    served?

10 St. Benedict laid down the strict Benedictine rule in Italy in the sixth
   century, and his disciple St. Maur brought the rule to France later in
   that century.
11 St. Augustine of Hippo (fifth century) criticized monks for their sloth.
   The question "How shall the world be served" means "Who will conduct
   the world's business". Since nearly all education was conducted by the
   religious foundations, and since educated men were needed to conduct
   the world's affairs, the Monk justifies his abstention from strict monastic
   rule because of his usefulness to society.

Lat Austyn have his swynk* to hym reserved!   labour
Therfore he was a prikasour* aright.   hard rider
Grehoundes he hadde as swift as fowel in
    flight;   *190*
Of prikyng* and of huntyng for the hare   riding
Was al his lust*; for no cost wolde he spare.   pleasure
I seigh* his sleves ypurfiled* at the hond   saw   trimmed
With grys*, and that the fyneste of a lond.   grey fur
And for to festne his hood under his chyn *195*
He hadde of gold ywroght* a ful curious*   made   very exquisite
    pyn;
A love knotte in the gretter* ende ther was.   larger
His heed was balled* that shoon as any glas,   bald
And eek* his face as it hadde been enoynt*.   also   anointed
He was a lord ful fat and in good poynt*;   condition
Hise eyen stepe* and rollynge in his heed,   protruding
That stemed* as a forneys* of a leed*;   *202*   shone   like a furnace be-
                                      neath a (lead) pot
His bootes souple, his hors in greet estaat*.   fine condition
Now certeinly, he was a fair prelaat;
He was nat pale as a forpyned goost*.   *205*   tormented ghost
A fat swan loved he best of any roost.
His palfrey* was as broun as is a berye.   saddle horse

A FRERE* ther was, a wantowne* and a   friar   playful
    merye,
A lymytour*,[12] a ful solempne* man.   *209*   limiter   pompous
In alle the ordres foure[13] is noon that kan*   knows

12 A "limiter" is someone, usually a mendicant friar, who has a licence to
    beg within certain prescribed limits.

13 The four orders (Franciscan, Dominican, Carmelite, and Augustinian)
    were originally founded in the thirteenth century to combat the tendency
    to worldliness within the earlier monastic orders and to give men a
    chance to lead a life of active service to mankind. The members em-
    braced poverty and devoted themselves to good works among the poor.
    The friars were eventually given licence to raise money by hearing con-
    fession and granting absolution, and thus they came into conflict with
    the parish priests whose duties they were now assuming. Chaucer makes
    it clear that in his day the orders of friars had once more become cor-
    rupted by worldliness.

So much of daliaunce* and fair langage; *flirtation
He hadde maad* ful many a mariage *arranged
Of yonge wommen at his owene cost.[14]
Unto his ordre he was a noble post*. *pillar
Ful wel biloved and famulier was he *215*
With frankeleyns* over al* in his contree*, *land-owners *everywhere *country
And eek* with worthy wommen of the toun, *also
For he hadde power of confessioun,
As seyde hym self, moore than a curat*, *parish priest
For of his ordre he was licenciat*. *220* *licensed
Ful swetely herde he confession,
And plesaunt was his absolucion.
He was an esy man to yeve* penaunce *give
Ther as* he wiste* to have a good pitaunce*; *where *knew *donation
For unto a poure ordre for to yive* *225* *give
Is signe that a man is wel yshryve*; *confessed
For if he yaf*, he dorste* make avaunt*, *gave *dared *boast
He wiste* that a man was repentaunt. *knew
For many a man so hard is of his herte
He may nat wepe, al thogh hym soore
    smerte*. *230* *suffers greatly
Therfore, in stede of wepynge and preyeres,
Men moote* yeve silver to the poure freres. *may
His typet* was ay* farsed* ful of knyves *cape *always *stuffed
And pynnes for yeven* yonge wyves. *give
And certeinly, he hadde a murye* note; *235* *merry
Wel koude* he synge and pleyen on a rote*; *knew how to *stringed in-
                                   strument
Of yeddynges* he baar outrely* the pris*. *ballads *completely *won *prize
His nekke whit was as the flour delys*. *fleur-de-lis
Therto* he strong was as a champion. *in addition
He knew the tavernes wel in al the toun, *240*
And every hostiler* and tappestere* *inn-keeper *bar-maid
Bet* than a lazar* or a beggestere*, *better *leper *female beggar
For unto swich* a worthy man as he *such
Acorded* nat, as by his facultee*, *244* *it was not proper *official
To have with sike* lazars aqueyntance – *sick *position

14 In other words, he provided dowries for the young girls he himself had
seduced and made pregnant.

It is nat honeste*, it may nat avance*   — fitting   benefit
For to deelen with no swich poraille*,   — poor people
But al with riche and selleres of vitaille*,   — food
And over al* ther as* profit sholde arise.   — everywhere   where
Curteis he was, and lowely of servyse*;   250   — humble in service
Ther was no man nowher so vertuous.
He was the beste beggere in his hous*,   — monastic house
For thogh a wydwe* hadde noght a sho*,   — widow   shoe
So plesaunt was his *In principio**15   254   — "In the beginning . . ."
Yet wolde he have a ferthyng er* he wente.   — before
His purchas* was wel* bettre than his rente*,   — takings   much   regular income
And rage* he koude as it were right a
    whelpe*.   — romp / just like a puppy
In lovedayes*16 ther koude he muchel*
    helpe,   — arbitration days   much
For ther he was nat lyk a cloystrer   259
With a thredbare cope*, as is a poure scoler,   — cloak
But he was lyk a maister* or a pope;   — Master of Arts
Of double worstede was his semycope*   — short cloak
That rounded as a belle* out of the presse*.   — (pleated) tunic   clothes-press
Somwhat he lipsed* for his wantownesse*   — lisped   playfulness
To make his Englissh sweete upon his tonge,
And in his harpyng, whan that he hadde
    songe,   266
His eyen twynkled in his heed aryght
As doon the sterres in the frosty nyght.
This worthy lymytour was cleped* Huberd.   — called

A MARCHANT was ther with a forked
    berd;   270
In motlee* and hye* on hors he sat;   — parti-coloured cloth   high
Upon his heed a Flaundryssh* bevere* hat,   — Flemish   beaver
His bootes clasped* faire and fetisly*.   — tied   neatly
Hise resons* he spak ful solempnely*,   — views   gravely

---

15 The first words of the Gospel of St. John were regarded with a peculiar, even superstitious, reverence in the Middle Ages.

16 On these special arbitration days legal disputes were settled out of court, and the clergy were active arbiters.

Sownynge* alway th'encrees* of his
    wynnyng*.   *275*   *proclaiming increase profit*
He wolde the see were kept for any thyng
Bitwixe Middelburgh and Orewelle.[17]
Wel koude he in eschaunge* sheeldes* selle.[18]   *exchange French crowns*
This worthy man ful wel his wit bisette*   *used his brains*
Ther wiste* no wight* that he was in dette,   *knew person*
So estatly* was he of his governaunce* *281*   *majestic demeanour*
With his bargaynes and with his chevy-
    saunce*.   *business deals*
For sothe, he was a worthy man withalle;
But sooth to seyn*, I noot* how men hym   *to tell the truth do not know*
    calle.

    A CLERK* ther was of Oxenford also, *285*   *scholar*
That unto logyk hadde longe ygo*.[19]   *turned long ago (to the study of)*
As leene was his hors as is a rake,
And he was nat right fat, I undertake*,   *guarantee*
But looked holwe* and therto sobrely*. *289*   *hollow gravely*
Ful thredbare was his overeste courtepy*,   *short outer cloak*
For he hadde geten hym yet no benefice*,   *church position*
Ne was so worldly for to have office,[20]
For hym was levere* have at his beddes heed   *he would rather*
Twenty bookes clad in blak or reed
Of Aristotle and his philosophie   *295*
Than robes riche, or fithele*, or gay sautrie*.   *fiddle small harp*
But al be that he was a philosophre,

17 Middelburg, Holland, and Orwell Harbour, England, were important ports in the wool trade.

18 The Merchant, in other words, exchanged currency on the black market to his own profit.

19 Logic, rhetoric, and grammar comprised the Trivium, while music, astronomy, arithmetic, and geometry made up the Quadrivium; in all, the Seven Liberal Arts. If the Oxford Scholar had taken to the study of logic "long ago", he must have been completing his M.A. degree when on the pilgrimage.

20 The Oxford Scholar did not take secular employment (usually of a legal nature), and hence he was able to devote himself fully to the pursuit of learning.

Yet hadde he but litel gold in cofre,[21]
But al that he myghte of his freendes hente*   receive
On bookes and on lernynge he it spente, *300*
And bisily gan for the soules preye
Of hem* that yaf* hym wher with to   them   gave
   scoleye*.   study
Of studie took he moost cure and moost
   heede;
Noght oo* word spak he moore than was   one
   neede,
And that was seyd in forme and reverence*,   with formality and respect
And short and quyk and ful of heigh
   sentence*;   *306*   great significance
Sownynge in* moral vertu was his speche,   tending toward
And gladly wolde he lerne and gladly teche.

A SERGEANT OF THE LAWE, war* and   cautious
   wys,
That often hadde been at the Parvys*,[22] *310*   porch of St. Paul's
Ther was also, ful riche of excellence.
Discreet he was and of greet reverence* –   reputation
He semed swich*, his wordes weren so wise. so
Justice he was ful often in assise
By patente and by pleyn commissioun.[23] *315*
For his science* and for his heigh* renoun*   knowledge good reputation
Of fees and robes hadde he many oon*.   a one
So greet a purchasour* was nowher noon;   buyer (of land)

21 Philosophy embraced both moral and physical science in the Middle
   Ages. Under the heading of natural philosophy came alchemy, whose
   aim was to discover the "Philosopher's Stone" which could convert base
   metals to gold. Chaucer's Scholar, it is clear, is not interested in this
   branch of "philosophy" and pursues learning for its own sake rather
   than for the material rewards it will bring him.

22 Lawyers frequently consulted their clients at the porch of St. Paul's (the
   "Parvys") in the afternoon when the law courts were closed.

23 The "patente" was an open letter of appointment from the king, and
   the "pleyn commissioun" gave the lawyer power to hear all kinds of
   cases when he acted as Justice of the Peace in the assizes or sessional
   courts.

Al was fee symple* to hym in effect;   freehold (as opposed to
His purchasyng myghte nat been infect*. 320 invalidated   leasehold)
Nowher so bisy a man as he ther nas* –   was not
And yet he semed bisier than he was.
In termes* hadde he caas* and doomes* alle accurately cases judgments
That from the tyme of Kyng William* were the Conqueror
    yfalle;   324
Therto he koude endite* and make a thyng* compose draw up an agree-
Ther koude no wight* pynchen* at his   person complain   ment
    writyng,
And every statut koude* he pleyn by roote*. knew by heart
He rood* but hoomly* in a medlee* coote rode plainly parti-coloured
Girt* with a ceint* of silk with barres smale; girdled belt
Of his array telle I no lenger tale.   330

A FRANKELEYN* was in his compaignye.   country land-owner
Whit was his berd as is the dayesye*;   daisy
Of his complexion he was sangwyn*.   ruddy
Wel loved he by the morwe* a sope* in wyn; in the morning piece of bread
To lyven in delit was evere his wone*,   335 custom
For he was Epicurus owene sone,
That heeld opinion that pleyn* delit   full
Was verray* felicitee parfit*.   true perfect
An housholdere, and that a greet, was he;
Seint Julian* was he in his contree.   340 patron saint of hospitality
His breed, his ale was alweys after oon*; of one (high) standard
A bettre envyned* man was nevere noon.   provided with wine
Withoute bake mete* was nevere his hous; baked food
Of fissh and flessh, and that so plentevous* plentiful
It snewed in his hous of mete and drynke, 345
Of alle deyntees* that men koude thynke delicacies
After the sondry* sesons of the yeer,   various
So chaunged he his mete and his soper*. diet
Ful many a fat partrich* hadde he in   partridge
    muwe*,   coop
And many a breem* and many a luce* in   bream (fish) pike
    stuwe*;   350 pond
Wo was his cook but if* his sauce were   unless
Poynaunt* and sharp, and redy al his geere*. pungent equipment

His table dormant in his halle alway
Stood redy covered al the longe day.[24]
At sessions* ther was he lord and sire;   355   sessions of the Justices of the Peace
Ful ofte tyme he was knyght of the shire*.   i.e., elected to Parliament
An anlaas* and a gipser* al of silk   dagger pouch
Heeng at his girdel, whit as morne mylk;
A shirreve* hadde he been and a contour*;   sheriff (shire) tax accountant
Was nowher swich* a worthy vavasour*.   360   such land-holder

An HABERDASSHERE and a CARPENTER,
A WEBBE*, a DYERE and a TAPYCER*,   weaver tapestry-maker
And they were clothed alle in o* lyveree*   one livery
Of a solempne and a greet fraternitee*.[25]   364   religious guild
Ful fressh and newe hir geere apiked* was;   arrayed
Hir knyves were chaped*, noght with bras,   mounted
But al with silver, wrought ful clene* and weel   elegantly
Hir girdles and hir pouches everydeel*.   altogether
Wel semed ech of hem* a fair burgeys*   them citizen
To sitten in a yeldehalle* on a deys*.   370   guild-hall dais
Everich* for the wisdom that he kan*   each knows
Was shaply* for to been an alderman,   suited
For catel* hadde they ynogh and rente*   property income
And eek* hir wyves wolde it wel assente,   also
And elles* certeyn were they to blame –   375   otherwise
It is ful fair to been ycleped* "Madame,"   called
And goon to vigilies al bifore*,   lead the procession on saints' eves
And have a mantel roialliche* ybore*.   royally borne

24 The dining table in the Middle Ages usually consisted of boards laid on trestles. It was generally dismantled at the end of the meal, but the Franklin's household makes use of the permanent table, an innovation which was being more widely used in Chaucer's day.

25 In addition to the trades guilds, there existed in the Middle Ages religious guilds which drew their membership from all the trades. The present-day service clubs with their varied membership, as opposed to craft unions, are a comparable modern counterpart.

A COOK they hadde with hem for the
  nones*,   379 occasion
To boille the chiknes* with the marybones*, chickens marrow-bones
And poudre marchant* tart and galyngale*. flavouring spice
Wel koude he knowe* a draughte of London judge
  ale.
He koude rooste and sethe* and broille and boil
  frye,
Maken mortreux* and wel bake a pye;   stew
But greet harm was it, as it thoughte me, 385
That on his shyne a mormal* hadde he.   running sore
For blankmanger*, that made he with the   creamed chicken with rice
  beste.

A SHIPMAN was ther wonynge* fer by   dwelling
  weste;
For aught I woot*, he was of Dertemouthe*. know Dartmouth (Devon)
He rood* upon a rouncy* as he kouthe*, 390 rode nag (best) could
In a gowne of faldyng* to the knee.   coarse cloth
A daggere hangynge on a laas* hadde he   lanyard
Aboute his nekke, under his arm adoun;
The hoote* somer hadde made his hewe al   hot
  broun.
And certeinly, he was a good felawe*; 395 good companion
Ful many a draughte of wyn hadde he
  ydrawe*   drawn
Fro Burdeuxward* while that the chapman* Bordeaux merchant
  sleepe*.   slept
Of nyce conscience* took he no keepe*.   foolish scruples paid no heed
If that he faught and had the hyer hond* 399 won
By water he sente hem* hoom to every lond*. them i.e., he threw his pris-
                                                  oners overboard
But of his craft* to rekene wel his tydes, skill
His stremes* and his daungers* hym bisydes*, currents shoals near him
His herberwe* and his moone, his   harbours
  lodemenage*,   pilotage
Ther nas* noon swich* from Hulle to   was not such
  Cartage*.   Cartagena (Spain)
Hardy he was and wys to undertake*; 405 conduct an enterprise

With many a tempest hadde his berd been
  shake.
He knew alle the havenes as they were
Fro Gootland* to the cape of Fynystere*,   Gotland (Sweden)   Finistere
And every cryke* in Britaigne* and in   (Spain)
  Spayne;   *409*   creek   Brittany
His barge* ycleped* was the Mawdelayne*.   ship   called   Magdalene

   With us ther was a DOCTOUR of PHISIK*,   medicine
In al this world ne was ther noon hym lik
To speke of phisik and of surgerye,
For he was grounded* in astronomye*.[26]   well versed   astrology
He kepte* his pacient a ful greet deel*   *415*   watched   very carefully
In houres* by his magyk natureel;   at (astrologically) critical
Wel koude* he fortunen the ascendent*   hours
Of hise ymages* for his pacient.   knew how   determine the
He knew the cause of everich* maladye, *419*   propitious moment
Were it of hoot or coold or moyste or drye,[27]   curative charms
And where they engendred and of what   every
  humour.
He was a verray*, parfit praktisour*.   true   practitioner

26 In medieval belief the stars and planets exerted an influence on human
   destiny. The physician treating a patient would thus have to know the
   patient's horoscope, and he would also have to be able to read the stars
   to discover what beneficent or maleficent influences were at work during
   the illness. In addition, the physician would have to know how to determine the astrologically propitious moment for making the curative
   charms or good-luck images that he gave the patient in the course of the
   treatment.

27 According to medieval theory, all things were created out of the four
   elements: earth, water, air, and fire. To each of these elements belonged
   certain properties: to earth, cold and dry; to water, cold and moist; to
   air, hot and dry; and to fire, hot and moist. The mixture of these qualities determined a person's temperament (known as "complexion" or
   "humour" in medieval terminology). Thus the melancholy temperament
   was preponderantly cold and dry; the phlegmatic, cold and moist; the
   choleric, hot and dry; and the sanguine, hot and moist. Disease was
   thought to be the result of an upset in the proper balance of these qualities in a person. The physician's task in treating the patient was to restore the balance of qualities proper to the patient's "complexion".

The cause yknowe* and of his harm* the roote, *known illness*

Anon* he yaf* the sike man his boote*; *immediately gave remedy*

Ful redy hadde he his apothecaries* *425* *pharmacists*

To sende hym drogges* and his letuaries*, *drugs remedies*

For ech of hem* made oother for to wynne*. *them gain*

Hir frendshipe nas nat* newe to bigynne. *was not*

Wel knew he the olde Esculapius*,[28] *Aesculapius*

And Deiscorides* and eek* Rufus, *430* *Dioscorides also*

Old Ypocras*, Haly and Galyen*, *Hippocrates Galen*

Serapion, Razis* and Avycen*, *Rhasis Avicenna*

Averrois*, Damascien* and Constantyn*, *Averroes Damascenus Constantinus*

Bernard and Gatesden* and Gilbertyn*. *Gaddesden Gilbert*

Of his diete mesurable* was he, *435* *moderate*

For it was of no superfluitee,

But of greet norissyng* and digestible*; *greatly nourishing easily digestible*

His studie was but litel on the Bible.

In sangwyn* and in pers* he clad was al, *red blue*

Lyned with taffata and with sendal*, *440* *silk*

And yet he was but esy* of dispence*. *cautious spending*

He kepte that he wan* in pestilence*, *gained time of plague*

For gold in phisik is a cordial* – *heart remedy*

Therfore he loved gold in special.[29]

28 The Physician was acquainted with all the most celebrated medical authorities. Aesculapius was the Greek god of medicine. Hippocrates, fifth and fourth centuries B.C., whose name and fame are preserved in the Hippocratic oath of medical practitioners, was regarded as the father of medicine. Dioscorides, first century A.D., and Rufus and Galen, both of the second century A.D., were also notable Greek medical practitioners. Haly, Serapion, Rhasis, Damascenus, Constantinus (the "cursed monk daun Constantyn" of line 598 of the Merchant's Tale), Avicenna, and Averroes were Arabic physicians who flourished between the ninth and twelfth centuries. Gaddesden, an Englishman, Bernard, and Gilbert were medical writers of the thirteenth and fourteenth centuries. Gaddesden served at the court of Edward III.

29 This ironical reference to the Physician's love of money is typically Chaucerian. Perhaps it is merely coincidental that Gaddesden (d. 1361), who is mentioned in line 434, had a reputation for thrift.

A good WIF* was ther OF BISIDE*   woman from near
 BATHE,   *445*
But she was som del* deef*, and that was somewhat deaf
 scathe*.   a pity
Of clooth makyng she hadde swich an haunt* such proficiency
She passed hem* of Ypres and of Gaunt*.[30] them Ghent
In al the parisshe wif ne was ther noon *449*
That to the offrynge bifore hire sholde goon,
And if ther dide, certeyn, so wrooth* was she angry
That she was out of alle charitee.
Hir coverchiefs* ful fyne were of ground*; head-dresses texture
I dorste* swere they weyeden* ten pound would dare weighed
That on a Sonday weren upon hir heed. *455*
Hir hosen weren of fyn scarlet reed,
Ful streit yteyd*, and shoes ful moyste* and tied tightly soft
 newe.
Boold was hir face and fair, and reed* of   ruddy
 hewe.
She was a worthy womman al hir lyve;
Housbondes at chirche dore[31] she hadde
 fyve –   *460*
Withouten* oother compaignye in youthe, besides
But therof nedeth nat to speke as nowthe*. at present
And thries* hadde she been at Jerusalem; thrice
She hadde passed many a straunge* strem. foreign
At Rome she hadde been and at Boloigne*,[32] Boulogne
In Galice* at Seint Jame and at Coloigne*; Galicia (Spain) Cologne
She koude* muchel* of wandrynge by the knew a great deal
 weye.   *467*
Gat-tothed* was she, soothly* for to seye. gap-toothed truly

---

30 Flemish cloth was regarded as superior to the English product. Doubt-
less the opinion expressed here is the Wife's own.

31 The marriage ceremony was usually performed at the church-porch, but
the nuptial mass would, of course, be celebrated at the altar.

32 The shrine of the Virgin at Boulogne, of Saint James of Compostella in
Galicia (Spain), and of the Three Kings at Cologne (Germany) were
favourite destinations for pilgrims.

Upon an amblere*³³ esily she sat,   pacer
Ywympled* wel, and on hir heed an hat *470* well hooded
As brood* as is a bokeler* or a targe*; broad buckler shield
A foot mantel* aboute hir hipes large, outer cloak
And on hire feet a paire of spores sharpe.
In felaweshipe* wel koude she laughe and company
 carpe*.   *474* joke
Of remedies of love* she knew par chaunce*, love charms by chance
For she koude* of that art the olde daunce. knew

 A good man was ther of religioun,
And was a poure PERSON* OF A TÓUN,   parson
But riche he was of holy thoght and werk.
He was also a lerned man, a clerk*, *480* scholar
That Cristes gospel trewely wolde preche;
His parisshens* devoutly wolde he teche. parishioners
Benygne* he was and wonder* diligent, kind wonderfully
And in adversitee ful pacient,   *484*
And swich* he was ypreved* ofte sithes*. such proven many times
Ful looth* were hym to cursen* for his reluctant excommunicate
 tithes,
But rather wolde he yeven* out of doute* give without doubt
Unto his poure parisshens aboute
Of his offrynge and eek* of his   also
 substaunce,   *489*
He koude* in litel thyng have suffisaunce. knew how to
Wyd was his parisshe and houses fer
 asonder*,   apart
But he ne lafte nat for reyn ne thonder
In siknesse ne in meschief* to visite misfortune
The ferreste* in his parisshe, muche and lite*, farthest great and small
Upon his feet, and in his hand a staf. *495*
This noble ensample* to his sheep he yaf*, example gave
That first he wroghte*, and afterward he worked
 taughte.
Out of the Gospel he tho* wordes caughte*, those took

33 The Wife rode a "pacer", a horse specially trained to lift both feet on
 the same side at the same time. The resultant ride was much smoother
 than that on an ordinary horse.

And this figure* he added eek therto,   parallel
That if gold ruste, what sholde iren do? *500*
For if a preest be foule on whom we truste,
No wonder is a lewed* man to ruste.   ignorant
And shame it is, if a preest take keep*,   will take heed
A shiten* shepherd and a clene sheep. *504* defiled
Wel oghte a preest ensample for to yive*   give
By his clennesse* how that his sheep sholde   purity
   lyve.
He sette* nat his benefice to hyre   let out
And leet* his sheep encombred in the myre   left
And ran to London unto Seint Poules*   St. Paul's
To seken* hym a chauntrie* for soules,[34] *510* seek chantry
Or with a bretherhed* to been withholde*, (religious) fraternity retained
But dwelte at hoom and kepte* wel his folde, watched
So that the wolf ne made it nat myscarie;
He was a shepherde and noght a mercenarie.
And thogh he hooly were and vertuous, *515*
He was noght to synful men despitous*,   contemptuous
Ne of his speche daungerous* ne digne*,   overbearing haughty
But in his techyng discreet and benygne*   kind
To drawen folk to hevene by fairnesse,
By good ensample, this was his bisynesse*.   endeavour
But it were any persone* obstinat, *521* if any person were
What so* he were of heigh or lowe estat,   whether
Hym wolde he snybben* sharply for the   rebuke
   nonys*.   for the occasion
A bettre preest I trowe* that nowher noon ys. believe
He waited after* no pompe and reverence,   looked for
Ne maked hym a spiced conscience*, *526* was not overly fastidious
But Cristes loore and his apostles twelve
He taughte, but first he folwed it hym selve.

With hym ther was a PLOWMAN was his
brother,

---

34 Rich men frequently left large sums to pay for the daily singing of
   mass for their souls. These chantries, as they were called, attracted
   priests who desired an easy life without responsibilities.

That hadde ylad* of donge* ful many a
    fother*.   *530*   driven manure cart-load

A trewe swynkere* and a good was he,   labourer
Lyvynge in pees and parfit charitee;
God loved he best with al his hoole herte
At alle tymes, thogh hym gamed or smerte*,   though it pleased him or pained him
And thanne his neighebore right as hym
    selve.   *535*
He wolde thresshe and therto dyke* and   make ditches
    delve*   dig
For Christes sake for every poure wight*,   person
Withouten hire, if it lay in his myght.
His tithes payde he ful faire and wel,
Bothe of his propre* swynk* and his catel*.   own labour goods
In a tabard* he rood upon a mere*.[35]   *541*   loose coat mare

Ther was also a REVE* and a MILLERE,   overseer (of an estate)
A SOMNOUR* and a PARDONER also,   summoner
A MAUNCIPLE* and my self; ther were   steward
    namo*.   no more

The MILLERE was a stout carl for the
    nones*;   *545*   exceedingly strong fellow
Ful big he was of brawn and eek* of bones,   also
That proved wel, for over al ther* he cam   everywhere
At wrastlynge, he wolde have alwey the ram*.   i.e., as prize
He was short sholdred*, brood, a thikke   with high shoulders
    knarre*;   muscular fellow
Ther was no dore that he nolde heve* of   heave
    harre*,   *550*   off its hinges
Or breke it at a rennyng* with his heed.   by running (at it)
His berd as any sowe or fox was reed,
And therto brood as though it were a spade.
Upon the cop right* of his nose he hade   right on the end
A werte*, and theron stood a toft of herys*   wart hairs
Reed as the brustles of a sowes erys*;   *556*   ears
His nosethirles* blake were and wyde.   nostrils

35 The mare was the least fashionable mount.

A swerd and a bokeler bar he by his syde.
His mouth as greet was as a greet forneys*;   furnace
He was a janglere* and a goliardeys*,   *560*   loud talker   jester
And that was moost of synne and harlotries*.   scurrilities
Wel koude* he stelen corn* and tollen   knew how   grain
   thries* –   charge thrice
And yet he hadde a thombe of gold,[36]
   pardee*!   certainly
A whit cote and a blew hood wered he;
A baggepipe wel koude he blowe and sowne*,   play
And ther with al* he broghte* us out of   with its music   led
   towne.   *566*

   A gentil MAUNCIPLE* was ther of a   steward
   temple,
Of which achatours* myghte take exemple   purchasers
For to be wise* in byynge* of vitaille*,   clever   buying   provisions
For wheither that he payde or took by taille*,   bought on credit
Algate* he wayted* so in his achaat*   *571*   always   looked out   purchas
That he was ay biforn* and in good staat.   ever ahead
Now is nat that of God a ful fair grace,
That swich* a lewed* mannes wit shal pace*   such   unlearned   (sur)pass
The wisdom of an heep of lerned men?   *575*
Of maistres* hadde he mo* than thries ten*   masters   more   thirty
That weren of lawe expert and curious*,   ingenious
Of which ther were a duszeyne* in that hous   dozen
Worthy to been stywardes of rente and lond
Of any lord that is in Engelond,   *580*
To make hym lyve by his propre good*   own property
In honour detteles*, but if he were wood*,   without debt   mad
Or lyve as scarsly* as hym list desire*,   frugally   as it pleased him to
And able for to helpen al a shire   *584*   wi
In any caas that myghte falle* or happe*;   befall   happen
And yet this Maunciple sette hir aller cappe*.   made fools of them all

36 An ironical reference to the proverb, "An honest miller has a thumb of gold."

The REVE* was a sclendre*, colerik* man;   *overseer thin irascible*

His berd was shave as ny* as ever he kan;   *close*

His heer was by his erys* ful round yshorn*;   *ears clipped*

His top was doked* lyk a preest byforn*;   *cut in front*

Ful longe were his legges and ful lene   *591*

Ylik* a staf; ther was no calf ysene*.   *like seen*

Wel koude* he kepe a gerner* and a bynne*;   *knew how to garner bin*

Ther was noon auditour koude on hym wynne.   *594*

Wel wiste* he by the droghte and by the reyn   *knew*

The yeldyng of his seed and of his greyn;

His lordes sheep, his neet*, his dayerye*,   *cattle dairy*

His swyn, his hors*, his stoor* and his pultrye   *horses stock*

Was hooly* in this reves governynge,   *wholly*

And by his covenant yaf* the rekenynge *600*   *gave*

Syn* that his lord was twenty yeer of age.   *since*

Ther koude no man brynge hym in arrerage*;   *prove him in arrears*

Ther nas* baillif*, ne hierde*, ne oother hyne*   *was not agent herdsman* / *labourer*

That he ne knew his sleighte and his covyne*.   *deceit*

They were adrad* of hym as of the deeth.   *afraid*

His wonyng* was ful fair upon an heeth; *606*   *dwelling*

With grene trees shadwed was his place.

He koude bettre than his lord purchace;

Ful riche he was astored pryvely*.   *furnished with stores secretly*

His lord wel koude he plesen* subtilly   *610*   *please*

To yeve* and lene* of his owene good*,   *give lend goods*

And have a thank and yet* a coote* and hood.   *also coat (i.e., in reward)*

In youthe he hadde lerned a good myster*;   *trade*

He was a wel* good wrighte*, a carpenter.   *very workman*

This Reve sat upon a ful good stot*   *615*   *horse*

That was al pomely* grey and highte* Scot;[37]   *dapple was called*

A long surcote* of pers* upon he hade,   *outer coat blue*

And by his syde he baar* a rusty blade.   *wore*

---

37 A common name for horses in this part of England.

Of Northfolk* was this Reve of which I telle, Norfolk
Biside a toun men clepen* Baldeswelle*. *620* call Bawdeswell
Tukked* he was as is a frere* aboute, girded about friar
And evere he rood* the hyndreste* of our rode hindmost
 route.

 A SOMNOUR*[38] was ther with us in that summoner
 place *623*
That hadde a fyr reed cherubynnes face,[39]
For saucefleem* he was with eyen narwe*; having a red, pimpled face
              close-set
As hoot* he was and lecherous as a sparwe, hot
With scaled* browes blake and piled* berd; scabby scanty
Of his visage children were aferd.
Ther nas* quyksilver, lytarge*, ne brymstoon, was not lead ointment
Boras*, ceruce*, ne oille of tartre* noon, *630* borax white lead cream of
              tartar
Ne oynement that wolde clense and byte,
That hym myghte helpen of his whelkes* sores
 white,
Nor of the knobbes sittynge on his chekes.
Wel loved he garleek, onyons and eek* also
 lekes*, leeks
And for to drynken strong wyn, reed as
 blood. *635*
Than wolde he speke and crie as he were
 wood*; mad
And whan that he wel dronken hadde the
 wyn,
Thanne wolde he speke no word but Latyn.
A fewe termes hadde he, two or thre,
That he hadde lerned out of som decre; *640*
No wonder is, he herde it al the day.
And eek ye knowen how that a jay

---

38 The Summoner's duty was to summon offenders to appear before the
 ecclesiastical court. Ecclesiastical courts enforced the payment of tithes
 and heard cases concerning adultery, fornication, and other vices which
 did not come under the common law.

39 In medieval wall paintings cherubs were generally painted red.

Kan clepen* "Watte*!" as wel as kan the pope.   call out   Walter!
But who so* koude* in oother thyng hym   whoever   knew how to
    grope*,   *644*   test
Thanne hadde he spent al his philosophie*.   learning
Ay* "*Questio quid juris?*"* wolde he crie.   always   "What says the law here?"
He was a gentil harlot* and a kynde;   fellow
A bettre felawe* sholde men noght fynde.   companion
He wolde suffre for a quart of wyn
A good felawe to have his concubyn   *650*
A twelf monthe, and excuse hym atte fulle*.   completely
Ful prively* a fynch eek koude he pulle*,   secretly   pull a clever trick
And if he foond* owher* a good felawe,   found   anywhere
He wolde techen hym to have noon awe*   no fear
In swich* caas of the ercedekenes curs*, *655*   such   archdeacon's excommunication
But if* a mannes soule were in his purs,   unless
For in his purs he sholde ypunysshed be.
"Purs is the ercedekenes helle," seyde he.
But wel I woot* he lyed right in dede;   know
Of cursyng oghte ech gilty man drede*, *660*   be afraid
For curs* wol slee*, right as assoillyng   excommunication   slay
    savith*;   absolution saves
And also* war* hym of a *significavit*.   therefore   beware   writ remanding to prison
In daunger* hadde he at his owene gise*   within his jurisdiction   as he pleased
The yonge girles* of the diocise,   young people
And knew hir conseil* and was al hir reed*.   their secrets   wholly their adviser
A gerland* hadde he set upon his heed   *666*   garland
As greet as it were for an ale stake*;   support for tavern sign
A bokeler hadde he maad hym of a cake.

With hym ther was a gentil PARDONER[40]

---

40 Pardoners sold indulgences or remissions for punishment. Originally the indulgence was the substitution of one kind of penance, usually a money payment, for a lengthy or arduous penance, such as a month on bread and water. In Chaucer's day, however, the indulgence was a recognized method of buying time off in purgatory for one's sins. Since the Pope alone had the authority to issue these indulgences or pardons, all pardoners would claim that they came straight from Rome. Needless to say, many pardoners in England in Chaucer's day were unlicensed and were in reality money-making frauds.

Of Rouncival,[41] his freend and his compeer*,   comrade
That streight was comen fro the court of
   Rome.   *671*
Ful loude he soong "Com hider*, love, to   hither
   me!"
This Somnour bar to hym a stif burdoun*;   sang the bass
Was nevere trompe* of half so greet a soun*.   trumpet   sound
This Pardoner hadde heer as yelow as wex,
But smothe it heeng as dooth a strike* of   hank
   flex.   *676*
By ounces* henge his lokkes that he hadde,   in thin clusters
And ther with he his shuldres overspradde,
But thynne it lay by colpons* oon and oon*;   strands   single
But hood for jollitee* wered he noon,   *680*   gaiety
For it was trussed* up in his walet*.   packed   travelling case
Hym thoughte* he rood al of the newe jet*;   it seemed to him   the latest style
Dischevelee*, save his cappe, he rood al bare.   hair hanging loose
Swich* glaryng eyen hadde he as an hare.   such
A vernycle*[42] hadde he sowed upon his   religious souvenir
   cappe,   *685*
His walet* biforn hym in his lappe,   travelling case
Bret ful* of pardon comen from Rome al   brim-full
   hoot.
A voys he hadde as smal as hath a goot*;   goat
No berd hadde he, ne nevere sholde have,
As smothe it was as it were late yshave.   *690*
I trowe* he were a geldyng or a mare.   believe
But of his craft*, fro Berwyk in to Ware*   trade   i.e., from one end of England to the other
Ne was ther swich another pardoner,
For in his male* he hadde a pilwe beer*   bag   pillow case
Which that he seyde was Oure Lady veyl.
He seyde he hadde a gobet* of the seyl   *696*   piece
That Seint Peter hadde whan that he wente

---

41 The religious establishment of St. Mary Rounceval in Charing, formerly
   a suburb but now a district of London.

42 The "vernycle" is a St. Veronica medal, an emblem signifying that the
   wearer had been to Rome. It is thus appropriate to support the Pardoner's claim that his pardons come "all hot" from Rome.

Upon the see til Jhesu Crist hym hente*.   caught hold of (Matt. 14:29)
He hadde a croys* of latoun* ful of stones,   cross   copper alloy
And in a glas he hadde pigges bones.   *700*
But with thise relikes whan that he fond
A poure person* dwellynge up on lond*,   parson   in the country
Upon a day he gat* hym moore moneye   got
Than that the person gat in monthes tweye.
And thus with feyned flaterye and japes* *705*   tricks
He made the person and the peple his apes*.   dupes
But trewely to tellen atte laste*,   in conclusion
He was in chirche a noble ecclesiaste*;   churchman
Wel koude* he rede a lesson or a storie,   knew how to
But alderbest* he song an offertorie*,   *710*   best of all   offertory
For wel he wiste* whan that song was songe,   knew
He moste* preche and wel affile his tonge*   had to   talk smoothly
To wynne silver, as he ful wel koude;
Therfore he song the murierly* and loude.   more merrily

Now have I toold yow soothly* in a   truly
   clause*   *715*   in short
Th'estaat*, th'array*, the nombre and eek*   station   mode of dress   also
   the cause
Why that assembled was this compaignye
In Southwerk at this gentil hostelrye
That highte* the Tabard faste* by the Belle.   was called   close
But now is tyme to yow for to telle   *720*
How that we baren* us that ilke* nyght   conducted   same
Whan we were in that hostelrie alyght,
And after wol I telle of oure viage*   journey
And al the remenaunt* of oure pilgrimage.   rest

But first, I pray yow of youre curteisye
That ye n'arette* it nat my vileynye*,   *726* not ascribe   to my low breed-
Thogh that I pleynly speke in this mateere,   ing
To telle yow hir wordes and hir cheere*,   behaviour
Ne thogh I speke hir wordes proprely*.   their very own words
For this ye knowen also* wel as I,   *730* as
Who so* shal telle a tale after a man,   whoever
He moot* reherce as ny* as evere he kan   must   close

Everich* a word, if it be in his charge,   every
Al* speke he nevere so rudeliche* and large*,   although   crudely   broadly
Or ellis he moot* telle his tale untrewe,   *735* must
Or feyne* thyng, or fynde wordes newe.   invent
He may nat spare al thogh he were his
   brother;
He moot* as wel seye o* word as* another.   must   one   as much as
Crist spak hym self ful brode in hooly writ,
And wel ye woot* no vileynye is it;   *740* know
Eek* Plato seith, who so kan hym rede,   also
The wordes mote* be cosyn* to the dede.   must   cousin
Also I pray yow to foryeve* it me   forgive
Al* have I nat set folk in hir degree*   *744* although   order of rank
Here in this tale as that they sholde stonde.
My wit is short, ye may wel understonde.

Greet chiere* made oure HOOST us   hospitality
   everichon*,   every one
And to the soper sette he us anon*;   forthwith
He served us with vitaille* at the beste;   food
Strong was the wyn and wel to drynke us
   leste*.   *750* it pleased us
A semely* man oure Hoost was withalle   fitting
For to been a marchal* in an halle.   marshal
A large man he was with eyen stepe*;   bright
A fairer burgeys* was ther noon in Chepe*.   better citizen   Cheapside, London
Boold of his speche and wys and wel ytaught,
And of manhode hym lakked right naught.
Eek* therto he was right a myrie* man,   *757* also   jovial
And after soper pleyen* he bigan,   jest
And spak of myrthe amonges othere thynges,
Whan that we hadde maad our rekenynges*,   paid our bills
And seyde thus: "Now lordynges*, trewely   gentlemen
Ye been to me right welcome hertely,   *762*
For by my trouthe, if that I shal nat lye,
I saugh* nat this yeer so myrie* a compaignye   saw   merry
At ones* in this herberwe* as is now.   *765* once   inn
Fayn* wolde I doon yow myrthe, wiste* I   gladly   knew
   how;

And of a myrthe* I am right now bythoght*   game   just thought of
To doon yow ese*, and it shal coste noght.   give you pleasure
Ye goon to Caunterbury, God yow spede*!   prosper
The blisful martir quite yow youre mede*!   grant you your reward
And wel I woot* as ye goon by the weye 771   know
Ye shapen* yow to talen* and to pleye*,   intend   tell stories   joke
For trewely, confort ne myrthe is noon
To ride by the weye doumb* as the stoon,   dumb
And therfore wol I maken yow disport*, 775   entertainment
As I seyde erst*, and doon yow som confort*,   at first   amuse you
And if yow liketh* alle by oon assent*,   it pleases you   common agree-
For to stonden at my juggement   ment
And for to werken* as I shal yow seye*,   do   tell you
To morwe whan ye riden by the weye,   780
Now by my fader* soule that is deed,   father's
But* ye be myrie, I wol yeve* yow myn heed;   unless   give
Hoold up youre hondes withouten moore
   speche!"

Oure conseil* was nat longe for to seche*;   decision   seek
Us thoughte* it was noght worth to make it   it seemed to us
   wys*,   785   deliberating about it
And graunted hym withouten moore avys*   consultation
And bad hym seye his voirdit* as hym leste*.   verdict   pleased him

"Lordynges," quod he, "now herkneth for
   the beste,   788
But taak it nought, I pray yow, in desdeyn*;   scorn
This is the poynt, to speken short and pleyn,
That ech of yow to shorte* with oure weye   shorten
In this viage* shal telle tales tweye*;   journey   two
To Caunterburyward I mene it so,
And homward he shal tellen othere two
Of aventures that whilom* have bifalle, 795   once
And which of yow that bereth* hym best of   conducts
   alle –
That is to seyn, that telleth in this caas
Tales of best sentence* and moost solaas* –   instruction   delight
Shal have a soper at oure aller cost*   the cost of all of us

Heere in this place, sittynge by this post, *800*
Whan that we come agayn fro Caunterbury.
And for to make yow the moore mury*,   merrier
I wol myself goodly with yow ryde
Right at myn owene cost and be youre gyde*,   guide
And who so* wole my juggement withseye*   whoever   resist
Shal paye al that we spende by the weye. *806*
And if ye vouche sauf* that it be so,   agree
Tel me anoon* withouten wordes mo,   at once
And I wol erly shape me* therfore."   prepare myself

    This thyng was graunted and oure othes
      swore   *810*
With ful glade herte, and preyden hym also
That he wolde vouche sauf for to do so,
And that he wolde been oure governour,
And of oure tales juge and reportour*,   critic
And sette a soper at a certeyn pris,   *815*
And we wol reuled been at his devys*   will
In heigh and lough*, and thus by oon* assent   high and low   one
We been acorded to* his juggement,   were agreed to
And therupon the wyn was fet* anon.   fetched
We dronken and to reste wente echon*   *820*   each one
Withouten any lenger taryynge.

    Amorwe*, whan that day gan for to   in the morning
      sprynge,
Up roos oure Hoost and was oure aller cok*   the cock for us all
And gadred* us togidre* in a flok,   gathered   together
And forth we riden* a litel moore than a   rode
      paas*   *825*   little faster than a foot pace
Unto the wateryng* of Seint Thomas.[43]   watering-place
And ther oure Hoost bigan his hors areste*,   stop
And seyde, "Lordynges! herkneth if yow
      leste*.   it pleases you

43 A watering-place for horses at the second milestone on the road to
    Canterbury.

Ye woot* youre forward*, and I it yow recorde*,   *know *agreement *recall

If even song and morwe* song accorde*, *830*   *morning *agree

Lat se now who shal telle the firste tale!

As evere mote* I drynke wyn or ale,   *may

Who so* be rebel to my juggement   *whoever

Shal paye for al that by the wey is spent. *834*

Now draweth cut* er that we ferrer twynne*;   *draw lots *depart further

He which that hath the shorteste shal bigynne.

Sire Knyght," quod he, "my mayster and my lord,

Now draweth cut, for that is myn accord*.   *opinion

Cometh neer," quod he, "my lady Prioresse,

And ye, sire Clerk; lat be youre shamefastnesse*,   *840   *modesty

Ne studieth noght; ley hond to, every man!"

Anon* to drawen every wight* bigan,   *at once *person

And shortly for to tellen as it was,

Were it by aventure* or sort* or cas*, *844*   *fate *destiny *chance

The sothe* is this, the cut fil* to the Knyght,   *truth *fell

Of which ful blithe and glad was every wyght,

And telle he moste* his tale as was reson   *had to

By forward* and by composicion*,   *agreement *contract

As ye han* herd. What nedeth wordes mo*?   *have *more

And whan this goode man saugh* that it was so,   *saw
                                                    850

As he that wys was and obedient

To kepe his forward by his free assent,

He seyde, "Syn* that I shal bigynne the game,   *since

What! welcome be the cut, a* Goddes name!   *in

Now lat us ryde and herkneth what I seye."

And with that word we ryden forth oure weye,   *856*

And he bigan with right a myrie cheere*   *merry mood

His tale anon, and seyde as ye may heere.

INTRODUCTION TO THE
WIFE OF BATH'S PROLOGUE AND TALE

The Wife of Bath's Prologue and Tale introduces a sequence of tales centring in the theme of marriage that long ago was identified, explored, and given the name the "Marriage Group" by the American scholar G. L. Kittredge.[1] This sequence is made up of the Wife's Prologue and Tale, the Clerk's Tale (not included in the present selection), the Merchant's Tale, and the Franklin's Tale. The central point in the dispute revolving around the theme of marriage concerns the question of which partner should dominate in the marriage relationship, husband or wife. The attitude of the Wife of Bath to this question need not be outlined here, since her Prologue and Tale are a long and eloquent testament to her position. The Clerk of Oxford, however, that quiet, modest, almost inconspicuous member of the Canterbury pilgrimage whose outward demeanour conceals a personality with strong convictions and a wry sense of humour, tells the story of Griselda, a patient woman who endures with incredible humility the fantastic trials her husband lays upon her obedience. And at the conclusion of his tale, in a final burst of superb irony and in an exceedingly complex verse form, the Oxford scholar puts paid to the strongly expressed feminist opinions of the forthright Wife of Bath. In turn, the Merchant, whose prosperous-looking exterior conceals far more than an accumulation of debts, discloses his own woe in marriage and while doing so displays in his tale an irony difficult to match elsewhere in literature for its savagery. The overt discussion of marriage seems to end with the Franklin's Tale, though certain passages in the Nun's Priest's Tale suggest that he too has followed the discussion on marriage with an attentive ear and feels compelled to add his own sly comments to the

---

1 See G. L. Kittredge, "Chaucer's Discussion of Marriage", *Modern Philology* IX (1913), 435-67.

subject. This kind of interaction among the pilgrims illustrates Chaucer's lively sense of the dramatic, his instinct to vivify his creations by bringing them into conflict with one another within the traditions and the conventions of the age in which he lived.

The Wife herself is a complex character who defies complete analysis and whose tale in some ways belies the personality revealed in both the General Prologue and the Prologue to her own tale. She is frankly sensual and aggressively feminist, or, as she herself puts it, "I am al Venerien/In feelying, and myn herte is Marcien",[2] and she led her five husbands a merry dance with her constant chiding and her real and feigned adulteries. But knowing what we do of the processes of medieval marriages – especially the marriages of women of some substance – in which young girls were often married off at puberty or before, we can have a certain amount of sympathy for this "gat-tothed" woman who loves good company, good travel, good living, and good lovers. For beneath the coarse exterior which expresses itself in flamboyant clothing and plain-speaking there flickers still an idealism and a yearning for a different kind of world. Or at least so her tale suggests.

No one doubts the intelligence of the Wife of Bath, and her conversation – if that is the right word for her long monologue that reveals all too much of her character – demonstrates that she would be a formidable adversary in debate. Like many women of strong character, she has a great fund of common sense, as well as a surprisingly large quantity of book-learning which she has picked up in the course of a varied and widely-travelled life. In fact, her recitation of her marital encounters indicates that she prefers intelligent men, men against whom she can match her wits. Her first three husbands were old and easily dominated, and though the revelation of the tactics used to subjugate them to her own will reveals a certain zest in her conquests, we sense that they never provided the kind of challenge that would occupy her full abilities. Her fourth husband, as she herself admits, was a different matter. Here the shoe was on the other foot; now she was the injured party in a marriage relation-

2 That is, she is influenced by the goddess of love, Venus, and the god of war, Mars.

ship that saw the husband casting abroad for his sexual pleasure. But the Wife was not without her own means of redress, and one does not like to contemplate too long the atmosphere of vicious hostility that must have existed in that household during his life-time. Fortunately he did not live too long, and his funeral provided the occasion for the Wife's choice of her fifth husband. Her fifth husband, a one-time Oxford scholar, twenty years old to the Wife's forty, proved to be an opponent whom it took all the Wife's skill to subdue. He is probably responsible for the literary allusions that frequently creep into her speech. But the story of Alison's victory over Jankin is one best told in her own words.

Some readers have complained that the long sermon on "gentillesse" near the end of the Wife's Tale is inappropriate and constitutes a blemish in the construction of the story as a whole. It is true that at first glance the Loathly Lady's strictures on what constitutes true gentility, to the knight who owes her his life but has unwillingly married her, seem unnecessarily long and serious in a story whose resolution turns on a neat trick of plot. These strictures seem out of place also in a story that is a notable *exemplum* illustrating the Wife's thesis that true happiness in marriage results only when the husband gives up his will to the domination of his wife. But the world of Chaucer's art, like the actual world in which Chaucer lived, possessed a vision of an underlying morality that determined the justice of events in this life. Without the sermon on "gentillesse", without the sinning knight's recognition of his sin, the tale told by the Wife of Bath would be a very immoral story. The knight who has committed rape passes through a year's suspenseful penance and in the end is rewarded with a beautiful wife who swears to be both true and beautiful. What Chaucer's art demands is some recognition on the part of this knight that he has learned something from his experience, some recognition of the fact that he has sinned. The sermon on the true nature of gentility constitutes this recognition which is so necessary to the morality of the tale. Without the sermon the tale would join the ranks of countless other smoking-room stories of epic good fortune. Far from being a blemish, the sermon on "gentillesse" is the very ingredient that gives moral significance to the tale.

A more penetrating criticism of this sermon is that which says it is perhaps not in keeping with the character of the Wife of Bath herself as we see that character revealed in the General Prologue and the Prologue to her tale. I use the word "perhaps" here deliberately. Surely the presence of this sermon in the Wife's tale suggests that the Wife herself subscribes to the sentiments expressed in it. If this is true, then we catch a glimpse of an idealism, an aspiration for something finer than what this world offers her, beneath the crude surface reality of the Wife of Bath. And who knows whether this loathly lady whom we call the Wife of Bath, had the proper circumstances been present, might not have turned out, like the woman in the tale, to be as faithful as she was beautiful?

The Wife of Bath's Prologue

"Experience, though noon auctoritee*   no authoritative book
Were in this world, is right ynogh for me
To speke of wo that is in mariage.
For lordynges, sith* I twelve yeer was of age,   since
Thonked be God that is eterne on lyve*,   5   everlasting
Housbondes at chirche dore¹ I have had
    fyve –
If I so ofte myghte have ywedded bee –
And alle were worthy men in hir* degree*.   their station
But me was toold, certeyn nat longe agoon is,
That sith that Crist ne wente nevere but onis*   once
To weddyng in the Cane* of Galilee*,   11   Cana John 2:1-2
That by the same ensample taughte he me
That I ne sholde wedded be but ones*.   once
Herke eek* which a sharp word for the   also
    nones*   for the occasion
Biside a welle Jhesus, God and Man,   15
Spak in repreeve* of the Samaritan*:   reproof John 4:6ff.
'Thou hast yhad* fyve housbondes,' quod he,   had
'And that man the which that hath now thee
Is nat thyn housbonde.' Thus seyde he,
    certeyn.
What that he mente therby I kan nat seyn;   20
But that I axe*, why that the fifthe man   ask
Was noon housbonde to thé Samaritan?
How many myghte she have in mariage?
Yet herde I nevere tellen in myn age
Upon this nombre diffinicioun.   25
Men may devyne* and glosen* up and doun,   speculate explain

1 See General Prologue, note 31, p. 40.

But wel I woot* expres* withouten lye   know   plainly
God bad us for to wexe* and multiplye;   increase
That gentil* text kan I wel understonde.   noble
Eek wel I woot, he seyde myn housbonde   *30*
Sholde lete* fader and mooder and take to   leave
  me,
But of no nombre mencioun made he,
Of bigamye* or of octogamye*.   second marriage   eighth
Why sholde men thanne speke of it vileynye*?   reproach
Lo, heere the wise kyng daun* Salomon*; *35*   sir   Solomon
I trowe* he hadde wyves mo* than oon*!   believe   more   one
As wolde* God it were leveful* unto me   would to   lawful
To be refreshed half so ofte as he,
Which yifte* of God hadde he for alle his   gift
  wyvys*;   wives
No man hath swich* that in this world alyve   such
  is.   *40*
God woot* this noble kyng, as to my wit*,   knows   understanding
The firste nyght had many a myrie fit*   experience
With ech of hem*, so wel was hym on lyve*!   them   his   life was so well off
Yblessed* be God that I have wedded fyve!   blessed
Welcome the sixte whan that evere he shal!
For sothe*, I wol nat kepe me chaast in al; *46*   in truth
Whan myn housbonde is fro the world ygon*,   gone
Som Cristen man shal wedde me anon*.   forthwith
For thanne th'apostle* seith that I am free   i.e., St. Paul (I Cor. 7:39)
To wedde a Goddes half* wher it liketh* me.   in God's name   pleases
He seith that to be wedded is no synne;   *51*
Bet* is to be wedded than to brynne*.   better   burn
What rekketh me* though folk seye vileynye   care I
Of shrewed* Lameth*[2] and his bigamye?   cursed   Lamech
I woot wel Abraham was an hooly man, *55*
And Jacob eek* as ferforth as I kan*,   also   as far as I know
And ech of hem hadde wyves mo than two,

2 Lamech is the first man mentioned in the Bible as having two wives (Gen.
  4:19). "Bigamye" in Middle English meant both having two mates simultaneously and marrying two mates in succession; Lamech is "cursed" because he had two wives at the same time.

And many another holy man also.
Wher kan ye seye, in any maner age,
That hye* God defended* mariage   60   high   prohibited
By expres* word? I pray yow, telleth me.   plain
Or where comanded he virginitee?
I woot as wel as ye, it is no drede*,   doubt
Th'apostle*, whan he speketh of   St. Paul (I Cor. 7:7)
     maydenhede*,   64   virginity
He seyde that precept therof he hadde noon.
Men may conseille* a womman to been oon*,   advise   single
But conseillyng is nat comandement;
He put it in oure owene juggement.
For hadde God comanded maydenhede,
Thanne hadde he dampned* weddyng with   condemned
     the dede,   70
And certein, if ther were no seed ysowe*,   sown
Virginitee, wherof thanne sholde it growe?
Poul* dorste nat comanden, atte leeste*,   St. Paul   at the very least
A thyng of which his maister yaf* noon   gave
     heeste*.   order
The dart is set up* for virginitee;   75   dart is offered as a prize
Cacche whoso may! Who renneth best, lat
     see!
But this word is nat taken of every wight*,   person
But ther as* God lust* gyve it of his myght.   where   wishes
I woot* wel that th'apostle was a mayde*,   know   virgin
But nathelees*, thogh that he wroot and sayde   nevertheless
He wolde that every wight were swich* as he,   such
Al nys but* conseil to virginitee.   82   is nothing but
And for to been a wyf he yaf* me leve   gave
Of indulgence; so it is no repreve*   shame
To wedde me* if that my make* dye,   85   marry   mate
Withouten excepcioun* of bigamye*.   objection   marrying twice
Al were it* good no womman for to touche,   although it were
He mente it as in his bed or in his couche,
For peril* is bothe fyr and tow* t'assemble*.   dangerous   pitch   bring to-
Ye knowe what this ensample may resemble;   gether
This is al and som, he heeld virginitee   91
Moore parfit* than weddyng in freletee* –   perfect   frailty (of the flesh)

Freletee clepe* I but if* that he and she   call   unless
Wolde leden* al hir lyf in chastitee.   lead
I graunte it wel, I have noon envie*,   *95*   ill-will
Thogh maydenhede* preferre* bigamye*;   virginity   be preferred to
                                                       marrying twice
It liketh hem* to be clene in body and goost*.   pleases them   spirit
Of myn estaat* ne wol I make no boost,   condition
For wel ye knowe a lord in his houshold
He nath nat* every vessel al of gold;   *100*   has not
Somme been of tree* and doon hir lord   wood
   servyse.

God clepeth* folk to hym in sondry wyse*,   calls   different ways
And everich* hath of God a propre yifte*,   everyone   individual gift
Som this, som that, as hym liketh shifte*.   it pleases him to assign
Virginitee is greet perfeccioun,   *105*
And continence eek* with devocioun,   also
But Crist, that of perfeccioun is welle,
Bad nat every wight he sholde go selle
Al that he hadde and yeve* it to the poore   give
And in swich wise* folwe hym and his foore*;   such manner   footsteps
He spak to hem that wolde lyve parfitly.   *111*
And lordynges*, by youre leve, that am nat I!   gentlemen
I wol bistowe* the flour of al myn age   bestow
In th'actes and in fruyt of mariage.
Telle me also to what conclusion*   *115*   end
Were membres maad of generacioun
And of* so parfit wys* a wright ywroght*?   by   perfectly wise   creator
                                                       created
Trusteth right wel, they were nat maad for
   noght.
Glose* whoso wole, and seye bothe up and   explain
   doun
That they were maad for purgacioun*   *120*   discharge
Of uryne, and oure bothe thynges smale
Was eek* to knowe a femele* from a male   also   female
And for noon oother cause; sey ye no?
Th'experience woot* wel it is noght so.   *124*   knows
So that the clerkes be nat with me wrothe*,   angry
I seye this, that they maked been for bothe;
That is to seye, for office* and for ese*   function   means
Of engendrure*, ther* we nat God displese.   procreation   wherein

Why sholde men ellis in hir* bookes sette *129*   their
That man shal yelde* to his wyf hire dette?   pay
Now, wherwith sholde he make his paiement
If he ne used* his sely* instrument?   did not use blessed
Thanne were they maad upon a creature
To purge uryne, and eek for engendrure. *134*
But I seye noght that every wight is holde*,   required
That hath swich* harneys* as I to yow tolde,   such equipment
To goon and usen hem in engendrure –
Thanne sholde men take of chastitee no
   cure*.   heed
Crist was a mayde* and shapen as a man,   virgin
And many a seint sith* that the world bigan,   since
Yet lyved they evere in parfit chastitee. *141*
I nyl* envye no virginitee;   will not
Lat hem be breed* of pured whete* seed,   bread refined wheat
And lat us wyves hoten* barly breed.   be called
And yet with barly breed, Mark* telle kan,   Mark 6:38ff.; also John 6:9
Oure Lord Jhesu refresshed many a man. *146*
In swich* estaat as God hath cleped* us   such called
I wol persevere; I n'am nat* precius*.   am not fastidious
In wyfhode I wol use myn instrument
As frely as my Makere hath it sent.   *150*
If I be daungerous*, God yeve* me sorwe!   aloof give
Myn housbonde shal it have bothe eve and
   morwe;
Whan that hym list*, com forth and paye his   it pleases him
   dette.
An housbonde wol I have, I nyl nat lette*,   hinder
Which shal be bothe my dettour and my
   thral*,   *155*   slave
And have his tribulacioun withal
Upon his flessh whil that I am his wyf.
I have the power durynge al my lyf
Upon his propre* body and noght he;   own
Right thus th'apostle tolde it unto me,   *160*
And bad oure housbondes for to love us
   weel*.   Ephesians 5:25

Al this sentence* me liketh* every deel*."   opinion please me entirely

    Up stirte* the Pardoner and that anon*;   started immediately

"Now dame," quod he, "by God and by Seint
    John,

Ye been* a noble prechour in this cas!   *165* are

I was aboute to wedde a wyf, allas!

What* sholde I bye* it on my flessh so   why buy
    deere*?   dearly

Yet hadde I levere* wedde no wyf to yeere*."   rather this year; i.e., never

    "Abyde!" quod she, "my tale is nat
    bigonne!   *169*

Nay, thou shalt drynken of another tonne*   cask

Er that I go, shal savoure* wors than ale,   taste

And whan that I have toold forth my tale

Of tribulacion in mariage,

Of which I am expert in al myn age*,   *174* life

This is to seyn, myself hath been the whippe,

Thanne maystow* chese* wheither thou wolt   may you choose
    sippe*   drink

Of thilke* tonne that I shal abroche*.   that same broach

Be war of it er thou to ny* approche,   too close

For I shal telle ensamples mo* than ten.   more

Whoso that nyl* be war by othere men,   *180* will not

By hym shul othere men corrected be.

The same wordes writeth Protholomee*;   Ptolemy

Rede in his Almageste[3] and take it there."

    "Dame, I wolde praye, if youre wyl it
    were,"

Seyde this Pardoner, "as ye bigan,   *185*

Telle forth youre tale. Spareth for no man,

And teche us yonge men of youre praktike*."   practice

---

3 Ptolemy (*fl.* A.D. 127-50) was a Graeco-Egyptian astronomer, mathematician, and geographer. His *Almagest* was widely influential in the Middle Ages, but the opinions attributed to that work by the Wife of Bath here and later in lines 326-7 are not found in it, though they probably represent later, unauthorized additions to Ptolemy's work.

"Gladly," quod she, "sith it may you like*. please
But that I praye to al this compaignye,
If that I speke after my fantasye*,   *190* i.e., as I please
As taketh nat agrief* of that I seye,   amiss
For myn entente* is but for to pleye.   intention
Now sire, now wol I telle forth my tale;
As evere moot* I drynke wyn or ale,   may
I shal seye sooth, tho* housbondes that I   those
    hadde,   *195*
As three of hem were goode and two were
    badde.
The thre men were goode and riche and olde;
Unnethe* myghte they the statut holde*   with difficulty   keep
In which that they were bounden unto me;
Ye woot* wel what I mene of this, pardee*! know   certainly
As help me God, I laughe whan I thynke *201*
How pitously a nyght I made hem swynke*,   labour
And by my fey*, I tolde of it no stoor*.   faith   took no account of it
They hadde me yeven* hir land and hir   given
    tresoor*.   wealth
Me neded nat do lenger* diligence   *205* longer
To wynne hir love or doon hem reverence.
They loved me so wel, by God above,
That I ne tolde no deyntee of* hir love.   set no store by
A wys womman wol bisye hire evere in oon*   always busy herself
To gete hire love, ye*, ther as* she hath   indeed   where
    noon.   *210*
But sith* I hadde hem hoolly* in myn hond, since   wholly
And sith they hadde me yeven all hir lond,
What sholde I taken heede hem for to plese,
But* it were for my profit and myn ese*?   unless   pleasure
I sette hem so awerke*, by my fey,   *215* to work
That many a nyght they songen* 'Weilawey*!' sang   alas
The bacon was nat fet* for hem, I trowe*,   fetched   trust
That som men han* in Essex at Dunmowe.⁴   have
I governed hem so wel after my lawe   *219*

4 A side of bacon (known as "the flitch of Dunmow") was offered annually to any couple proving conjugal harmony for a year and a day.

That ech of hem ful blisful was and fawe* glad
To brynge me gaye thynges fro the fayre*. fair
They were ful glad whan I spak to hem
 faire*, pleasantly
For God it woot*, I chidde* hem spitously*. knows scolded spitefully
Now herkneth hou I baar me* proprely, conducted myself
Ye wise wyves, that kan understonde. *225*
Thus sholde ye speke and bere hem wrong on
 honde*, accuse them falsely
For half so boldely kan ther no man
Swere and lyen as a womman kan.
I sey nat this by wyves that been wyse,
But if* it be whan they hem mysavyse*. *230* except make a mistake
A wys wyf, if that she kan* hir good, knows
Shal beren hym on hond* the cow⁵ is wood*, persuade chough is mad
And take witnesse of hir owene mayde
Of hir assent*; but herkneth how* I sayde: agreement listen to what

" 'Sire olde kaynard*, is this thyn array? dotard
Why is my neighebores wyf so gay? *236*
She is honoured over al ther* she gooth. wherever
I sitte at hoom; I have no thrifty clooth*. decent clothes
What dostow* at my neighebores hous? do you do
Is she so fair? Artow* so amorous? *240* are you
What rowne* ye with oure mayde? whisper
 Benedicite*! by heaven!
Sire olde lecchour, lat thy japes* be! games
And if I have a gossib* or a freend god-parent
Withouten gilt*, ye chiden* as a feend guiltlessly scold
If that I walke or pleye unto his hous. *245*
Thou comest hoom as dronken as a mous
And prechest on thy bench, with yvel preef*! bad luck to you!
Thou seist to me it is a greet meschief* misfortune

---

5 A reference to the folk-tale in which a jealous husband sets the bird
to watch over his wife's conduct. By a trick the guilty wife persuades
the husband that the bird has gone mad, and he wrings its neck. A story
similar to the one alluded to here is related by the Manciple later in the
Canterbury Tales.

To wedde a poure womman, for costage*; *because of expense*
And if that she be riche of heigh parage*, *lineage*
Thanne seistow* that it is a tormentrie *251* *you say*
To soffren hire pride and hir malencolie.
And if that she be fair, thou verray knave,
Thou seyst that every holour* wol hire have; *lecher*
She may no while in chastitee abyde* *255* *remain*
That is assailled upon ech a syde*. *every side*
Thou seyst som folk desiren us for richesse;
Somme for oure shap, somme for oure
 fairnesse,
And somme for she kan outher synge or
 daunce, *259*
And somme for gentillesse* and daliaunce*, *nobility coquetry*
Somme for hir handes and hir armes smale.
Thus goth al to the devel by thy tale*! *reckoning*
Thou seyst men may nat kepe a castel wal,
It may so longe assailled been over al*. *everywhere*
And if that she be foul* thou seist that she *ugly*
Coveiteth every man that she may se, *266*
For as a spaynel* she wol on hym lepe *spaniel*
Til that she fynde som man hir to chepe*; *win*
Ne noon so grey goos gooth ther in the lake
As, seistow*, wol be withoute make*. *270* *you say mate*
And seyst it is an hard thyng for to welde* *control*
A thyng that no man wol his thankes* helde*. *willingly hold*
Thus seistow, lorel*, whan thou goost to *wretch*
 bedde,
And that no wys man nedeth for to wedde,
Ne no man that entendeth* unto hevene. *275* *strives*
With wilde thonder dynt* and firy levene* *thunder-bolt fiery lightning*
Moot* thy welked* nekke be to-broke*! *may withered broken*
Thow seyst that droppyng* houses and eek* *falling also*
 smoke
And chidyng* wyves maken men to flee *279* *scolding*
Out of hir owene houses; a, benedicitee*! *by heaven*
What eyleth swich* an old man for to chide? *such*
Thou seyst that we wyves wol oure vices
 hide

Til we be fast*, and thanne we wol hem   securely wedded
   shewe*.   show
Wel may that be a proverbe of a shrewe*! *284*   scoundrel
Thou seist that oxen, asses, hors and houndes,
They been assayed* at diverse stoundes*;   tested   times
Bacynes*, lavours* er that men hem bye*;   basins   bowls   buy
Spoones, stooles and al swich housbondrye,
And so be pottes, clothes and array.
But folk of wyves maken noon assay*   *290*   test (of character)
Til they be wedded, olde dotard shrewe*!   foolish old scold
And thanne, seistow*, we wol oure vices   you say
   shewe.

Thou seist also that it displeseth me
But if that thou wolt preyse my beautee,
And but that thou poure* alwey upon my   gaze
   face,   *295*
And clepe* me faire dame in every place,   call
And but thou make a feeste on thilke* day   that
That I was born, and make me fressh and
   gay,
And but thou do to my norice* honour,   nurse
And to my chambrere* withinne my bour*,   chambermaid   bedroom
And to my fadres folk and his allyes*.   *301*   kinsmen
Thus seistow, olde barel ful of lyes!
And yet of oure apprentice Janekyn,
For his crispe heer*, shynynge as gold so fyn,   curly hair
And for he squiereth* me bothe up and   escorts
   doun,   *305*
Yet hastow* caught a fals suspecioun;   you have
I wol* hym nat, thogh thou were deed   want
   tomorwe!
But tel me this: why hidestow* with sorwe   do you hide
The keyes of thy cheste awey fro me?
It is my good* as wel as thyn, pardee*!   *310*   property   certainly
What! Wenestow* make an ydiot of oure   do you think to
   dame?
Now by that lord that called is Seint Jame,
Thou shalt nat bothe, thogh thou were wood*,   mad
Be maister of my body and of my good*!   property

That oon* thou shalt forgo, maugree* thyne   the one   in spite of
  eyen!   *315*
What helpeth it of me enquere* and spyen*?   ask after   spy on
I trowe* thou woldest loke* me in thy chiste.   believe   lock
Thou sholdest seye, "Wyf, go wher thee
  liste*.   please
Taak youre disport*. I nyl leve* no talys;   pleasure   will not believe
I knowe yow for a trewe wyf, dame Alys."

   " 'We love no man that taketh kepe or
    charge*   *321* is concerned about
Wher that we goon; we wol ben at oure
  large*.   free
Of alle men, yblessed* moot* he be,   blessed   may
The wise astrologien* daun Protholome*,   astrologer   Sir Ptolemy
That seith this proverbe in his Almageste:[6]
"Of alle men his wysdom is the hyeste*   *326* highest
That rekketh* nevere who hath the world on   cares
  honde*."   has great wealth
By this proverbe thou shalt understonde
Have thou ynogh. What thar thee* rekke or   why is it necessary for you
  care
How myrily* that othere folkes fare?   *330* merrily
For certeyn, olde dotard, by youre leve,
Ye shal han* queynte* right ynogh at eve.   have   i.e., love-making
He is to greet a nygard that wolde werne*   refuse
A man to lighte a candle at his lanterne; *334*
He shal have never the lasse* light, pardee!   less
Have thou ynogh; thee thar nat pleyne thee*.   it is not necessary for you to complain
Thou seyst also that if we make us gay
With clothyng and with precious array,
That it is peril of* oure chastitee.   a danger to
And yet with sorwe thou most enforce*   make an effort
  thee,   *340*
And seye thise wordes in th'apostles* name: I Timothy 2:9
"In habit* maad with chastitee and shame*   clothing   modesty
Ye wommen shul apparaille yow," quod he,

6 See note 3 on p. 63.

"And noght in tressed* heer and gay perree*,   (elaborately) dressed   jewel-
As perles, ne with gold, ne clothes riche."   lery
After thy text ne after thy rubriche*   346   rubric
I wol nat wirche* as muchel* as a gnat!   work   much
Thou seydest this, that I was lyk a cat;
But whoso wolde senge* a cattes skyn,   singe
Thanne wolde the cat wel dwellen in his in*. prefer to remain at home
And if the cattes skyn be slyk* and gay, 351 sleek
She wol nat dwelle in house half a day,
But forth she wole er any day be dawed*   dawned
To shewe hir skyn and goon a
   caterwawed* –   go caterwauling
This is to seye, if I be gay, sir shrewe, 355
I wol renne out, my borel* for to shewe.   clothes
Sire olde fool, what helpeth thee t'espyen*? spy
Thogh thou preye Argus with his hundred
   eyen
To be my wardecors* as he kan best,   body-guard
In feith, he shal nat kepe me but me lest*. unless it please me
Yet koude I make his berd*, so moot* I 361 delude him may
   thee*!   prosper
Thou seydest eek* that ther been thynges also
   three,[7]
The whiche thynges troublen al this erthe,
And that no wight may endure the ferthe*. fourth
O leve* sire shrewe*! Jhesu shorte thy lyf! dear scold
Yet prechestow* and seyst an hateful wyf you preach
Yrekened* is for oon* of thise
   meschaunces*.   367 considered one / misfortunes
Been ther none othere resemblaunces
That ye may likne* youre parables to, liken
But if a sely* wyf be oon of tho*? 370 hapless one of them
Thou liknest eek wommenes love to helle,
To bareyne* lond ther* water may nat barren where
   dwelle.

7 A reference to Proverbs 30: 21-3. The three things are a slave who is
king, a fool well fed, and a maid who succeeds her mistress. The fourth,
referred to in line 364, is "an odious woman who is married".

Thou liknest it also to wilde fyr –
The moore it brenneth*, the moore it hath   burns
   desyr   *374*
To consume every thyng that brent* wole be.   burned
Thou seyst, right as wormes shende* a tree,   destroy
Right so a wyf destroyeth hire housbonde.
This knowe they that been to wyves bonde*.'   bound

  "Lordynges, right thus as ye have
understonde
Baar I stifly myne olde housbondes on
   honde*   *380*   I boldly asserted to my old
That thus they seyden in hir dronkenesse.   husbands
And al was fals, but that I took witnesse
On Janekyn and on my nece also.
O Lord! The peyne I dide hem and the wo!
Ful giltlees, by Goddes swete pyne*!   *385*   suffering
For as an hors I koude byte and whyne.
I koude pleyne*, and I was in the gilt,   complain
Or elles often tyme hadde I been spilt*.   destroyed
Who so that first to mille comth, first grynt*; grinds
I pleyned first, so was oure werre* stynt*.   war checked
They were ful glade to excuse hem blyve*   promptly
Of thyng of which they nevere agilte* hir   were guilty
   lyve*.   *392*   in their lives
Of wenches wolde I beren hem on honde*   accuse
Whan that for syk* they myghte unnethe*   illness hardly
   stonde;
Yet tikled I his herte for that he   *395*
Wende* that I hadde of hym so greet   thought
   chiertee*.   fondness
I swoor that al my walkynge out by nyghte
Was for t'espye wenches that he dighte*. *398* had intercourse with
Under that colour hadde I many a myrthe,
For al swich* wit is yeven* us in oure byrthe. such given
Deceite, wepyng, spynnyng God hath yeve
To wommen kyndely* whil that they may   naturally
   lyve,
And thus of o* thyng I avaunte me*:   *403*   one boast

Atte ende* I hadde the bet* in ech degree, at the end better
By sleight or force or by som maner thyng,
As by continueel murmure or grucchyng*. complaining
Namely, abedde hadden they meschaunce*; misfortune
Ther wolde I chide* and do hem no   scold
 pleasaunce.
I wolde no lenger* in the bedde abyde   longer
If that I felte his arm over my syde 410
Til he had maad his raunson unto me.
Thanne wolde I suffre hym do his nycetee*. foolishness
And therfore, every man this tale I telle:
Wynne who so may, for al is for to selle;
With empty hand men may none haukes* hawks
 lure.   415
For wynnyng wolde I al his lust endure
And make me a feyned appetit,
And yet in bacon* hadde I nevere delit. i.e., old meat; therefore, old
That made me that evere I wolde hem chide,   men
For thogh the pope had seten hem biside,
I wolde noght spare hem at hir owene bord*. table
For by my trouthe, I quitte hem word for
 word,   422
As help me verray God omnipotent.
Though I right now sholde make my
 testament*,   will
I ne owe hem nat a word that it nys* quit. is not
I broghte it so aboute by my wit 426
That they moste* yeve* it up as for the beste, had to give
Or elles hadde we nevere been in reste.
For thogh he looked as a wood leoun* mad lion
Yet sholde he faille of his conclusioun. 430
Thanne wolde I seye, 'Goode lief*, taak darling
 keep*   notice
How mekely looketh Wylkin oure sheep.
Com neer, my spouse, let me ba* thy cheke. kiss
Ye sholde been al pacient and meke,
And han* a swete, spiced conscience*, 435 have nice disposition
Sith* ye so preche of Jobes pacience. since
Suffreth alwey, syn ye so wel kan preche,

And but* ye do, certein, we shal yow teche   unless
That it is fair to have a wyf in pees.
Oon* of us two moste bowen*, doutelees,   one yield
And sith a man is moore resonable   *441*
Than womman is, ye moste been suffrable.
What eyleth yow to grucche* thus and   complain
  grone?
Is it for ye wolde have my queynte* allone?   sexual organ
Wy, taak it al! Lo, have it every deel*!   *445*   entirely
Peter, I shrewe* yow but ye love it weel.   curse
For if I wolde selle my *bele chose**,   sexual organ
I koude walke as fressh as is a rose;   *448*
But I wol kepe it for youre owene tooth;
Ye be to blame, by God; I seye yow sooth*.'   truth
Swiche manere wordes hadde we on honde.
Now wol I speke of my fourthe housbonde.

    "My fourthe housbonde was a revelour;
This is to seyn, he hadde a paramour*,   mistress
And I was yong and ful of ragerye*,   *455*   passion
Stibourne* and strong and joly as a pye*.   stubborn magpie
How koude I daunce to an harpe smale
And synge, ywis*, as any nyghtyngale   certainly
Whan I hadde dronke a draughte of swete
  wyn!
Metellius,[8] the foule cherl, the swyn,   *460*
That with a staf birafte* his wyf hir lyf   deprived
For she drank wyn, though I hadde been his
  wyf,
He sholde nat han daunted* me fro drynke.   intimidated
And after wyn, on Venus moste I thynke,
For al so siker* as coold engendreth hayl,   just as sure as
A likerous* mouth moste han a likerous*   gluttonous lecherous
  tayl.   *466*
In womman vinolent* is no defence;   addicted to wine
This knowen lecchours by experience.

8 The story is taken from Valerius Maximus, a Latin author of a book of
  historical anecdotes. Further use of this source is made in lines 643-9, and
  he is referred to in the Wife's Tale, line 309.

But Lord Crist, whan that it remembreth me
Upon my yowthe and on my jolytee*,   470   merriment
It tikleth me about myn herte roote!
Unto this day it dooth myn herte boote*   good
That I have had my world as in my tyme!
But age, allas, that al wole envenyme*,   poison
Hath me biraft* my beautee and my pith*.   deprived   vigour
Lat go, fare wel, the devel go therwith!   476
The flour is goon; ther is namoore to telle;
The bren* as I best kan now moste I selle.   bran
But yet to be right myrie* wol I fonde*.   merry   try
Now wol I telle of my fourthe housbonde.
I seye I hadde in herte greet despit   481
That he of any oother had delit.
But he was quit, by God and by Seint Joce*!   a Breton saint
I made hym of the same wode a croce*.   stick; i.e., I made him jealous
Nat of my body in no foul manere,   485   too
But certeinly, I made folk swich cheere*   entertained people in such a
That in his owene grece I made hym frye   way
For angre and for verray jalousye.
By God, in erthe I was his purgatorie,
For which I hope his soule be in glorie.   490
For God it woot*, he sat ful ofte and song   knows
Whan that his shoo ful bitterly hym wrong*.   pinched
Ther was no wight save God and he that
    wiste*   knew
In many wise* how soore I hym twiste*.   many ways   tortured
He deyde whan I cam fro Jerusalem   495
And lith ygrave* under the roode beem*.   lies buried   beam bearing a
Al* is his tombe noght so curyous*   although   costly   crucifix
As was the sepulcre of hym, Daryus*,   Darius, Persian emperor
Which that Appelles⁹ wroghte subtilly.   499   (d. 330 B.C.)
It nys* but wast* to burye hym preciously*.   is not   waste   expensively
Lat hym fare wel; God gyve his soule reste!
He is now in his grave and in his cheste*.   coffin

9 In the once popular *Alexandreis* of Gautier de Chatillon (*c.* 1135-1201),
  a Latin poem on the exploits of Alexander the Great, a wholly fictitious
  Jewish architect named Apelles is introduced as the designer of the elaborate tombs of both the wife of Darius and Darius himself.

"Now of my fifthe housebonde wol I telle.
God lat his soule nevere come in helle!
And yet he was to me the moste shrewe*;   ill-tempered man
That feele I on my ribbes al by rewe*,   *506* one after another
And evere shal unto myn endyng day.
But in oure bed he was so fressh and gay
And therwithal so wel koude he me glose*   coax
Whan that he wolde han my *bele chose*,   sexual organ
That thogh he hadde me bet* on every bon,   beaten
He koude wynne agayn my love anon*.   *512* straightway
I trowe* I loved hym best for that he   believe
Was of his love daungerous* to me.   chary
We womman han, if that I shal nat lye,   *515*
In this matere a queynte* fantasye: artful
Wayte what* thyng we may nat lightly have,   whatever
Ther after wol we crie al day and crave.
Forbede us thyng and that desiren we;   *519*
Presse on us faste and thanne wol we fle.
With daunger* oute we al oure chaffare*.   reluctantly   we set out all
                                                            our wares
Greet prees* at market maketh deere ware*,   crowd   expensive goods
And to greet cheep* is holde at litel prys;   too much abundance
This knoweth every womman that is wys.   *524*
My fifthe housbonde, God his soule blesse,
Which that I took for love and no richesse,
He som tyme was a clerk of Oxenford
And hadde left scole and wente at hom to
    bord   *528*
With my gossib*, dwellynge in oure toun.   close friend
God have hir soule, hir name was Alisoun.
She knewe myn herte and eek* my privetee*   also   private affairs
Bet* than oure parissh preest, as mot I   better
    thee*.   *532* so may I prosper
To hire biwreyed* I my conseil al,   reveal
For hadde myn housbonde pissed on a wal
Or doon a thyng that sholde han cost his lyf,
To hire, and to another worthy wyf,   *536*
And to my nece which that I loved weel,
I wolde han toold his conseil every deel*,   every bit
And so I dide ful often, God it woot*.   knows

That made his face often reed and hoot *540*
For verray shame, and blamed hym self for
    he
Hadde toold to me so greet a pryvetee*.   secret
And so bifel that ones* in a Lente,   once
So often tymes I to my gossyb* wente,   close friend
For evere yet I loved to be gay *545*
And for to walke in March, Averill and May
From hous to hous to heere* sondry tales,   hear
That Jankyn clerk and my gossyb, dame Alys,
And I myself into the feeldes wente –
Myn housbonde was at Londoun al that
    Lente – *550*
I hadde the bettre leyser* for to pleye,   leisure
And for to se and eek* for to be seye*   also seen
Of lusty* folk. What wiste* I wher my grace   pleasure-loving knew
Was shapen* for to be or in what place?   destined
Therfore I made my visitacions *555*
To vigilies* and to processions,   celebrations on saints' eves
To prechyng eek and to thise pilgrimages,
To pleyes of myracles* and to mariages,   dramatized Biblical stories
And wered upon my gaye scarlet gytes*.   dresses
Thise wormes, ne thise motthes, ne thise
    mytes* *560*   insects
Upon my peril frete* hem nevere a deel*.   ate not at all
And wostow* why? For they were used   do you know
    weel!

    "Now wol I tellen forth what happed me.
I seye that in the feeldes walked we
Til trewely we hadde swich* daliaunce*, *565*   such flirtation
This clerk* and I, that of my purveiaunce*   scholar foresight
I spak to hym and seyde hym how that he,
If I were wydwe*, sholde wedde me.   widow
For certeinly, I seye for no bobaunce*   boast
Yet was I nevere withouten purveiaunce *570*
Of mariage, n'of* othere thynges eek.   nor of
I holde a mouses herte nat worth a leek*   not worth anything

That hath but oon* hole for to sterte* to,   one   run
And if that faille, thanne is al ydo*.   finished
I bar hym on honde* he hadde enchanted   accused him
   me –   575
My dame taughte me that soutiltee* –   trick
And eek I seyde I mette* of hym al nyght;   dreamed
He wolde han* slayn me as I lay upright   have
And al my bed was ful of verray blood;
But yet I hope that he shal do me good,   580
For blood bitokeneth gold, as me was taught.
And al was fals; I dremed of it
   right naught*,   not at all
But as I folwed ay my dames loore*   instruction
As wel of this as of othere thynges moore.

   "But now, sire; lat me se. What shal I
   seyn?   585
A, ha! by God, I have my tale ageyn!
Whan that my fourthe housbonde was on
   beere*,   in his bier
I weep algate* and made sory cheere*   continually   sorrowful looks
As wyves mooten*, for it is usage*,   589 must   custom
And with my coverchief covered my visage.
But for that I was purveyed of* a make*   provided with   mate
I wepte but smal, and that I undertake*.   guarantee
To chirche was myn housbonde born
   amorwe*   in the morning
With neighebores that for hym maden
   sorwe,   594
And Jankyn oure clerk was oon* of tho*.   one   them
As help me God, whan that I saw hym go
After the beere, me thoughte he hadde a
   paire
Of legges and of feet so clene and faire
That al myn herte I yaf* unto his hoold*.   gave   keeping
He was, I trowe*, a twenty wynter oold,   600 believe
And I was fourty if I shal seye sooth*;   truth
But yet I hadde alwey a coltes tooth*.   always had youthful desires

Gat-tothed*10 I was, and that bicam me weel; teeth wide apart
I hadde the preynte of seynt Venus seel*. imprint of St. Venus's seal;
    i.e., birthmark
As help me God, I was a lusty oon, 605
And fair and riche and yong and wel bigon*, lucky
And trewely, as myn housbondes tolde me,
I had the beste *quonyam* myghte be. sexual organ
For certes, I am al Venerien*11 influenced by Venus
In feelyng, and myn herte is Marcien*. 610 influenced by Mars
Venus me yaf my lust*, my likerousnesse*, passion lecherousness
And Mars yaf me my sturdy hardynesse.
Myn ascendent was Taur and Mars therinne.
Allas, allas, that evere love was synne!
I folwed ay myn inclinacioun 615
By vertu of my constellacioun*, conjunction of stars at birth
That made me I koude noght withdrawe
My chambre of Venus from a good felawe.
Yet have I Martes* mark upon my face, Mars'
And also in another pryvee* place. 620 secret
For God so wyse be my savacioun*, salvation
I ne loved nevere by no discrecioun,
But evere folwed myn appetit,
Al were he* short or long or blak or whit; whether he were
I took no kepe*, so that he liked me*, 625 paid no heed pleased me
How poure he was, ne eek of what degree.
What sholde I seye but at the monthes ende
This joly clerk Jankyn that was so hende* pleasant
Hath wedded me with greet solempnytee,
And to hym yaf* I al the lond and fee* 630 gave property
That evere was me yeven* ther-bifoore, given
But afterward repented me ful soore.
He nolde* suffre nothyng of my list*; would not pleasure

10 Different associations are connected with widely spaced teeth. It may
    mean that the person will be lucky and travel, or it may be a sign of a
    bold, lascivious nature. Both sets of associations fit the Wife of Bath.

11 The astrological references here explain the Wife's propensity for love
    and also her militancy. At the time of her birth Taurus (line 613), one
    of the mansions or houses of Venus, was in the ascendant with Mars in
    it; thus both Venus and Mars together influenced her character.

By God, he smoot me ones* on the lyst*   once   ear
For that I rente* out of his book a leef   635   tore
That of the strook myn ere wax* al deef.   grew
Stibourne* I was as is a leonesse*,   stubborn   lioness
And of my tonge a verray jangleresse*,   chatterbox
And walke I wolde as I hadde doon biforn
From hous to hous, although he hadde it
    sworn*,   640   i.e., forbidden
For which he wolde often tymes preche,
And me of olde Romayn geestes* teche: stories
How he Symplicius Gallus¹² lefte his wyf
And hire forsook for terme of al his lyf,
Noght but for open-heveded* he hir say*   bare-headed   saw
Lokynge out at his dore upon a day!   646
Another Romayn tolde he me by name,
That for* his wyf was at a someres game*   because   mid-summer's day
Withouten his wityng*, he forsook hire eke*;   knowledge   also   festival
And thanne wolde he upon his Bible seke
That ilke* proverbe of Ecclesiaste,¹³   651   same
Where he comandeth and forbedeth faste
Man shal nat suffre his wyf go roule aboute*.   roaming about
Thanne wolde he seye right thus withouten
    doute,   654
'Who so that buyldeth his hous al of salwes*   willow-twigs
And priketh* his blynde hors over the falwes*   gallops   fallow ground
And suffreth his wyf to go seken halwes*   shrines; i.e., go on pilgrimages
Is worthy to been hanged on the galwes*.'   gallows
But al for noght; I sette noght an hawe*   put no store
Of* his proberbes, n'of his olde sawe,   660   in
Ne I wolde nat of hym corrected be.
I hate hym that my vices telleth me,
And so doo mo*, God woot*, of us than I.   more   knows
This made hym with me wood al outrely*;   completely enraged
I nolde* noght forbere* hym in no cas*.   665   would not   put up with   at all

12 This story is from Valerius Maximus; see note 8, p. 72. "Another Romayn" of line 647 is Sempronius Sophus, who is mentioned in the same
   chapter by Valerius.
13 The Book of Ecclesiasticus of the Apocrypha is intended, 25:25.

"Now wol I seye yow sooth, by Seint
   Thomas,
Why that I rente* out of his book a leef,   tore
For which he smoot* me so that I was deef.   struck
He hadde a book that gladly nyght and day
For his disport* he wolde rede alway.   670   pleasure
He cleped it Valerie and Theofraste,[14]
At which book he lough* alwey ful faste.   laughed
And eek* ther was som tyme a clerk* at   also   scholar
   Rome,
A cardinal, that highte Seint Jerome,
That made a book agayn Jovinian,   675
In which book ther was eek Tertulan,
Crisippus*, Trotula and Helowys*,   Chrysippus   Héloïse
That was abbesse nat fer fro Parys,
And eek the Parables of Salomon*,   Solomon
Ovydes *Art* and bookes many on*,   680 Ovid's *Art of Love*   many a   one
And alle of thise were bounden in o* volume.   one
And every nyght and day was his custume,
Whan he hadde leyser* and vacacion   leisure
From oother worldly occupacion,
To reden on this book of wikked wyves.   685
He knew of hem mo legendes and lyves
Than been of goode wyves in the Bible.
For trusteth wel, it is an impossible*   impossibility
That any clerk* wol speke good of wyves,   scholar
But if it be of holy seintes lyves,   690
N'of noon oother womman never the mo*.   more

14 Jankin's book contained the most celebrated anti-feminist literature of
the Middle Ages. "Valerie" (line 671) is "Valerius' Letter to Rufinus on
the Subject of Not Marrying" by Walter Map (twelfth century); "Theofraste" is "The Golden Book on Marriage" by Theophrastus (third
century B.C.), an author known to the Middle Ages in later translations.
St. Jerome (line 674, fifth century A.D.) wrote a "Letter against Jovinian" which contained anti-feminist passages. Tertullian (line 676, third
century A.D.), a church father, wrote works on chastity, monogamy, and
sexual modesty. Héloïse (line 677, twelfth century) is the celebrated
mistress of Abélard. Nothing certain is known of Chrysippus and Trotula (line 677). The Latin poet Ovid's *Art of Love* and the Book of
Proverbs were also represented in Jankin's "book of wikked wives".

Who peynted the leoun*?[15] Telle me who! lion
By God, if wommen hadde writen stories
As clerkes han* withinne hir oratories*, have chapels
They wolde han writen of men moore
    wikkednesse   *695*
Than all the mark of Adam* may redresse. all males
The children* of Mercurie and Venus[16] i.e., born under
Been in hir wirkyng* ful contrarius*. working completely different
Mercurie loveth wysdam and science*, knowledge
And Venus loveth ryot* and dispence*,   *700* riotous living extravagance
And for hir diverse disposicion*, different influence as result of
  different position in horoscope
Ech falleth in otheres exaltacion.[17]
And thus, God woot*, Mercurie is desolat* knows destitute
In Pisces* wher Venus is exaltat*,   *704* the (astrological) sign of the
  Fish exalted
And Venus falleth ther* Mercurie is reysed. where
Therfore no womman of no clerk is preysed.
The clerk, wham he is oold and may noght do
Of Venus werkes worth his olde sho,
Thanne sit he doun and writ in his dotage* senility
That wommen kan nat kepe hir mariage.   *710*

    "But now to purpos why I tolde thee
That I was beten for a book, pardee!
Upon a nyght, Jankyn, that was oure sire,
Redde on his book as he sat by the fire,
Of Eva first that for hir wikkednesse   *715*
Was al mankynde broght to wrecchednesse,

15 A reference to Aesop's fable in which a man shows a lion a painting of
    a lion being killed by a man. The lion asks, "Who painted the lion?",
    the question implying that a painting by a lion would reverse the situ-
    ation.
16 In astrology Mercury signifies science and philosophy, Venus happiness
    and physical pleasure.
17 According to astrological belief, when one planet is "exalted" (i.e., in
    the astrological sign in which its influence is greatest), another planet of
    contrary nature is at its point of least influence. Thus when Venus is in
    Pisces (line 704), it is at its most influential point, and its contrary
    Mercury is depressed. When Mercury is exalted, Venus is depressed (line
    705).

For which that Jhesu Crist hymself was slayn,
That boghte us with his herte blood agayn.
Lo, heere expres* of womman may ye fynde   explicitly
That womman was the los* of al mankynde!   ruin
Tho* redde he me how Sampson loste his   then
    heres* –   *721*   hair
Slepynge, his lemman* kitte* it with hir   sweetheart   cut
    sheres –
Thurgh which treson loste he bothe his
    eyen*.   eyes
Tho redde he me, if that I shal nat lyen,
Of Hercules and of his Dianyre*[18]   *725*   Deianira
That caused hym to sette hymself afyre.
No thyng forgat he the sorwe and wo
That Socrates[19] hadde with his wyves two,
How Xantippa* caste pisse upon his heed;   Xantippe
This sely* man sat stille as he were deed. *730*   poor
He wiped his heed; namoore dorste* he seyn   dared
But er that thonder stynt* comth a reyn.   stops
Of Phasipha*[20] that was the queene of Crete,   Pasiphaë
For shrewednesse* hym thoughte the tale   wickedness
    was swete –
Fy, namoore! It is a grisly thyng   *735*
Of hire horrible lust and hir likyng*.   pleasure
Of Clitermystra*[21] for hir lecherye   Clytemnestra
That falsly made hir housbonde for to dye,
He redde it with ful good devocion.
He tolde me eek* for what occasion   *740*   also

18 According to Greek legend, Deianira, wife of Hercules, gave him a
   magical robe when she thought his love was waning. The robe, however,
   was the shirt of Nessus, a centaur whom Hercules had previously killed,
   and it caused Hercules' death by burning.

19 Socrates (469-399 B.C.) the Athenian philosopher is meant. His wife
   Xantippe had a reputation as a shrew.

20 Pasiphaë, in Greek legend, was the wife of Minos, King of Crete. She
   conceived a passion for a bull, and the monster called the Minotaur
   was the offspring of this union.

21 Clytemnestra with her lover Aegisthus slew her husband Agamemnon on
   his return home from the Trojan war.

Amphiorax*[22] at Thebes loste his lyf;   Amphiaraos
Myn housbonde hadde a legende* of his wyf,   story
Eriphilem*, that for an ouche* of gold   Eriphyle   jewelled ornament
Hath prively* unto the Grekes told   secretly
Wher that hir housbonde hidde hym in a
     place,   *745*
For which he hadde at Thebes sory grace.
Of Lyvia[23] tolde he me, and of Lucye;[24]
They bothe made hir housbondes for to dye,
That oon* for love, that oother was for hate.   one
Lyvia hir housbonde on an even late   *750*
Empoysoned hath for that she was his fo*.   enemy
Lucya, likerous*, loved hir housbonde so   lascivious
That for he sholde alwey upon hire thynke,
She yaf* hym swich a maner* love-drynke*   gave   such a kind of   love-
That he was deed er it were by the morwe*;   morning   potion
And thus algates* housbondes han* sorwe.   continually   have
Thanne tolde he me how oon* Latumyus[25]   one
Compleyned unto his felawe Arrius   *758*
That in his gardyn growed swich a tree
On which he seyde how that his wyves thre
Hanged hem self for hertes despitus*.   *761* spiteful
'O leeve* brother,' quod this Arrius,   dear
'Yif* me a plante of thilke* blessed tree,   give   that same
And in my gardyn planted shal it bee!'
Of later date of wyves hath he red   *765*
That som han* slayn hir housbondes in hir   have
     bed

22 Amphiaraos was persuaded by his wife Eriphyle, who had been bribed
   to do so, to join a fatal expedition against Thebes which resulted in his
   death.

23 At the instigation of Sejanus, Livia poisoned her husband Drusus, A.D.
   23.

24 Lucia, wife of the Roman poet Lucretius, accidentally poisoned her husband with a love-potion intended to revive his waning love.

25 The name has not been identified, and the same story is told of other
   persons also not identified. This story and the previous two are taken
   from "Valerius' Letter to Rufinus" (see note 14, page 79).

And lete hir lechour* dighte* hire al the nyght   *lecher *have intercourse with
Whan that the corps lay in the floor upright.
And somme han dryve nayles in hir brayn
Whil that they slepte, and thus they han hem slayn.   770
Somme han hem yeve* poysoun in hir drynke.   *given
He spak moore harm than herte may bithynke,
And ther-with-al he knew of mo* proverbes   *more
Than in this world ther growen gras or herbes.
'Bet* is,' quod he, 'thyn habitacioun   775 *better
Be with a leoun or a foul dragoun
Than with a womman usynge* for to chyde*.   *always *scold
Bet is,' quod he, 'hye* in the roof abyde   *high
Than with an angry wyf doun in the hous.
They been so wikked and contrarious*   780 *hostile
They haten that* hir housbondes loveth ay*.'   *what *constantly
He seyde a womman cast hir shame away
Whan she cast of* hir smok*, and forther mo*,   *off *smock *furthermore
A fair womman, but* she be chaast also,   *unless
Is lyk a gold ryng in a sowes nose.   785
Who wolde leeve*, or who wolde suppose*   *believe *imagine
The wo that in myn herte was and pyne*?   *pain
And whan I saugh* he wolde nevere fyne*   *saw *cease
To reden on this cursed book al nyght,
Al sodeynly thre leves have I plyght*   790 *ripped
Out of his book right as he radde*, and eke*   *read *also
I with my fest* so took hym on the cheke   *fist
That in oure fyr he fil bakward adoun.
And he up stirte* as dooth a wood* leoun,   *jumped *enraged
And with his fest he smoot* me on the heed   *struck
That in the floor I lay as I were deed.   796
And whan he saugh* how stille that I lay,   *saw
He was agast* and wolde han* fled his way,   *frightened *have
Til atte laste* out of my swogh* I breyde*.   *finally *faint *regained consciousness

'O hastow* slayn me, false theef?' I seyde,   have you
'And for my land thus hastow mordred* me.   murdered
Er I be deed*, yet wol I kisse thee.'   *802*   before I die
And neer he cam and kneled faire adoun
And seyde, 'Deere suster* Alisoun,   sister
As helpe me God, I shal thee nevere smyte.
That I have doon, it is thy self to wyte*;   *806*   it is your own fault
Foryeve* it me, and that I thee biseke.'   forgive
And yet eft soones* I hitte hym on the cheke   afterwards
And seyde, 'Theef, thus muchel* am I   much
    wreke*.   avenged
Now wol I dye; I may no lenger* speke.' *810*   longer

    "But atte laste*, with muchel care and wo   finally
We fille acorded* by us selven two.   became reconciled
He yaf* me al the bridel in myn hond   gave
To han* the governance of hous and lond,   have
And of his tonge and of his hond also,   *815*
And made hym brenne* his book anon right   burn
    tho*.   right then
And whan that I hadde geten unto me*   gotten for myself
By maistrie* al the soveraynetee*,   skill   supremacy
And that he seyde, 'Myn owene trewe wyf,
Do as thee lust* the terme of al thy lyf;   *820*   it pleases
Keep thyn honour, and keepe eek* myn   also
    estaat*,'   property
After that day we hadden never debaat*.   quarrel
God helpe me so, I was to hym as kynde
As any wyf from Denmark unto Ynde*,   India
And also trewe, and so was he to me.   *825*
I prey to God that sit in magestee*,   majesty
So blesse his soule for his mercy deere.
Now wol I seye forth my tale, if ye wol
    heere."

    The Frere lough* whan that he hadde herd   laughed
    al this.
"Now dame," quod he, "so have I joye or
    blis,   *830*

This is a long preamble of a tale!"
And whan the Somonour herde the Frere
    gale*,   *cry out*
"Lo!" quod the Somonour, "Goddes armes
    two!
A frere wol entremette* hym evere mo*!   *meddle   more*
Lo, goodè men, a flye and eek* a frere   835   *also*
Wol falle in every dyssh and eek mateere.
What spekestow* of preambulacioun?   *do you speak*
What, amble*, or trotte, or pees, or go sit   *walk*
    doun!
Thou lettest* oure disport* in this manere."   *hinder entertainment*
"Ye, woltow* so, sire Somonour?" quod the   *will you*
    Frere,   840
"Now by my feith, I shal er that I go
Telle of a somonour swich* a tale or two   *such*
That al the folk shal laughen in this place."
"Now elles, Frere, I wol bishrewe* thy face,"   *curse*
Quod this Somonour, "and I bishrewe me
But if* I telle tales two or thre   846   *unless*
Of freres er I com to Sidyngborne*,²⁶   *Sittingbourne*
That I shal make thyn herte for to morne*,   *grieve*
For wel I woot* thy pacience is gon."   849   *know*

  Oure Hoost cride, "Pees! and that anon*,"   *at once*
And seyde, "Lat the womman telle hire tale.
Ye fare as folk that dronken ben of ale.
Do, dame, telle forth youre tale, and that is
    best."
"Al redy, sire," quod she, "right as yow lest*,   *it pleases you*
If I have licence of this worthy Frere."   855
"Yis, dame," quod he, "tel forth and I wol
    heere."

---

26 Sittingbourne is about forty miles from London.

The Wife of Bath's Tale

In th'olde dayes of Kyng Arthour,
Of which that Britons* speken greet honour,   Welshmen
Al was this land fulfild of fairye.
The elf queene* with hir joly compaignye   queen of fairy
Daunced ful ofte in many a grene mede*.   *5* meadow
This was the olde opinion, as I rede –
I speke of manye hundred yeres ago –
But now kan no man se none elves mo*.   more
For now the grete charitee* and prayeres   Christian love
Of lymytours* and othere hooly freres   *10* limiters (friars licensed to
That serchen every lond and every streem   beg with prescribed limits)
As thikke as motes in the sonne beem,
Blessynge halles, chambres, kichenes,
    boures*,   bedrooms
Citees, burghes*, castels, hye* toures,   towns high
Thropes*, bernes*, shipnes*, dayeryes* –   villages barns stables
This maketh that ther been no fairyes.   *16*   dairies
For ther as wont to walken* was an elf,   where used to walk
Ther walketh now the lymytour hym self
In undermeles* and in morwenynges*,   afternoons mornings
And seyth his matyns* and his hooly thynges morning prayers
As he gooth in his lymytacioun*.   *21* area to which he was limited
Wommen may go saufly* up and doun   safely
In every busssh or under every tree –
Ther is noon oother incubus* but he,   evil spirit
And he ne wol doon hem but dishonour.   *25*
And so bifel* that this Kyng Arthour   it happened
Hadde in his hous a lusty bacheler*   young knight
That on a day cam ridynge fro ryver*,   from (the hawking ground by
And happed that allone as he was born   *29*   the) river
He saugh* a mayde walkynge hym biforn,   saw

Of which mayde anoon* maugree hir heed*   at once   without her consent
By verray force he rafte* hire maydenhed.   took away
For which oppression* was swich* clamour   violation   such
And swich pursute unto the Kyng Arthour
That dampned* was this knyght for to be
    deed   35   condemned
By cours of lawe, and sholde han* lost his
    heed –   was to have
Paraventure* swich* was the statut tho* –   perhaps   such   then
But that* the queene and othere ladyes mo*   except that   more
So longe preyden the kyng of grace
Til he his lyf hym graunted in the place,   40
And yaf* hym to the queene al at hir wille   gave
To chese* wheither she wolde hym save or   choose
    spille*.   kill
The queene thanked the kyng with al hir
    myght,
And after this thus spak she to the knyght
Whan that she saugh* hir tyme upon a day: saw
"Thou standest yet," quod she, "in swich
    array*   46   such condition
That of thy lyf yet hastow* no suretee*.   you have   surety
I grante thee lyf if thou kanst tellen me
What thyng is it that wommen moost desiren.
Be war* and keep thy nekke boon* from   beware   bone
    iren*!   50   iron
And if thou kanst nat tellen it anon*,   forthwith
Yet wol I yeve* thee leve for to gon   give
A twelf-month and a day to seche and leere*   learn
An answere suffisant in this mateere,
And suretee wol I han er that thou pace*   55   pass (forth)
Thy body for to yelden in this place."

Wo was this knyght and sorwefully he
    siketh*,   sighs
But he may nat do al as hym liketh*   pleases
And at the laste he chees* hym for to wende*   chose   go
And come agayn right at the yeres ende   60

With swich answere as God wolde hym
   purveye*,   *provide*
And taketh his leve and wendeth forth his
   weye.
He seketh every hous and every place
Where as he hopeth for to fynde grace*   *good fortune*
To lerne what thyng wommen loven moost,
But he ne koude arryven in no coost*   *66* *coast; i.e, place*
Where as he myghte fynde in this mateere
Two creatures accordynge in feere*.   *agreeing together*
Somme seyde wommen loven best richesse,
Somme seyde honour, somme seyde
   jolynesse*,   *70* *merriment*
Somme riche array*, somme seyden lust*   *clothing pleasure*
   abedde,
And ofte tyme to be wydwe* and wedde.   *widow*
Somme seyde that oure hertes been moost
   esed
Whan that we been yflatered* and   *flattered*
   yplesed* –   *pleased*
He gooth ful ny* the sothe*, I wol nat lye; *close to   truth*
A man shal wynne us best with flaterye, *76*
And with attendance* and with bisynesse* *attentions solicitude*
Been we enlymed* bothe moore and lesse* – *ensnared great and small*
And somme seyn that we loven best
For to be free and do right as us lest*,   *80* *pleases*
And that no man repreve* us of oure vice, *reprove*
But seye that we be wise and no thyng nyce*; *foolish*
For trewely, ther is noon of us alle,
If any wight* wol clawe* us on the galle*, *person scratch · sore spot*
That we nel kike* for he seith us sooth*. *85* *will not kick truth*
Assay* and he shal fynde it that so dooth, *try*
For be we nevere so vicious withinne,
We wol be holden wise and clene* of synne. *pure*
And somme seyn that greet delit han* we *have*
For to been holden stable and eek* secree*, *also trusty*
And in o* purpos stedefastly to dwelle, *91* *one*
And nat biwreye* thyng that men us telle. *betray*

But that tale is nat worth a rake stele*!   rake-handle
Pardee*, we wommen konne no thyng hele*! certainly conceal
Witnesse on Myda*; wol ye heere the tale? Midas
Ovyde[1], amonges othere thynges smale, *96*
Seyde Myda hadde under his longe heres* hair
Growynge upon his heed two asses eres*, ears
The which vice he hydde as he best myghte
Ful subtilly from every mannes sighte, *100*
That save his wyf ther wiste* of it namo*. knew no more
He loved hire moost and trusted hire also;
He preyde hire that to no creature
She sholde tellen of his disfigure*. deformity
She swoor hym nay; for al this world to
 wynne   *105*
She nolde* do that vileynye or synne would not
To make hir housbonde han* so foul a name. have
She nolde nat telle it for hir owene shame.
But nathelees*, hir thoughte* that she dyde* nevertheless it seemed to her
That she so longe sholde a conseil* hyde. *110* secret   died
Hir thoughte it swal* so soore aboute hir swelled
 herte
That nedely* som word hir moste* asterte*, necessarily had to escape
And sith* she dorste* telle it to no man, since dared
Doun to a mareys* faste by she ran. marsh
Til she cam there hir herte was afyre; *115*
And as a bitore* bombleth* in the myre, bittern booms
She leyde hir mouth unto the water doun.
"Biwreye* me nat, thou water, with thy betray
 soun*,"   sound
Quod she, "to thee I telle it and namo*: *119* no more
Myn housbonde hath longe asses erys* two! ears
Now is myn herte all hool; now is it oute!
I myghte no lenger* kepe it, oute of doute*." longer certainly
Heere may ye see, thogh we a tyme abyde,

---

1 The story of Midas is from the Latin poet Ovid's *Metamorphoses,* xi,
174-93. In Ovid's version it is Midas' barber, not his wife, who reveals the
secret. It has been suggested that the Wife of Bath's fifth husband, the
Oxford scholar, deliberately altered the story.

Yet out it moot*; we kan no conseil hyde.   must
The remenant of the tale, if ye wol heere,
Redeth Ovyde, and ther ye may it leere*. *126*   learn

This knyght, of which my tale is specially,
Whan that he saugh* he myghte nat come   saw
   therby –
This is to seye, what wommen love moost –
Withinne his brest ful sorweful was the
   goost*,   *130*   spirit
But hoom he gooth, he myghte nat sojourne.
The day was come that homward moste he
   tourne,
And in his wey it happed hym to ryde
In al this care under a forest syde
Wher as he saugh upon a daunce go   *135*
Of ladyes foure and twenty and yet mo*;   more
Toward the whiche daunce he drow* ful   drew
   yerne*   eagerly
In hope that som wysdom sholde he lerne,
But certeinly, er he cam fully there,
Vanysshed was this daunce, he nyste* where. knew not
No creature saugh he that bar lyf,   *141*
Save on the grene he saugh sittynge a wyf*.   woman
A fouler* wight* ther may no man devyse.   uglier   creature
Agayn the knyght thise olde wyf gan ryse
And seyde, "Sire Knyght, heer forth* ne lith*   past here   lies
   no wey.   *145*
Tel me what that ye seken*, by youre fey*!   seek   faith
Paraventure* it may the bettre be;   perhaps
Thise olde folk kan* muchel thyng*," quod   know   many things
   she.
"My leeve* mooder," quod this knyght,   dear
   "certeyn,
I n'am but deed* but if that I kan seyn   *150*   dead
What thyng it is that wommen moost desire.
Koude ye me wisse*, I wolde wel quite youre   instruct
   hire*."   repay you

"Plight me thy trouthe heere in myn hand,"
  quod she;
"The nexte thyng that I requere* thee   ask
Thou shalt it do, if it lye in thy myght,   *155*
And I wol telle it yow er it be nyght."
"Have heer my trouthe," quod the knyght; "I
  graunte."
"Thanne," quod she, "I dar me wel avaunte* boast
Thy lyf is sauf*, for I wol stonde therby.   safe
Upon my lyf, the queen wol seye as I.   *160*
Lat se which is the proudeste of hem alle
That wereth on* a coverchief or a calle* has on head-dress
That dar seye nay of that I shal thee teche.
Lat us go forth withouten lenger* speche." longer
Tho* rowned* she a pistel* in his ere   *165* then whispered message
And bad hym to be glad and have no fere*. fear
Whan they be comen to the court, this knyght
Seyde he had holde his day as he hadde
  hight*,   promised
And redy was his answere as he sayde.   *169*
Ful many a noble wyf and many a mayde
And many a wydwe*, for that they ben wise, widow
The queene hirself sittynge as justise*, judge
Assembled been his answere for to heere,
And afterward this knyght was bode* commanded to
  appeere.
To every wight* comanded was silence, *175* person
And that the knyght sholde telle in audience* legal assembly
What thyng that worldly wommen loven best.
This knyght ne stood nat stille as doth a
  best*,   beast
But to his questioun anon* answerde at once
With manly voys that al the court it herde:
"My lige* lady, generally," quod he, *181* liege
"Wommen desiren have sovereynetee
As wel over hir housbond as hir love,
And for to been in maistrie hym above.
This is youre mooste* desir, thogh ye me greatest
  kille!   *185*

Dooth as yow list*. I am here at youre wille."   *it pleases*
In al the court ne was ther wyf, ne mayde,
Ne wydwe* that contraried* that he sayde,   *widow* *contradicted*
But seyden he was worthy han* his lyf.   *to have*
And with that word up stirte* the olde wyf   *jumped*
Which that the knyght saugh* sittynge on the   *saw*
    grene.   *191*
"Mercy!" quod she, "my sovereyn lady
    queene!
Er that youre court departe, do me right!
I taughte this answere unto the knyght,
For which he plighte* me his trouthe there,   *pledged*
The firste thyng I wolde hym requere*   *196*   *demand*
He wolde it do, if it lay in his myght.
Bifore the court thanne preye I thee, Sire
    Knyght,"
Quod she, "that thou me take unto thy wyf,
For wel thou woost* that I have kept* thy   *know* *saved*
    lyf.   *200*
If I sey fals, sey nay, upon thy fey*!"   *faith*
This knyght answerde, "Allas and
    weylawey*!   *alas*
I woot* right wel that swich* was my   *know* *such*
    biheste*.   *promise*
For Goddes love, as chees* a newe requeste!   *choose*
Taak al my good* and lat my body go."   *205*   *property*
"Nay thanne," quod she, "I shrewe* us bothe   *curse*
    two!
For thogh that I be foul, oold and poore,
I nolde* for al the metal ne for oore*   *would not care*   *ore*
That under erthe is grave* or lith* above,   *buried* *lies*
But if* thy wyf I were and eek* thy love."   *unless* *also*
"My love?" quod he; "nay, my dampnacion!
Allas, that any of my nacion   *212*
Sholde evere so foule disparaged* be!"   *socially disgraced (for marry-ing below one's rank)*
But al for noght; th'ende is this, that he
Constreyned* was; he nedes moste* hire   *compelled* *had to*
    wedde,   *215*
And taketh his olde wyf and gooth to bedde.

Now wolden som men seye, paraventure*,   perhaps
That for my necligence I do no cure*   do not care
To tellen yow the joye and al th'array*   festivities
That at the feeste* was that ilke* day.   220   celebration same
To which thyng shortly answere I shal:
I seye ther nas no* joye ne* feeste* at al;   was not any nor rejoicing
Ther nas but hevynesse and muche sorwe,
For prively* he wedded hire on a morwe*   secretly the next morning
And al the day after hidde hym as an owle,
So wo* was hym his wyf looked so foule*.   sorrowful ugly
Greet was the wo the knyght hadde in his
   thoght   227
Whan he was with his wyf abedde ybroght*;   brought
He walweth* and he turneth to and fro.   tosses
His olde wyf lay smylynge everemo*   230   continually
And seyde, "O deere housbonde, benedicitee*!   bless us
Fareth every knyght thus with his wyf as ye?
Is this the lawe of Kyng Arthures hous?
Is every knyght of his so dangerous*?   unapproachable
I am youre owene love and youre wyf;   235
I am she which that saved hath youre lyf.
And certes*, yet dide I yow nevere unright*.   certainly wrong
Why fare ye thus with me this firste nyght?
Ye faren* lyk a man had lost his wit.   behave
What is my gilt*? For Goddes love, tel it, 240   offence
And it shal been amended, if I may."
"Amended?" quod this knyght, "allas! nay,
   nay!
It wol nat been amended never mo*.   more
Thou art so loothly* and so oold also,   ugly
And therto comen of so lough a kynde*,   245   base-born parentage
That litel wonder thogh I walwe* and   toss
   wynde*.   turn
So wolde God myn herte wolde breste*!"   would to God my heart would
                                             break
"Is this," quod she, "the cause of youre
   unreste?"
"Ye, certeinly," quod he, "no wonder is."
"Now sire," quod she, "I koude amende al
   this,   250

If that me liste*, er it were dayes thre,   *pleased me*
So wel ye myghte bere* yow unto me.   *behave*
But for ye speken of swich* gentillesse*   *such nobility*
As is descended out of old richesse*,   *wealth*
That therfore sholden ye be gentil* men, *255*   *noble*
Swich arrogance is nat worth an hen!
Looke who* that is moost vertuous alway,   *whoever*
Pryvee* and apert*, and moost entendeth   *privately publicly*
   ay*   *always strives*
To do the gentil* dedes* that he kan,   *noble deeds*
Taak hym for the grettest gentil man.   *260*
Crist wol* we clayme of hym oure   *desires that*
   gentillesse,
Nat of oure eldres* for hire olde richesse.   *parents*
For thogh they yeve* us al hir heritage*,   *give inheritance*
For which we clayme to been of heigh
   parage*,   *high lineage*
Yet may they nat biquethe for no thyng *265*
To noon of us hir vertuous lyvyng,
That made hem gentil men ycalled* be,   *called*
And bad us folwen hem in swich degree*.   *condition*
Wel kan the wise poete of Florence
That highte* Dant[2] speken in this sentence.   *is called*
Lo, in swich maner rym is Dantes tale: *271*
'Ful selde* up riseth by his branches smale   *rarely*
Prowesse* of man, for God of his goodnesse   *excellence*
Wole* that of hym we clayme oure   *intends*
   gentillesse.'   *274*
For of oure eldres* may we no thyng clayme   *parents*
But temporel* thyng that man may hurte and   *perishable*
   mayme.
Eek* every wight* woot* this as wel as I;   *also person knows*
If gentillesse* were planted natureelly*   *nobility innate*
Unto a certeyn lynage* doun the lyne   *family*
Pryvee* and apert*, thanne wolde they   *privately publicly*
   never fyne*   *280*   *cease*

2 The quotation (lines 272-4) is translated from Dante's *Divine Comedy,*
  Purgatorio, vii, 121-3.

To doon of gentillesse the faire office*. *perform noble deeds
They myghte do no vileynye or vice.
Taak fyr* and bere it in the derkeste hous *fire
Bitwix this and the mount of Kaukasous*, *the Caucasian mountain
And let men shette* the dores and go *shut
   thenne*,   285 *thence
Yet wole the fyr as faire lye* and brenne* *blaze burn
As twenty thousand men myghte it biholde.
His office natureel ay wol it holde*, *i.e., it will always behave naturally as a fire
Up peril of my lyf*, til that it dye. *I'll stake my life on it
Heere may ye se wel how that genterye* 290 *nobility of character
Is nat annexed* to possession*, *joined *wealth
Sith* folk ne doon hir operacion* *since *behave according to their rank
Alwey as doth the fyr, lo, in his kynde*. *nature
For God it woot*, men may wel often fynde *knows
A lordes sone* do shame and vileynye. 295 *son
And he that wole han* pris* of his gentrye* *have *the reputation *nobility
For* he was born of a gentil* hous, *because *noble
And hadde his eldres* noble and vertuous, *parents
And nel* hym selven do no gentil dedis* *will not *deeds
Ne folwen his gentil auncestre* that deed* is, *noble ancestor *dead
He nys* nat gentil, be he duc or erl, 301 *is not
For vileyns* synful dedes make a cherl*. *rude *villain
For gentillesse nys but renomee* *renown
Of thyn auncestres for hire heigh bountee*, *great virtues
Which is a strange thyng to* thy persone. *something foreign to
For gentillesse cometh fro God allone. 306
Thanne comth oure verray gentillesse* of *true nobility
   grace*; *by God's favour
It was no thyng biquethe us with oure place*. *station in life
Thenketh hou noble, as seith Valerius,[3]
Was thilke* Tullius Hostillius, 310 *that same
That oute of poverte roos* to heigh* *rose *great
   noblesse.

3 Valerius Maximus; see the Wife's Prologue, note 8. Tullus Hostillius was
the third legendary king of Rome.

Redeth Senek and redeth eek* Boece;⁴   also
Ther shul ye seen expres* that no drede is*   plainly   there is no doubt
That he is gentil* that dooth gentil dedis.   noble
And therfore, leeve* housbonde, I thus   dear
    conclude,   *315*
Al were it* that myne auncestres weren   even if it were
    rude*   low-born
Yet may the hye* God, and so hope I,   exalted
Grante me grace to lyven vertuously.
Thanne am I gentil whan that I bigynne
To lyven vertuously and weyve* synne.   *320*   put aside

    "And ther as ye of poverte me repreeve*,   reproach
The hye God, on whom that we bileeve,
In wilful poverte chees* to lyve his lyf.   chose
And certes*, every man, mayden, or wyf   certainly
May understonde that Jhesu hevene kyng
Ne wolde nat chese* a vicious lyvyng.   *326*   choose
Glad* poverte is an honeste thyng, certeyn;   cheerfully borne
This wole Senec and othere clerkes* seyn.   scholars
Who so that halt hym payd* of his poverte,   is contented
I holde hym riche, al* hadde he nat a   even if
    sherte*.   *330*   shirt
He that coveiteth* is a pouere* wight*,   covets   poor   person
For he wolde han* that is nat in his myght;   have
But he that noght hath, ne coveiteth have,
Is riche, althogh ye holde hym but a knave*.   peasant
Verray* poverte, it syngeth proprely*.   *335*   true   appropriately
Juvenal⁵ seith of poverte myrily*   happily
The poure man, whan he goth by the weye
Bifore the theves, he may synge and pleye.
Poverte is hateful good, and as I gesse,
A ful greet bryngere out* of bisynesse*, *340*   producer   endeavour

---

4 Seneca (d. A.D. 65), Roman dramatist and Stoic philosopher; Boethius
(c. 475-525), Roman philosopher whose *Consolation of Philosophy,* a
justly famous work, was translated by Chaucer.

5 Juvenal (first and second centuries A.D.), Roman satirist.

A greet amendere* eek* of sapience* — promoter also wisdom
To hym that taketh it in pacience.
Poverte is al this, although it seme alenge*, — tedious
Possession that no wight wol chalenge*. — dispute
Poverte ful ofte when a man is lowe 345
Maketh his God and eek hym self to knowe.
Poverte a spectacle* is, as thynketh me*, — optic glass it seems to me
Thurgh which he may his verray* freendes — true
  see.
And therfore sire, syn* that I noght yow — since
  greve*, 349 — injure
Of my poverte namoore ye me repreve*. — reproach

"Now sire, of elde* ye repreve me, — age
And certes*, sire, thogh noon auctoritee* — certainly (authoritative) text
Were in no book, ye gentils* of honour — noblemen
Seyn* that men sholde an oold wight* doon — say person
  favour,
And clepe* hym fader*, for youre gentillesse, — call father
And auctors* shal I fynden, as I gesse. 356 — authorities
Now ther ye seye that I am foul* and old; — ugly
Thanne drede* yow noght to been a — fear
  cokewold*. — cuckold
For filthe* and eelde*, al so mote* I thee*, — ugliness age may prosper
Been gret wardeyns* upon chastitee. 360 — guardians
But nathelees*, syn* I knowe youre delit*, — nevertheless since pleasure
I shal fulfille youre worldly* appetit. — fleshly
Chese* now," quod she, "oon* of thise — choose one
  thynges tweye*: — two
To han* me foul* and old til that I deye*, — have ugly die
And be to yow a trewe, humble wyf, 365
And nevere yow displese in al my lyf,
Or elles ye wol han me yong and fair,
And take youre aventure* of the repair* — chance resort (of visitors)
That shal be to youre hous by cause of me,
Or in som oother place, may wel be. 370
Now chese your selven wheither* that yow — whichever
  liketh*." — pleases

This knyght avyseth hym* and sore siketh*,   considers   sighs
But atte laste* he seyde in this manere,   finally
"My lady and my love, and wyf so deere,
I put me in youre wise governance.   375
Cheseth youre self which may be moost
    plesance
And moost honour to yow and me also.
I do no fors* the wheither* of the two,   am indifferent   whichever
For as yow liketh*, it suffiseth me."   it pleases you
"Thanne have I gete of yow maistrie*," quod   sovereignty
    she,   380
"Syn* I may chese and governe as me lest*."   since   pleases
"Ye, certes*, wyf," quod he, "I holde it best."   certainly
"Kys me," quod she, "we be no lenger*   longer
    wrothe*,   angry
For by my trouthe, I wol be to yow bothe.
This is to seyn, ye, bothe fair and good.   385
I prey to God that I moote* sterven* wood*,   may   die   mad
But I to yow be al so good and trewe
As evere was wyf syn that the world was
    newe.
And but* I be tomorn* as fair to seene   unless   tomorrow
As any lady, emperice, or queene   390
That is bitwix the est and eek the west,
Do with my lyf and deth right as yow lest.
Cast up the curtyn*; looke how that it is!"   curtain
And whan the knyght saugh* verraily* al   saw   truly
    this,
That she so fair was and so yong therto,   395
For joye he hente* hire in his armes two.   clasped
His herte bathed in a bath of blisse.
A thousand tyme arewe* he gan hir kisse.   in a row
And she obeyed hym in every thyng
That myghte doon hym plesance or likyng.
And thus they lyve unto hir lyves ende   401
In parfit* joye, and Jhesu Crist us sende   perfect
Housbondes meeke, yonge, and fressh a
    bedde,

And grace t'overbyde* hem that we wedde.   outlive
And eek* I preye Jhesu shorte* hir lyves 405   also   shorten
That nat wol be governed by hir wyves!
And olde and angry nygards of dispence*,   misers in spending
God sende hem soone verray pestilence*!   real disaster

INTRODUCTION TO THE
MERCHANT'S PROLOGUE AND TALE

The Merchant's Tale is third in the sequence known as the Marriage Group of tales. It follows immediately after the Clerk's Tale (not represented in this selection) which relates the incredible patience of the wife Griselda in the face of her husband Walter's inhuman demands. In the brief prologue to his tale the Merchant quotes a few phrases from the concluding lines of the Clerk's Tale and applies them in heart-felt fashion to his own case. The Wife of Bath and the Clerk had presented in their tales exactly opposite views of what constituted the role of the woman in marriage. The Merchant takes neither side in the discussion of marriage. Though married but two months, his experience is enough to convince him of all "The sorwe and woo that is in mariage" (to quote "Lenvoy de Chaucer a Bukton"), and so he relates a tale which is a condemnation of the institution of marriage itself.

The contrast between the depiction of the Merchant's character in the General Prologue and its presentation in the brief introduction to his tale comes as a surprise. In the General Prologue our attention is concentrated on the Merchant as a cunning business man whose business deals, especially in foreign currency, are not always honest, and whose commercial empire rests on a foundation of debt. But at this point in the *Canterbury Tales* we discover that the pretentious exterior of his character in the General Prologue conceals not only financial insecurity but also domestic problems. And it is the festering rancour engendered by these domestic problems that dictates the nature of the tale related by the Merchant.

In the brief prologue to his tale the Merchant's true confessions concerning his unhappy marriage are a surprising indiscretion. A man who is capable of conducting black-market deals in foreign currency and who likes to talk about the profits he has made, while at the same time maintaining strict silence on his debts, is not one to confess openly the mistake he has made in a two-month-old marriage. But the indiscretion can be explained, I think, partly by the pervasive and infectious atmosphere of confession generated by the Wife of Bath's startingly frank revelations, and partly by the fact that like many of the other males on the Canterbury pilgrimage he has been wounded by the Wife of Bath in his most sensitive point, his sexual vanity. This wound momentarily throws him off balance, and he is unable to restrain his exasperated anger. He recovers himself, however, when invited by the Host to continue his tale of marital woe, and his regained sense of discretion puts an end to the exhibition of himself he was about to make. But his wounded vanity and the frustrations of his marriage combine in a tale that is a savage attack on men desiring marriage, faithless wives, and the institution of marriage itself. The tale functions as a vehicle for the outraged feelings of the Merchant, and it also allows him to objectify those feelings by expressing them in this way.

The Merchant's attack on marriage follows a pattern familiar to the modern reader. The Merchant adapts the love triangle to his purpose, and in this story we have the commonplace theme of a husband and wife and a suitor to the wife. But the familiar situation contains certain complications in the Merchant's handling of it. The husband is depicted as old and repulsively lecherous; the wife is young and victimized by the husband's lechery; the suitor is a young squire in a position of trust in the husband's household. In a situation such as this one's sympathies would naturally swing towards the young couple, and the delineation of old January's grotesque lechery assists this reaction. But as the action of the story proceeds, the reader finds that he has little reason to sympathize with any one of the characters. January, who married to satisfy physical lust, alienates sympathy by his bedside behaviour with the young May and by his aged antics with her in his carefully enclosed garden where things not done abed are performed. May at first engages our sympathy since she is January's tender victim, but the haste with which, out of the nobility of her heart we are told, she decides to take pity on the squire Damian and break her marriage vows leaves little doubt in the reader's mind concerning the essential nature of her character. And the love-sick Damian, whose sexual opportunism leads him to betray his position of trust in his master's household, also loses his claim to our sympathy. Thus the Merchant turns what might have been a poignant story of love defeated by the circumstances of the world into a squalid little domestic scandal, and the sordidness of the tale brings the institution of marriage itself into disrepute.

At the end of the Merchant's Tale the blind old January has his sight restored by the god Pluto and is thus able to catch a glimpse of his wife and the squire in the pear tree above his head. It has been noted by some readers that the physical blindness endured by January is symbolic of his spiritual blindness, of his immersion in the world of sense experience, indeed sexual experience, to the exclusion of any other values. But the restoration of his sight at the end of the tale does not signify a spiritual regeneration in the old man. The wife May, with the help of Pluto's wife Proserpina, is able to convince her aged husband that what was going on in the pear tree was something he only thought he saw when his sight was first restored. In other words, nothing in the action is made clear to the old man; the plot against the sanctity of his marriage remains concealed. The three principal actors in this little drama of lust and adultery remain in their essential natures. This ironical ending is necessary to the over-all impression of cynicism and despair about the relationship between the sexes that lies behind the Merchant's Tale. The irony is also in keeping with the savage irony at the beginning of the story in the praise of marriage, and thus the tale reveals a surprising symmetry.

The Merchant's Prologue and Tale

"Wepyng and waylyng, care and oother
sorwe
I knowe ynogh*, on even and amorwe*,"   enough   night and morning
Quod the Marchant, "and so doon othere mo*   more
That wedded been. I trowe* that it be so,   believe
For wel I woot*, it fareth so with me.   5   know
I have a wyf, the worste that myghte be,
For thogh the feend to hire ycoupled were,
She wolde hym overmacche, I dar wel swere.
What sholde I yow reherce* in special*   repeat   in particular
Hir hye* malice? She is a shrewe at al*!   10 great   complete scold
Ther is a long and large difference
Bitwix* Grisildis*¹ grete pacience   between   Griselda's
And of my wyf the passyng crueltee.
Were I unbounden, also moot I thee*,   as I may prosper
I wolde nevere eft* come in the snare.   15 again
We wedded men lyve in sorwe and care.
Assaye* who so wole, and he shal fynde   try
That I seye sooth, by Seint Thomas of Ynde*,   India
As for the moore* part, I seye nat alle.   greater
God shilde* that it sholde so bifalle!   20 forbid
A, goode sire Hoost, I have ywedded be
Thise monthes two, and moore nat, pardee*!   certainly
And yet I trowe* he that al his lyve   believe
Wyflees hath been, though that men wolde
   hym ryve*   pierce

---

1 Griselda, heroine of the Clerk's Tale, which immediately precedes the
Merchant's Tale, exhibits superhuman patience in the face of unbelievable
adversity. The opening line of the Prologue of the Merchant's Tale is an
echo of the closing line of the Clerk's Tale.

Unto the herte, ne koude in no manere   *25*

Tellen so muchel* sorwe as I now heere   much

Koude tellen of my wyves cursednesse!"

   "Now," quod oure Hoost, "Marchant, so
God yow blesse,

Syn ye so muchel knowen of that art,

Ful hertely I pray yow, telle us part."   *30*

   "Gladly," quod he, "but of myn owene
soore

For sory herte I telle may namoore*."   no more

   Whilom* ther was dwellynge in Lumbardye   once

A worthy knyght that born was of Pavye*,   Pavia (Italy)

In which he lyvede in greet prosperitee,   *35*

And sixty yeer a wyflees man was hee,

And folwed ay* his bodily delyt   always

On wommen ther as was his appetyt,

As doon thise fooles that been seculeer*.[2]   secular

And whan that he was passed sixty yeer,   *40*

Were it for hoolynesse or for dotage*,   foolishness

I kan nat seye, but swich* a greet corage*   such desire

Hadde this knyght to been a wedded man

That day and nyght he dooth al that he kan

T'espien* where he myghte wedded be,   *45*   discover

Preyinge oure Lorde to granten hym that he

Mighte ones* knowe of thilke* blisful lyf   once that

That is bitwixe an housbonde and his wyf,

And for to lyve under that hooly boond

With which that first God man and womman
bond.   *50*

"Noon oother lyf," seyde he, "is worth a
bene*.   bean

For wedlock is so esy and so clene*   pure

---

2 The Merchant's Tale, in the scheme of the *Canterbury Tales* as a whole,
seems to have been originally intended for a cleric, perhaps the Monk.
In rearranging the tales and assigning this one to the Merchant, Chaucer
probably overlooked this incidental comment which indicates a cleric
speaking. Further similar oversights occur at lines 110 and 178.

That in this world it is a paradys."
Thus seyde this olde knyght that was so wys.
And certeinly, as sooth* as God is kyng,   55   true
To take a wyf, it is a glorious thyng;
And namely, whan a man is oold and hoor*   grey
Thanne is a wyf the fruyt of his tresor*.   i.e., his choicest possession
Thanne sholde he take a yong wyf and a feir,
On which he myghte engendren* hym an heir,   beget
And lede his lyf in joye and in solas*.   61   pleasure
Where as thise bacheleris synge "Allas!"
Whan that they fynden any adversitee
In love, which nys* but childyssh vanytee.   is not
And trewely, it sit* wel to be so   65   suits
That bacheleris have often peyne and wo;
On brotel* ground they buylde, and   fragile
    brotelnesse*   insecurity
They fynde whan they wene* sikernesse*.   think (to find)   security
They lyve but as a bryd* or as a beest   bird
In libertee and under noon arreest*,   70   restraint
Ther as* a wedded man in his estaat   whereas
Lyveth a lyf blisful and ordinaat*   regulated
Under this yok* of mariage ybounde.   yoke
Wel may his herte in joye and blisse
    habounde*,   abound
For who kan be so buxom* as a wyf,   75   obedient
Who is so trewe and eek* so ententyf*   also   attentive
To kepe* hym syk or hool, as is his make*?   care for   mate
For wele or wo*, she wol hym nat forsake;   joy or sorrow
She nys nat* wery* hym to love and serve,   is not   weary
Thogh that he lye bedrede* til he sterve*.   80   bedridden   die
And yet som clerkes seyn it nys nat so,
Of which he, Theofraste*,³ is oon of tho.   Theophrastus
What force* though Theofraste liste* lye?   what matter   it please
"Ne take no wyf," quod he, "for
    housbondrye*.   economy

3 Theophrastus (third century B.C.), author of "The Golden Book on Marriage" and known to the Middle Ages through later translations; see **Wife
   of Bath's Prologue**, note 14, p. 79.

As for to spare in houshold thy dispence*, 85 reduce household expenses
A trewe servant dooth moore diligence
Thy good* to kepe than thyn owene wyf, property
For she wol clayme half part al hir lyf.
And if thou be syk, so God me save,
Thy verray* freendes or a trewe knave* 90 true servant
Wol kepe thee bet* than she that waiteth* better waits for
 ay* always
After thy good*, and hath doon many a day. property
And if thou take a wyf unto thyn hoold*, keeping
Ful lightly* maystow* been a cokewold*." easily may you cuckold
This sentence, and an hundred thynges worse
Writeth this man, ther God his bones corse*! curse
But take no kepe of* al swich* vanytee; 97 pay no attention to such
Deffie* Theofraste and herke* me. defy listen to
A wyf is Goddes yifte*, verraily*. gift truly
Alle othere manere yiftes, hardily*, 100 certainly
As londes, rentes, pasture or commune,
Or moebles*, alle been yiftes of fortune movable possessions
That passen as a shadwe* upon a wal, shadow
But drede* nat if pleynly speke I shal, fear
A wyf wol laste, and in thyn hous endure 105
Wel lenger* than thee list*, paraventure*! much longer pleases perhaps
Mariage is a ful greet sacrement.
He which that hath no wyf, I holde hym
 shent*. ruined
He lyveth helplees and al desolat –
I speke of folk in seculer estaat*. 110 lay folk
And herke* why, I seye nat this for noght, listen
That womman is for mannes helpe ywroght*. made
The hye God, whan he hadde Adam maked
And saugh* hym al allone, bely naked, saw
God of his grete goodnesse seyde than, 115
"Lat us now make an helpe unto this man
Lyk to hym self." And thanne he made hym
 Eve.
Heere may ye se and heer-by may ye preve* prove
That wyf is mannes helpe and his confort,
His paradys terrestre and his disport*; 120 entertainment

So buxom* and so vertuous is she,   *obedient*
They moste nedes* lyve in unitee.   *must*
O* flessh they been and o flessh, as I gesse, *one*
Hath but oon herte, in wele* and in distresse. *prosperity*
A wyf, a, Seinte Marie benedicite!   *125*
How myghte a man han* any adversitee   *have*
That hath a wyf? Certes*, I kan nat seye.   *certainly*
The blisse which that is bitwixe hem tweye
Ther may no tonge telle or herte thynke. *129*
If he be poure, she helpeth hym to swynke*. *labour*
She kepeth his good* and wasteth never a   *property*
   deel*.   *part*
Al that hir housbonde lust*, hire liketh* weel. *is pleasing to it pleases*
She seith nat ones* "Nay" whan he seith   *once*
   "Ye".
"Do this," seith he. "Al redy, sire," seith she.
O blisful ordre of wedlok precious!   *135*
Thou art so murye* and eek* so vertuous   *pleasant also*
And so commended and appreved eek,
That every man that halt* hym worth a leek, *considers*
Upon his bare knees oughte al his lyf
Thanken his God that hym hath sent a wyf,
Or elles preye to God hym for to sende   *141*
A wyf to laste unto his lyves ende.
For thanne his lyf is set in sikernesse*;   *security*
He may nat be deceyved, as I gesse,
So that he werke after his wyves* reed*. *145* *wife's advice*
Thanne may he boldely beren up his heed.
They been so trewe and ther with al so wyse,
For which, if thou wolt werken as the wyse,
Do alwey so as wommen wol thee rede*.   *advise*
Lo, how that Jacob*, as thise clerkes* rede, *as in Genesis 27:1-29 scholars*
By good conseil of his mooder Rebekke*, *151* *Rebecca*
Boond the kydes skyn aboute his nekke,
For which his fadres* benyson* he wan*.   *father's blessing won*
Lo, Judith*, as the storie eek* telle kan,   *Apocryphal Book of Judith,*
By wys conseil she Goddes peple kepte, *155*   *chs. 11-13 also*
And slow* hym Olofernus* whil he slepte.   *slew Holofernes*
Lo, Abigayl*, by good conseil how she   *Abigail, I Samuel 25:1-35*

Saved hir housbonde Nabal whan that he
Sholde han* be slayn; and looke Ester* also, have Esther 7:1-10
By good conseil delyvered out of wo *160*
The peple of God and made hym Mardochee* Mordecai
Of Assuere* enhaunced* for to be. Ahasuerus exalted
Ther nys* no thyng in gree superlatyf*, is not of higher rank
As seith Senek,[4] above an humble wyf.
Suffre thy wyves tonge as Caton*[5] bit*; *165* Cato bids
She shal comaunde and thou shalt suffren it.
And yet she wol obeye of curteisye.
A wyf is kepere of thyn housbondrye*. household goods
Wel may the sike* man biwaille and wepe sick
Ther as* ther nys no wyf the hous to kepe. where
I warne thee, if wisely thou wolt wirche*, *171* work
Love wel thy wyf, as Crist loved his chirche.
If thou lovest thy self, thou lovest thy wyf.
No man hateth his flessh, but in his lyf
He fostreth it, and therfore bidde I thee *175*
Cherisse thy wyf, or thou shalt nevere thee*. prosper
Housbonde and wyf, what so* men jape* or however joke
 pleye,
Of worldly* folk holden the siker* weye. lay more secure
They been so knyt* ther may noon harm joined
 bityde*, befall
And namely upon the wyves syde. *180*
For which this Januarie, of whom I tolde,
Considered hath inwith his dayes olde
The lusty* lyf, the vertuous quyete* pleasurable peace
That is in mariage hony swete,
And for hise freendes on a day he sente *185*
To tellen hem th'effect of his entente.

---

4 Seneca (d. A.D. 65), Roman dramatist and Stoic philosopher.

5 The *Distichs of Cato*, a once-popular set of moral apophthegms dating
from the third or fourth century A.D., is meant. The Middle Ages attributed the work to Cato the Elder (d. 149 B.C.), but they are connected
with an almost unknown Dionysius Cato.

With face sad* his tale he hath hem toold. serious
He seyde, "Freendes, I am hoor* and oold, grey
And almoost, God woot*, on my pittes* knows grave's
 brynke.
Upon my soule somwhat moste I thynke. *190*
I have my body folily* despended*; foolishly wasted
Blessed be God that it shal been amended!
For I wol be, certeyn, a wedded man,
And that anoon* in al the haste I kan, at once
Unto som mayde fair and tendre of age. *195*
I pray yow, shapeth* for my mariage prepare
Al sodeynly*, for I wol nat abyde*. promptly wait
And I wol fonde* t'espien* on my syde try discover
To whom I may be wedded hastily.
But, for as muche as ye been mo* than I, *200* more (in number)
Ye shullen* rather swich* a thyng espyen will such
Than I, and where me beste were to allyen*. i.e., marry
But o* thyng warne I yow, my freendes one
 deere:
I wol noon oold wyf han* in no manere. have
She shal nat passe twenty yeer, certayn. *205*
Oold fissh and yong flessh wolde I have fayn.
Bet* is," quod he, "a pyk than a pykerel*, better young pike
And bet than olde boef* is the tendre veel*. beef veal
I wol han no womman thritty yeer of age.
It is but benestraw* and greet forage*, *210* bean-husk rough fodder
And eek* thise olde wydwes*, God it woot*, also widows knows
They konne so muchel craft* on Wades have so much skill in
 boot*,[6] boat
So muchel broken harm* whan that hem so many petty grievances
 leste*, it pleases
That with hem sholde I nevere lyve in reste.
For sondry scoles maken sotile* clerkis*; *215* subtle scholars
Womman of many scoles half a clerk is.
But certeynly, a yong thyng may men gye* guide

---

6 Wade was a legendary hero whose exploits are alluded to in medieval romance, but of whom we know almost nothing.

Right as men may warm wex with handes
    plye*.   mould
Wherfore I sey yow pleynly in a clause*,   briefly
I wol noon oold wyf han* right for this   have
    cause.   220
For if so were that I hadde swich*   such
    myschance*   misfortune
That I in hire ne koude han no plesance,
Thanne sholde I lede my lyf in avoutrye*,   adultery
And go streight to the devel whan I dye*,   die
Ne children sholde I none upon hire geten.
Yet were me levere* houndes* hadde me   I had rather   dogs
    eten*   226   eaten
Than that myn heritage* sholde falle   inheritance
In straunge hand, and this I telle yow alle.
I dote nat*, I woot* the cause why   am not foolish   know
Men sholde wedde, and forthermoore woot I
Ther speketh many a man of mariage   231
That woot namoore of it than woot my page
For whiche* causes man sholde take a wyf.   what
If he ne may nat lyven chaast his lyf,
Take hym a wyf with greet devocion,   235
By cause of leveful* procreacion   lawful
Of children to th'onour of God above,
And nat oonly for paramour* or love,   passion
And for they sholde leccherye eschue*   239   avoid
And yelde* hir dette* whan that it is due,   pay i.e., marriage debt
Or for that ech of hem sholde helpen oother
In meschief* as a suster shal the brother,   trouble
And lyve in chastitee ful holily.
But sires, by youre leve, that am nat I,
For God be thanked, I dar make avaunt*,   boast
I feele my lymes* stark* and suffisaunt   246   limbs strong
To do al that a man bilongeth to*.   befits a man
I woot my selven best what I may do,
Though I be hoor*, I fare as dooth a tree   grey
That blosmeth* er that fruyt ywoxen* be,   250   blossoms grown
And blosmy* tree nys neither* drye ne deed.   blossoming isn't either
I feele me nowher hoor but on myn heed.

Myn herte and alle my lymes been as grene
As laurer* thurgh the yeer is for to sene.   laurel
And syn* that ye han* herd al myn entente*,   since   have   intention
I prey yow to my wil ye wol assente."   *256*

Diverse men diversely hym tolde
Of mariage manye ensamples olde.
Somme blamed it, somme preysed it, certeyn.
But atte laste*, shortly for to seyn,   *260*   finally
As alday* falleth altercacion   everyday
Bitwixen freendes in disputison*,   argument
Ther fil a stryf* bitwixe his bretheren two,   dispute
Of which that oon* was cleped* Placebo;   one   called
Justinus soothly called was that oother.   *265*
Placebo seyde, "O Januarie brother,
Ful litel nede hadde ye, my lord so deere,
Conseil to axe* of any that is heere.   ask
But that ye been so ful of sapience
That yow ne liketh* for youre heigh*   it doesn't please you   great
    prudence   *270*
To weyven* fro the word of Salomon[7] –   depart
This word seyde he unto us everychon*,   every one
'Wirk alle thyng by conseil,' thus seyde he,
'And thanne shaltow* nat repente thee' –   you will
But though that Salomon spak swich* a   such
    word,   *275*
Myn owene deere brother and my lord,
So wysly* God my soule brynge at reste,   as certainly as
I holde youre owene conseil is the beste.
For brother myn, of me taak this motyf*.   suggestion
I have now been a court man al my lyf,   *280*
And God it woot*, thogh I unworthy be,   knows
I have stonden in ful greet degree
Abouten lordes of ful heigh estaat*,   great position
Yet hadde I nevere with noon of hem
    debaat*.   argument

7 The quotation (lines 273-4) is really from the Book of Ecclesiasticus (Apocrypha) 32:24.

I nevere hem contraried*, trewely.   285   contradicted
I woot wel that my lord kan* moore than I.   knows
What* that he seith, I holde it ferme and   whatever
    stable.
I seye the same, or elles thyng semblable*.   something similar
A ful grèet fool is any conseillour
That serveth any lord of heigh honour   290
That dar presume or elles thenken it
That his conseil sholde passe his lordes wit*.   intelligence
Nay, lordes been no fooles, by my fay!
Ye han your selven shewed heer to day
So heigh sentence*, so holily and weel   295   such good judgment
That I consente and conferme every deel*   completely
Youre wordes alle and youre opinioun.
By God, ther nys* no man in al this toun,   is not
Ne in Ytaille*, that koude bet* han* sayd.   Italy   better   have
Crist halt hym of this conseil ful wel apayd*,   was well pleased with
And trewely, it is an heigh corage*   301   spirit
Of any man that stapen* is in age   advanced
To take a yong wyf, by my fader kyn*!   father's kin
Youre herte hangeth on a joly pyn*!   is merry
Dooth now in this matiere right as yow
    leste*,   305   it pleases you
For fynally, I holde it for the beste."

Justinus, that ay stille sat and herde,
Right in this wise he to Placebo answerde:
"Now brother myn, be pacient, I preye,
Syn* ye han* seyd, and herkneth* what I   since   have   listen to
    seye.   310
Senek,8 amonges othere wordes wyse,
Seith that a man oghte hym right wel avyse*   consider carefully
To whom he yeveth* his lond or his catel*,   gives   property

8 Whether the reference is to the *De Beneficiis* (chs. 14-16) of Seneca, or
  whether Chaucer got it from Valerius Maximus (see Wife of Bath's Prologue, note 8), the passage is a good illustration of the medieval habit of
  arguing from "auctoritees" or authoritative texts. See also below, lines
  445-6.

And syn I oghte avysen me* right wel   *consider*
To whom I yeve my good awey fro me,   *315*
Wel muchel moore* I oghte avysed be   *very much better*
To whom I yeve my body for alwey.
I warne ye wel, it is no childes pley
To take a wyf withouten avysement.
Men moste* enquere*, this is my assent*, *320*   *must inquire opinion*
Wher* she be wys or sobre or dronkelewe*,   *whether addicted to drink*
Or proud, or elles ootherweys a shrewe*,   *scold*
A chidestere*, or wastour of thy good*,   *(female) nagger property*
Or riche or poore or elles mannysh wood*.   *man-crazy*
Al* be it so that no man fynden shal   *325*   *although*
Noon in this world that trotteth hool in al,
Ne man ne beest swich* as men koude   *such*
  devyse*,   *imagine*
But nathelees*, it oghte ynough suffise   *nevertheless*
With any wyf, if so were that she hadde
Mo* good thewes* than hire vices badde.   *more traits*
And al this axeth* leyser* for t'enquere. *331*   *requires leisure*
For God it woot*, I have wept many a teere   *knows*
Ful pryvely* syn that I hadde a wyf.   *in secret*
Preyse who so wole a wedded mannes lyf,
Certeyn, I fynde in it but cost and care   *335*
And observances*, of alle blisses bare.   *obligations*
And yet, God woot, my neighebores aboute,
And namely, of wommen many a route*, *338*   *large number*
Seyn that I have the mooste stedefast wyf,
And eek* the mekeste oon* that bereth lyf.   *also one*
But I woot best where wryngeth me my sho*.   *my shoe pinches*
Ye mowe* for me right as yow liketh* do.   *may it pleases you*
Avyseth yow*, ye been a man of age,   *consider*
How that ye entren into mariage,
And namely, with a yong wyf and a fair. *345*
By hym that made water, erthe and air,
The yongest man that is in al this route*   *company*
Is bisy ynough to bryngen it aboute
To han* his wyf allone, trusteth me.   *have*
Ye shul nat plesen hire fully yeres thre;   *350*
This is to seyn, to doon hire ful plesance.

A wyf axeth* ful many an observance*;   requires   attention
I pray yow that ye be nat yvele apayd*."   ill pleased
"Wel," quod this Januarie, "and hastow*   have you
   ysayd?
Straw for thy Senek*, and for thy proverbes   Seneca
I counte nat a panyer* ful of herbes!   *356*   basket
Of scole termes wyser men than thow,
As thou hast herd, assenteden right now
To my purpos. Placebo, what sey ye?"
"I seye it is a cursed man," quod he,   *360*
"That letteth* matrymoigne*, sikerly*."   hinders   matrimony   certain
And with that word they rysen sodeynly
And been assented* fully that he sholde   agreed
Be wedded whanne hym liste* and wher he   it pleased him
   wolde.   *364*

Heigh fantasye* and curious* bisynesse*   imagination   eager   attention
Fro day to day gan in the soule impresse*   make in the soul an impression
Of Januarie aboute his mariage.
Many fair shap and many a fair visage
Ther passeth thurgh his herte nyght by nyght,
As who so* tooke a mirour polisshed bryght   whoever
And sette it in a commune market place, *371*
Thanne sholde he se ful many a figure pace*   pass
By his mirour, and in the same wyse
Gan Januarie inwith* his thoght devyse*   within   imagine
Of maydens whiche that dwelten hym bisyde.
He wiste* nat wher that he myghte abyde,   knew
For if that oon* have beaute in hir face, *377*   one
Another stant* so in the peples grace   stands
For hir sadnesse* and hir benyngnytee*   seriousness   kindness
That of the peple grettest* voys* hath she,   most   acclaim
And somme were riche and hadden badde
   name.   *381*
But nathelees*, bitwixe ernest and game,   nevertheless
He atte laste* apoynted* hym on oon   finally   settled
And leet* alle othere from his herte goon,   let
And chees* hire of his owene auctoritee, *385*   chose
For love is blynd al day* and may nat see.   always

And whan that he was in his bed ybroght,
He purtreyede* in his herte and in his thoght   depicted
Hir fresshe beautee and hir age tendre,
Hir myddel smal, hir armes longe and
   sklendre*,   390   slender
Hir wise governance*, hir gentillesse*,   demeanour   gentility
Hir wommanly berynge and hir sadnesse*.   seriousness
And whan that he on hire was
   condescended*,   settled
Hym thoughte* his choys myghte nat ben   it seemed to him
   amended.   394
For whan that he hym self concluded hadde,
Hym thoughte ech oother mannes wit so
   badde
That inpossible it were to repplye
Agayn his choys; this was his fantasye*.   fancy
His freendes sente he to at his instance,   399
And preyed hem to doon hym that plesance
That hastily they wolden to hym come.
He wolde abregge* hir labour alle and some.   shorten
Nedeth namoore* for hym to go ne ryde;   no more
He was apoynted* ther* he wolde abyde. 404   resolved   where
Placebo cam, and eek* his freendes soone,   also
And alderfirst* he bad* hem alle a boone*,   first of all   asked   favour
That noon of hem none argumentes make
Agayn the purpos which that he hath take,
Which purpos was plesant to God, seyde he,
And verray* ground of his prosperitee. 410   true
He seyde ther was a mayden in the toun
Which that of beautee hadde greet renoun*.   reputation
Al* were it so she were of smal degree*,   although   low station in life
Suffiseth hym hir yowthe and hir beautee.
Which mayde, he seyde, he wolde han* to his   have
   wyf,   415
To lede in ese and hoolynesse his lyf,
And thanked God that he myghte han hire al,
That no wight his blisse parten shal.
And preyde hem to laboure in this nede
And shapen* that he faille nat to spede*, 420   contrive   succeed

For thanne, he seyde, his spirit was at ese.
"Thanne is," quod he, "no thyng may me
    displese,   *422*
Save o* thyng priketh in* my conscience,   one disturbs
The which I wol reherce* in youre presence. recount
I have," quod he, "herd seyd ful yoore ago* very long ago
Ther may no man han parfit blisses two –
This is to seye, in erthe and eek in hevene.
For though he kepe hym fro the synnes
    sevene⁹
And eek from every branche of thilke* tree, that same
Yet is ther so parfit felicitee   *430*
And so greet ese* and lust* in mariage, delight pleasure
That evere I am agast* now in myn age afraid
That I shal lede now so myrie* a lyf, merry
So delicat* withouten wo and stryf, delightful
That I shal han myn hevene in erthe heere.
For sith* that verray hevene is boght so since
    deere   *436*
With tribulacion and greet penance,
How sholde I thanne, that lyve in swich* such
    plesance
As alle wedded men doon with hire wyvys,
Come to the blisse ther* Crist eterne on lyve where
    ys?   *440*
This is my drede*, and ye, my bretheren fear
    tweye,
Assoileth* me this question*, I preye." resolve problem

Justinus, which that hated his folye,
Answerde anon* right in his japerye*, at once joking
And for he wolde his longe tale abregge*, shorten
He wolde noon auctoritee allegge*, *446* adduce
But seyde, "Sire, so ther be noon obstacle

9 The Seven Deadly Sins so popular in medieval and renaissance tradition
are pride, envy, wrath, sloth, avarice, gluttony, and lechery. A large part
of the Parson's Tale is devoted to these sins.

Oother than this, God of his hygh myracle
And of his mercy may so for yow wirche*   provide
That er ye have youre right of hooly chirche,
Ye may repente of wedded mannes lyf,   *451*
In which ye seyn ther is no wo ne stryf.
And elles God forbede but* he sente   unless
A wedded man hym grace to repente
Wel ofte rather than a sengle man.   *455*
And therfore, sire, the beste reed* I kan*,   advice   know
Dispeire yow noght, but have in youre
    memorie
Paraunter* she may be youre purgatorie.[10]   perhaps
She may be Goddes meene* and Goddes   means
    whippe.
Thanne shal youre soule up to hevene skippe
Swifter than dooth an arwe out of the bowe.
I hope to God herafter shul ye knowe   *462*
That ther nys* noon so greet felicitee   is not
In mariage, ne nevere mo* shal bee,   more
That yow shal lette* of youre savacion*,   hinder you   salvation
So that ye use as skile* is and reson   *466*   good sense
The lustes* of youre wyf attemprely*,   desires   moderately
And that ye plese hire nat to amorously,
And that ye kepe yow eek* from oother   also
    synne.
My tale is doon, for my wit is thynne.   *470*
Beth nat agast herof*, my brother deere,   afraid of this
But lat us waden out of* this mateere.   pass from
The Wyf of Bathe,[11] if ye han understonde,
Of mariage which we have on honde*,   are discussing
Declared hath ful wel in litel space.   *475*
Fareth now wel; God have yow in his grace!"

10 Compare the Wife of Bath's statement concerning her fourth husband:
   "in erthe I was his purgatorie", Wife of Bath's Prologue, line 489.

11 Chaucer seems to imply here that the characters in the Merchant's Tale
   have heard the Wife of Bath's discourse on marriage.

And with that word this Justyn and his
   brother
Han take hir leve, and ech of hem of oother.
For whan they saughe* that it moste nedes   saw
   be,
They wroghten* so by sly and wys tretee*   brought it about   skilful
That she, this mayden which that Mayus   agreement
   highte*,   *481*   was called
As hastily as ever that she myghte
Shal wedded be unto this Januarie.
I trowe* it were to longe yow to tarie   believe
If I yow tolde of every scrit* and bond   *485*   deed
By which that she was feffed* in his lond,   put in possession
Or for to herknen* of hir riche array,   listen to
But fynally, ycomen* is the day   come
That to the chirche bothe be they went*   gone
For to receyve the hooly sacrement.   *490*
Forth comth the preest with stole aboute his
   nekke
And bad hire be lyk Sarra* and Rebekke*[12]   Sarah   Rebecca
In wysdom and in trouthe of mariage,
And seyde his orisons* as is usage*,   prayers   custom
And croucheth hem* and bad* God sholde   made sign of cross over them
   hem blesse,   *495*   prayed
And made al siker* ynogh with hoolynesse.   secure
Thus been they wedded with solempnitee*,   ceremony
And at the feeste* sitteth he and she   marriage feast
With othere worthy folk upon the deys*.   raised platform
Al ful of joye and blisse is the paleys,   *500*
And ful of instrumentz and of vitaille*,   food
The mooste deyntevous* of al Ytaille*.   daintiest   Italy
Biforn hem stoode instrumentz of swich*   such
   soun*   sound

---

12 The prayers in the marriage ceremony – a "hooly sacrement" (line 490)
   in the medieval church – mention Isaac and Sarah, and Abraham and
   Rebecca.

That Orpheus, ne of Thebes Amphioun,[13]
Ne maden nevere swich a melodye.   *505*
At every cours* thanne cam loud   course (of meal)
   mynstralcye,
That never tromped Joab[14] for to heere,
Ne he, Theodamas,[15] yet half so cleere
At Thebes whan the citee was in doute.
Bacus* the wyn hem shynketh* al aboute,   Bacchus   pours out
And Venus laugheth upon every wight*, *511*   person
For Januarie was bicome hir knyght
And wolde bothe assayen* his corage*   try   ardour
In libertee and eek* in mariage,   also
And with hire fyrbrond in hire hand aboute
Daunceth biforn the bryde and al the route*.   company
And certeinly, I dar right wel seyn* this, *517*   say
Ymeneus* that god of weddyng is   Hymen
Saugh* nevere his lyf so myrie* a wedded   saw   merry
   man.
Hoold thou thy pees*, thou poet Marcian*,[16]   peace   Martianus Capella
That writest us that ilke* weddyng murie   same
Of hire Philologie and hym Mercurie,   *522*
And of the songes that the Muses songe,
To* smal is bothe thy penne and eek thy   too
   tonge

---

13 Orpheus was the celebrated musician of Greek mythology whose melo-
dies so charmed the king of the underworld that he agreed to release
Orpheus' wife Eurydice to the upper world. Amphion, also of Greek
mythology, played his lyre during the building of the walls of Thebes,
and the stones moved into place of their own accord.

14 Joab is mentioned as sounding his trumpet in II Samuel 2:28, 18:16,
and 20:22.

15 Thiodamus is a priest in the *Thebaid* of Statius, a first-century Latin
author. Thiodamus does not actually blow a trumpet himself, but
trumpets are sounded at the conclusion of his prayers.

16 Martianus Capella (fifth century A.D.) wrote a poem on the marriage of
Philology and Mercury (*De Nuptiis Philologiae et Mercurii*).

For to discryven of* this mariage.   *525*   describe
Whan tendre youthe hath wedded stoupyng
   age,
Ther is swich* myrthe that it may nat be   such
   writen.
Assayeth* it youre self; thanne may ye witen*   try know
If that I lye or noon in this matiere.
Mayus, that sit with so benyngne* a chiere*,   gracious face
Hire to biholde it semed fairye*.   *531*   enchantment
Queene Ester[17] looked nevere with swich an
   eye
On Assuer*; so meke a look hath she   Ahasuerus
I may yow nat devyse* al hir beautee,   describe
But thus muche of hir beautee telle I may,
That she was lyk the brighte morwe of May
Fulfild of alle beautee and plesance.   *537*
This Januarie is ravysshed in a trance
At every tyme he looked on hir face.
But in his herte he gan hire to manace* *540* threaten
That he that nyght in armes wolde hire
   streyne
Harder than evere Parys dide Eleyne*.[18]   Helen
But nathelees*, yet hadde he greet pitee   nevertheless
That thilke* nyght offenden hire moste* he,   same must
And thoughte, "Allas, o tendre creature! *545*
Now wolde God ye myghte wel endure
Al my corage*, it is so sharpe and keene.   ardour
I am agast* ye shul it nat susteene.   afraid
But God forbede that I dide al my myght.
Now wolde God that it were woxen nyght*,   night had come
And that the nyght wolde lasten everemo.
I wolde that al this peple were ygo*!"   *552* gone
And fynally he dooth al his labour
As he best myghte, savynge his honour,
To haste* hem fro the mete* in subtil wyse.   hasten food

---

17 Esther's beauty attracted the notice of King Ahasuerus; see Esther 5:2.
18 The Trojan prince Paris and Helen of Troy are meant.

The tyme cam that reson was to ryse,   *556*
And after that men daunce and drynken
   faste,
And spices al aboute the hous they caste,
And ful of joye and blisse is every man,
Al but a squyer highte* Damyan,   *560*   called
Which carf* biforn the knyght ful many a   carved
   day.
He was so ravysshed on his lady May
That for the verray peyne he was ny wood*.   nearly mad
Almoost he swelte* and swowned* ther* he   died   fainted   where
   stood,
So soore hath Venus hurt hym with hire
   brond   *565*
As that she bar it daunsynge in hire hond,
And to his bed he wente hym hastily.
Namoore* of hym at this tyme speke I,   no more
But ther I lete hym wepe ynogh and pleyne*   lament
Til fresshe May wol rewen* on his peyne. *570*   have pity

   O perilous fyr, that in the bedstraw
   bredeth!
O famulier* foo*, that his servyce bedeth*!   household   foe   offers
O servant traytour, false hoomly hewe*,   domestic servant
Lyk to the naddre* in bosom sly untrewe,   adder
God shilde* us alle from youre aqueyntance!   defend
O Januarie, dronken in plesance   *576*
In mariage, se how thy Damyan,
Thyn owene squier and thy born man,
Entendeth* for to do thee vileynye!   intends
God graunte thee thyn hoomly fo* t'espye*,   enemy in the house   to dis-
For in this world nys* worse pestilence   *581*   is not   cover
Than hoomly foo al day* in thy presence.   always
Parfourned* hath the sonne his ark diurne*;   performed   daily round
Ne lenger* may the body of hym sojurne   longer
On th'orisonte* as in that latitude.   *585*   horizon
Night with his mantel that is derk and rude
Gan oversprede the hemysperie* aboute,   hemisphere
For which departed is this lusty route*   joyous company

Fro Januarie with thank on every syde.
Hoom to hir houses lustily* they ryde   *590*   happily
Where as they doon hir thynges as hem leste*,   it pleased them
And whan they sye* hir tyme, goon to reste.   saw
Soone after that this hastif* Januarie   impatient
Wolde go to bedde; he wolde no lenger tarye.
He drynketh ypocras*, clarree* and vernage*   wine cordial   spiced wine
Of spices hoote* t'encressen* his corage*,   Italian white win
And many a letuarie* hath he ful fyn   *597*   hot   increase   ardour
Swich as the cursed monk daun Constantyn[19]   medicine mixed with syrup;
Hath writen in his book *De Coitu*.   i.e., an aphrodisia
To eten hem alle he nas no thyng eschu*. *600*   did not shun at all
And to his privee* freendes thus seyde he: intimate
"For Goddes love, as soone as it may be,
Lat voyden* al this hous in curteys wyse."   empty
And they han doon right as he wol devyse.
Men drynken and the travers* drawe anon.   curtain
The bryde was broght a bedde as stille as
  stoon,   *606*
And whan the bed was with the preest
  yblessed,
Out of the chambre hath every wight* hym   person
  dressed*,   gone
And Januarie hath faste in armes take
His fresshe May, his paradys, his make*. *610*   mate
He lulleth* hire, he kisseth hire ful ofte   soothes
With thikke brustles* of his berd unsofte,   bristles
Lyk to the skyn of houndfyssh*, sharp as   dogfish
  brere*,   briar
For he was shave al newe in his manere.
He rubbeth hire aboute hir tendre face   *615*
And seyde thus, "Allas, I moot* trespace*   must   offend
To yow, my spouse, and yow greetly offende
Er tyme come that I wil doun descende.
But nathelees*, considereth this," quod he;   nevertheless
"Ther nys* no werkman, what so evere he be,   is not

---

19 "Constantyn" is one of the medical authorities cited in the description of
  the Monk in the General Prologue, line 433.

That may bothe werke wel and hastily. *621*

This wol be doon at leyser* parfitly*.   leisure   perfectly

It is no fors* how longe that we pleye;   it doesn't matter

In trewe wedlok coupled be we tweye,

And blessed be the yok* that we be inne, *625*   yoke

For in oure actes we mowe* do no synne.   can

A man may do no synne with his wyf,

Ne hurte hym selven with his owene knyf,

For we han* leve to pleye us* by the lawe."   have   enjoy ourselves

Thus laboureth he til that the day gan*   began

   dawe*,   *630*   to dawn

And thanne he taketh a sop* in fyn clarree*,   piece of bread   spiced wine

And upright in his bed thanne sitteth he.

And after that he sang ful loude and cleere

And kiste his wyf and made wantowne

   cheere*.   behaved amorously

He was al coltissh*, ful of ragerye*,   *635*   frisky   ardour

And ful of jargon* as a flekked* pye*.   talk spotted magpie

The slakke skyn aboute his nekke shaketh

Whil that he sang, so chaunteth* he and   sings

   craketh*.   croaks

But God woot* what that May thoughte in   knows

   hir herte

Whan she hym saugh* up sittynge in his   saw

   sherte,   *640*

In his nyght cappe and with his nekke lene*.   thin

She preyseth nat his pleyyng worth a bene.

Thanne seyde he thus: "My reste wol I take.

Now day is come I may no lenger* wake."   longer

And doun he leyde his heed and sleepe til

   pryme*,   *645*   9 a.m.

And afterward, whan that he saugh his tyme,

Up ryseth Januarie, but fresshe May

Heeld hire chambre unto the fourthe day,

As usage* is of wyves for the beste.   custom

For every labour* som tyme moot* han reste labourer   must

Or elles longe may he nat endure.   *651*

This is to seyn, no lyves* creature,   living

Be it of fyssh or bryd* or beest or man.   bird

Now wol I speke of woful Damyan
That langwissheth for love as ye shul heere;
Therfore I speke to hym in this manere. *656*

    I seye, o sely* Damyan, allas!   wretched
Andswere to my demaunde* as in this cas.   question
How shaltow* to thy lady fresshe May   will you
Telle thy wo? She wol alwey seye nay.   *660*
Eek* if thou speke, she wol thy wo biwreye*. also betray
God be thyn helpe, I kan no bettre seye.
This syke* Damyan in Venus fyr   ailing
So brenneth* that he dyeth for desyr,   burns
For which he putte his lyf in aventure*. *665* hazard
No lenger* myghte he in this wise endure,   longer
But prively* a penner* gan he borwe,   secretly writing case
And in a lettre wroot he al his sorwe,
In manere of a compleynt[20] or a lay*,   song
Unto his faire fresshe lady May,   *670*
And in a purs of sylk heng* on his sherte hung
He hath it put and leyd it at his herte.

    The moone, that at noon was thilke* day   that same
That Januarie hath wedded fresshe May, *674*
In two of Tawr* was in to Cancre* glyden,[21] second degree of Taurus
                                          Cancer
So longe hath Mayus in hir chambre byden*, remained
As custume is unto thise nobles alle.
A bryde shal nat eten in the halle
Til dayes foure, or thre dayes atte leeste*, *679* at least
Ypassed ben*; thanne lat hire go to feeste. have passed
The fourthe day compleet fro noon to noon,
Whan that the heighe masse was ydoon,
In halle sit this Januarie and May
As fressh as is the brighte someres day.
And so bifel* how that this goode man   *685* it happened

---

20 The complaint and lay were types of short poem; a humorous example
   of the former is Chaucer's "Complaynt to his Purse".

21 The moon had passed from the second degree of Taurus through Gemini
   into Cancer. The frequent astrological references in Chaucer's poetry
   indicate the extreme importance of astrological lore in the Middle Ages.

Remembred hym upon this Damyan,
And seyde, "Seynte Marie, how may this be,
That Damyan entendeth* nat to me?   attends
Is he ay syk, or how may this bityde?"
Hise squieres whiche that stooden ther bisyde
Excused hym by cause of his siknesse,   *691*
Which letted* hym to doon his bisynesse;   prevented
Noon oother cause myghte make hym tarye.
"That me forthynketh*," quod this Januarie,   I regret that
"He is a gentil squier, by my trouthe.   *695*
If that he deyde* it were harm and routhe*;   died   pity
He is as wys, discreet and secree*   able to keep secrets
As any man I woot* of his degree*,   know   station
And therto manly and eek servysable*,   willing to serve
And for to be thrifty* man right able.   *700* proper
But after mete*, as soone as evere I may,   food
I wol my self visite hym, and eek* May,   also
To doon hym al the confort that I kan."
And for that word hym blessed every man,
That of his bountee and his gentillesse   *705*
He wolde so conforten in siknesse
His squier, for it was a gentil* dede.   noble
"Dame," quod this Januarie, "taak good hede,
At after mete* ye with youre wommen alle,   right after dinner
Whan ye han been in chambre out of this
    halle,   *710*
That alle ye go se this Damyan.
Dooth hym disport*; he is a gentil man,   entertain him
And telleth hym that I wol hym visite,
Have I no thyng but rested me a lite.
And spede yow faste*, for I wol abyde*   *715* make haste   wait
Til that ye slepe faste by my syde."
And with that word he gan to hym calle
A squier that was marchal of his halle*,   i.e., head butler
And tolde hym certeyn thynges what he
    wolde.
This fresshe May hath streight hir wey
    yholde*   *720* held
With alle hir wommen unto Damyan.

Doun by his beddes syde sit* she than,   sits
Confortynge hym as goodly as she may.
This Damyan whan that his tyme he say*,   saw
In secree wise* his purs and eek his bille*,   secret manner   letter
In which that he ywriten hadde his wille, *726*
Hath put into hire hand withouten moore,
Save that he siketh* wonder* depe and   sighs   very
    soore*.   sorrowfully
And softely to hire right thus seyde he:
"Mercy, and that ye nat discovere me!   *730*
For I am deed if that this thyng be kyd*."   known
This purs hath she inwith* hir bosom hyd   within
And wente hire wey; ye gete namoore of me.
But unto Januarie ycomen is* she   has come
That on his beddes syde sit ful softe.   *735*
He taketh hire and kisseth hire ful ofte,
And leyde hym doun to slepe, and that anon*.   at once
She feyned hire* as that she moste gon   pretended
Ther as ye woot* that every wight* moot   know   person
    neede*,   must
And whan she of this bille* hath taken heede,   letter
She rente it al to cloutes* atte laste,   *741*   shreds
And in the pryvee softely it caste.

    Who studieth* now but faire fresshe May?   ponders
Adoun by olde Januarie she lay
That sleep til that the coughe hath hym
    awaked.   *745*
Anon he preyde hire strepen hire al naked;
He wolde of hire, he seyde, han som
    plesance,
And seyde hir clothes dide hym encombrance,
And she obeyeth, be hire lief or looth*.   whether she wants to or not
But lest that precious* folk be with me   fastidious
    wrooth*,   *750*   angry
How that he wroghte* I dar nat to yow telle,   what he did
Or wheither hire thoughte it* paradys or   it seemed to her
    helle.
But heere I lete hem werken in hir wyse

Til evensong rong, and that they moste aryse.
Were it by destynee or by aventure*,   *755*   chance
Were it by influence* or by nature*,   i.e., by magic   naturally
Or constellacion*, that in swich estaat   conjunction of the stars
The hevene stood that tyme fortunaat[22]
Was for to putte a bille* of Venus werkes,   plea
For alle thyng hath tyme, as seyn thise clerkes,
To any womman for to get hire love,   *761*
I kan nat seye, but grete God above
That knoweth that noon act is causelees,
He deme* of al, for I wol holde my pees.   let him judge
But sooth is this, how that this fresshe May
Hath take swich* impression that day   *766* such
Of pitee of this syke Damyan,
That from hire herte she ne dryve kan
The remembrance for to doon hym ese.
"Certeyn," thoghte she, "whom that this thyng
   displese   *770*
I rekke* noght, for heere I hym assure   care
To love hym best of any creature,
Thogh he namoore hadde than his sherte."
Lo, pitee renneth* soone in gentil* herte![23]   runs noble
Heere may ye se how excellent franchise*   generosity
In wommen is whan they hem narwe avyse*.   consider closely
Som tyrant* is as ther be many oon*   *777* i.e., hard-hearted woman
                                   a one
That hath an herte as hard as any stoon
Which wolde han lat hym sterven* in the   die
   place
Wel rather than han graunted hym hire grace,
And hem rejoysen in hir crueel pryde,   *781*
And rekke nat to been* an homycide.   care not if they are
This gentil May, fulfilled* of pitee,   filled full
Right of hire hand* a lettre made she   *784* in her own hand
In which she graunted hym hire verray grace.

22 There were astrologically propitious moments for undertaking any enterprise; see the General Prologue, lines 417-18, for another example.

23 A cynical repetition, almost word for word, of a line occurring in a
   more romantic context in the Knight's Tale.

Ther lakketh noght oonly but day and place,
Wher that she myghte unto his lust suffise*, satisfy his pleasure
For it shal be right as he wol devyse*. arrange
And whan she saugh* hir tyme upon a day, saw
To visite this Damyan gooth May, 790
And sotilly this lettre doun she threste* thrust
Under his pilwe*, rede it if hym leste*. pillow   it pleases him
She taketh hym by the hand and harde hym
    twiste,
So secrely* that no wight* of it wiste*, secretly   person   knew
And bad hym be al hool*, and forth she recover fully
    wente 795
To Januarie whan that he for hir sente.

    Up riseth Damyan the nexte morwe*; morning
Al passed was his siknesse and his sorwe.
He kembeth hym*, he preyneth hym* and combs his hair   preens
    pyketh*, makes himself neat
He dooth al that his lady lust* and lyketh*, delights   pleases
And eek* to Januarie he gooth as lowe* 801 obedient
As evere dide a dogge for the bowe*. i.e., trained for hunting
He is so plesant unto every man,
For craft is al, who so that do it kan,
That every wight* is fayn* to speke hym person   glad
    good. 805
And fully in his lady* grace he stood. lady's
Thus lete* I Damyan aboute his nede, leave
And in my tale forth I wol procede.
Somme clerkes holden that felicitee
Stant* in delit* and therfore, certeyn, he, resides   pleasure
This noble Januarie with al his myght 811
In honeste wise* as longeth to* a knyght, honourably   befits
Shoope* hym to lyve ful deliciously*. arranged   pleasurably
His housynge*, his array* as honestly* household   arrangements
To his degree* was maked as a kynges. 815 for his station in life   worthily
Amonges othere of his honeste* thynges worthy
He made a gardyn walled al with stoon;
So fair a gardyn woot* I nowher noon. know
For oute of doute*, I verraily* suppose without doubt   truly

That he that wroot *The Romance of the
   Rose*[24]   *820*
Ne koude of it the beautee wel devyse*.   describe
Ne Priapus[25] ne myghte nat suffise,
Thogh he be god of gardyns, for to telle
The beautee of the gardyn and the welle
That stood under a laurer* alwey grene. *825* laurel-tree
Ful ofte tyme he, Pluto, and his queene
Proserpina and al hire fairye
Disporten hem* and maken melodye   amuse themselves
Aboute that welle and daunced as men tolde.
This noble knyght, this Januarie the olde, *830*
Swich* deyntee* hath in it to walke and pleye such pleasure
That he wol no wight suffre bere the keye,
Save he hym self, for of the smale wyket*   wicket-gate
He baar* alwey of silver a clyket*   carried   latch-key
With which, whan that hym leste*, he it   it pleased him
   unshette*,   *835* unlocked
And whan he wolde paye his wyf hir dette
In somer seson, thider* wolde he go   thither
And May his wyf, and no wight* but they   person
   two.
And thynges whiche that were nat doon
   abedde,
He in the gardyn parfourned* hem and   performed
   spedde*.   *840* accomplished
And in this wise many a murye* day   happy
Lyved this Januarie and fresshe May.
But worldly joye may nat alwey endure
To Januarie, ne to no creature.

24 A celebrated allegorical poem in Old French of the thirteenth century.
The unfinished first part by Guillaume de Lorris was continued to
enormous length by Jean de Meun later in the century. Chaucer translated a part of the poem.

25 Priapus in Greek legend was guardian of gardens and a fertility deity;
extreme lasciviousness is also associated with his name.

O sodeyn hap*, o thou fortune unstable,   sudden chance
Lyk to the scorpion so deceyvable*,   846 deceitful
That flaterest with thyn heed whan thou wolt
    stynge!
Thy tayl is deeth thurgh thyn envenymynge*. poisoning
O brotil* joye, o swete venym queynte*!   fragile sly poison
O monstre, that so subtilly kanst peynte* 850 paint
Thy yiftes* under hewe* of stidefastnesse   gifts colour
That thou deceyvest bothe moore and lesse*, great and small
Why hastow* Januarie thus deceyved,   have you
That haddest hym for thy ful freend
    receyved?
And now thou hast biraft* hym bothe his   deprived
    eyen,   855
For sorwe of which desireth he to dyen.
Allas, this noble Januarie free*   generous
Amydde his lust* and his prosperitee   pleasure
Is woxen* blynd, and that al sodeynly.   has grown
He wepeth and he waileth pitously,   860
And ther with al the fyr of jalousie,
Lest that his wyf sholde falle in som folye,
So brente* his herte that he wolde fayn*   burned gladly
That som man bothe hire and hym had
    slayn.
For neither after his deeth nor in his lyf 865
Ne wolde he that she were love* ne wyf,   sweetheart
But evere lyve as wydwe* in clothes blake,   widow
Soul* as the turtle* that hath lost hire make*. solitary turtle-dove mate
But atte laste, after a monthe or tweye,
His sorwe gan aswage*, sooth* to seye. 870 lessen truth
For whan he wiste* it may noon oother be*, knew not otherwise
He paciently took his adversitee,
Save oute of doute* he may nat forgoon*   without doubt give up
That he nas jalous everemoore in oon*.   constantly
Which jalousye, it was so outrageous,   875
That neither in halle nyn* noon oother hous, nor in
Nyn noon oother place neverthemo
He nolde* suffre hire for to ryde or go,   would not
But if that he had hand on hire alway.

For which ful ofte wepeth fresshe May   *880*
That loveth Damyan so benyngnely*   graciously
That she moot* outher* dyen sodeynly,   must either
Or elles she moot han hym as hir leste*;   it pleases her
She wayteth whan* hir herte wolde breste*.   expects that break
Upon that oother syde Damyan   *885*
Bicomen is the sorwefulleste man
That evere was, for neither nyght ne day
Ne myghte he speke a word to fresshe May
As to his purpos of no swich mateere,
But if that Januarie moste it heere   *890*
That hadde an hand upon hire everemo.
But nathelees*, by writyng to and fro
And privee* signes wiste* he what she mente,   secret knew
And she knew eek* the fyn* of his entente*.   also aim intention

  O Januarie, what myghte it thee availle
Thogh thou myghtest se* as fer as shippes   see
    saille,   *896*
For as good is blynd deceyved be
As to be deceyved whan a man may se.
Lo, Argus[26] which that hadde an hondred
    eyen,
For al that he koude poure* or pryen*,   *900* gaze pry
Yet was he blent*, and God woot*, so been   deceived knows
  mo*,   more
That wenen* wisly that it be nat so;   believe
Passe over is an ese*; I seye namoore.   to overlook it is an easy way
This fresshe May, that I spak of so yoore*,   long ago   out
In warm wex hath emprented the clyket*   latch-key
That Januarie bar* of the smale wyket*,   *906* carried wicket-gate
By which into his gardyn ofte he wente.
And Damyan, that knew al hire entente,
The clyket countrefeted pryvely*.   secretly
Ther nys* namoore to seye, but hastily   *910* isn't

---

26 In Greek legend, Argus of the hundred eyes was set to watch over Io, the favourite of Zeus, by his wife Hera, who hoped to prevent her husband's intended adultery.

Som wonder by this clyket shal bityde*,   befall
Which ye shul heeren if ye wol abyde.
O noble Ovyde,[27] ful sooth* seistou*, God   truly you say
  woot*,   knows
Which sleighte* is it, thogh it be long and   trick
  hoot,
That he nyl* fynde it out in som manere. *915*   will not
By Pyramus and Tesbee* may men leere*,   Thisbe learn
Thogh they were kept ful longe streite
  overal*,   guarded strictly in every way
They been accorded* rownynge* thurgh a   reached agreement whisper-
  wal,   ing
Ther* no wight koude han founde out swich   where
  a sleighte*.   trick
But now to purpos; er that dayes eighte *920*
Were passed er the monthe of Juyl bifille*,[28]   arrived
That Januarie hath caught so greet a wille,
Thurgh eggyng* of his wyf, hym for to pleye   urging
In his gardyn, and no wight but they tweye,
That in a morwe* unto his May seith he: morning
"Rys up, my wyf, my love, my lady free! *926*
The turtle* voys is herd, my dowve sweete;   turtle-dove's
The wynter is goon with his reynes* weete*.   rains wet
Com forth now with thyn eyen columbyn*.   like a dove
How fairer been thy brestes than is wyn! *930*
The gardyn is enclosed al aboute;
Com forth, my white spouse, out of doute*   without a doubt
Thou hast me wounded in myn herte, o wyf.
No spot of thee ne knew I al my lyf.   *934*
Com forth, and lat us taken som disport*;   amusement
I chees* thee for my wyf and my confort."   chose

27 The story of Pyramus and Thisbe is in the Latin poet Ovid's *Metamorphoses*, iv, 55ff.

28 The first eight days of June are clearly meant since the astrological conjunction mentioned later in line 1010 could occur only before June 12 in Chaucer's day. It is difficult, however, to explain the "July" ("Juyl").

Swiche olde lewed wordes used he.[29]
On Damyan a signe made she
That he sholde go biforn with his cliket*. *939*   latch-key
This Damyan thanne hath opened the wyket*,   wicket-gate
And in he stirte* and that in swich manere   leapt
That no wight myghte it se* neither yheere*,   see   hear
And stille he sit* under a bussh anon*.   sits   at once
This Januarie as blynd as is a stoon
With Mayus in his hand and no wight mo*   more
In to his fresshe gardyn is ago*   *946*   has gone
And clapte to* the wyket sodeynly.   shut
"Now wyf," quod he, "heere nys* but thou   is not
     and I
That art the creature that I best love;
For by that lord that sit in hevene above, *950*
Levere* ich* hadde to dyen* on a knyf   rather   I   die
Than thee offende, trewe deere wyf.
For Goddes sake, thenk how I thee chees*,   chose
Noght for coveitise*, doutelees,   avarice
But oonly for the love I had to thee.   *955*
And though that I be oold and may nat see,
Beth to me trewe, and I shal telle yow why.
Thre thynges, certes, shal ye wynne ther by:
First, love of Crist, and to youre self honour,
And al myn heritage*, toun and tour   *960*   inheritance
I yeve* it yow, maketh chartres* as yow   give   draw up documents
     leste*.   it pleases you
This shal be doon tomorwe er sonne reste*,   before sundown
So wisly* God my soule brynge in blisse.   as certainly
I prey yow first in covenant ye me kisse.
And thogh that I be jalous, wyte* me noght;   blame
Ye been so depe enprented in my thoght, *966*
That whan I considere youre beautee,
And ther with al the unlikly elde* of me,   age
I may nat, certes, though I sholde dye*,   die

29 Many of January's "olde lewed wordes" are from the Biblical Song of
Solomon.

Forbere to been out of youre compaignye
For verray love; this is with outen doute. *971*
Now kisse me, wyf, and lat us rome aboute."
   This fresshe May, whan she thise wordes
   herde,
Benyngnely* to Januarie answerde,   graciously
But first and forward she bigan to wepe, *975*
"I have," quod she, "a soule for to kepe
As wel as ye, and also myn honour,
And of my wyfhod thilke* tendre flour*   that flower
Which that I have assured* in youre hond   pledged
Whan that the preest to yow my body bond;
Wherfore I wol answere in this manere *981*
By the leve of yow, my lord so deere.
I prey to God that nevere dawe* the day   dawn
That I ne sterve* as foule womman may,   die
If evere I do unto my kyn* that shame, *985* relatives
Or elles I empeyre* so my name   injure
That I be fals, and if I do that lakke*,   sin
Do strepe* me and put me in a sakke*   strip sack
And in the nexte ryver do me drenche*.   drown me
I am a gentil womman and no wenche*. *990* strumpet
Why speke ye thus but men been evere
   untrewe,
And wommen have repreve* of yow ay   reproof
   newe*?   ever anew
Ye han* noon oother contenance*, I leeve*, have constancy believe
But speke to us of untrust and repreeve*." reproof
   And with that word she saugh* wher   saw
   Damyan   *995*
Sat in the bussh, and coughen she bigan,
And with hir fynger signes made she
That Damyan sholde clymbe up on a tree
That charged was with fruyt, and up he
   wente,
For verraily* he knew al hire entente*, *1000* truly purpose
And every signe that she koude make
Wel bet* than Januarie hir owene make*,   much better mate
For in a lettre she hadde toold hym al

Of this matere, how he werchen* shal. *1004*   behave
And thus I lete hym sitte up on the pyrie*,   pear-tree
And Januarie and May romynge myrie*.   happily

Bright was the day and blew* the   blue
    firmament;
Phebus hath of gold his stremes doun ysent*   sent
To gladen every flour with his warmnesse.
He was that tyme in Geminis*, as I gesse,   Gemini (sign of the zodiac)
But litel fro his declynacion   *1011*
Of Cancer, Jovis* exaltacion.[30]   Jupiter's
And so bifel* that brighte morwe* tyde*   it happened   morning   time
That in the gardyn in the ferther syde,
Pluto that is kyng of fairye,   *1015*
And many a lady in his compaignye,
Folwynge his wyf the queene Proserpyne*,   Proserpina
Ech after oother right as a lyne
Whil that she gadered* floures* in the mede.   gathered   flowers
In Claudyan*[31] ye may the stories rede, *1020*   Claudian
And in his grisely* carte he hire sette.   terrible
This kyng of fairye thanne adoun hym sette
Upon a bench of turves* fressh and grene,   made of turf
And right anon* thus seyde he to his queene: straightway
"My wyf," quod he, "ther may no wight
    seye* nay;   *1025*   say
Th'experience so preveth* every day   proves
The tresons whiche that wommen doon to
    man.
Ten hondred thousand* tellen I kan   i.e., stories
Notable of youre untrouthe and brotilnesse*.   frailty
O Salomon, wys and richest of richesse, *1030*
Fulfild of sapience and of worldly glorie,
Ful worthy been thy wordes to memorie

---

30 The "exaltation" of a planet is its point of greatest influence; see Wife
   of Bath's Prologue, note 17, also note 28 above.

31 Claudius Claudianus, fourth-century author of an unfinished poem en-
   titled *De Raptu Proserpinae* (*The Abduction of Proserpina*).

To every wight that wit and reson kan*:   knows
Thus preiseth he yet the bountee* of man: goodness
'Amonges a thousand men yet foond* I oon*,   found one
But of wommen alle foond I noon*.'   *1036*   from Ecclesiastes 7:28
Thus seith the kyng that knoweth youre
   wikkednesse,
And Jhesus, *filius Syrak*,[32] as I gesse,
Ne speketh of yow but seelde* reverence.   seldom
A wylde fyr* and a corrupt pestilence   *1040*   erysipelas (skin disease pro-
                                          ducing red blotches)
So falle upon youre bodyes yet to nyght!
Ne se* ye nat this honourable knyght?   see
By cause, allas, that he is blynd and old,
His owene man shal make hym cokewold.
Lo, heere he sit, the lechour in the tree! *1045*
Now wol I graunten of my magestee
Unto this olde blynde worthy knyght
That he shal have ageyn his eyen syght. *1048*
Whan that his wyf wolde doon hym vileynye,
Thanne shal he knowen al hire harlotrye,
Bothe in repreve of hire and othere mo*."   more
"Ye shal?" quod Proserpyne, "Wol ye so?
Now by my moodres* sires* soule I swere   mother's father's (i.e.,
                                          Saturn)
That I shal yeven* hire suffisant answere,   give
And alle wommen after for hire sake,   *1055*
That though they be in any gilt* ytake*,   sin taken
With face boold they shulle hem self excuse
And bere hem doun* that wolden hem accuse.   overcome them
For lakke of answere noon of hem shal
   dyen*,   die
Al* hadde man seyn* a thyng with bothe   even if seen
   hise eyen,   *1060*
Yit shul we wommen visage* it hardily*,   bluff boldly
And wepe and swere and visage it subtilly
So that ye men shul been as lewed* as gees.   ignorant
What rekketh me* of youre auctoritees*?   do I care authoritative wri-
                                          ters
I woot* wel that this Jew, this Salomon, *1065*   know
Foond* of us wommen fooles many oon*.   found many a one

32 Jesus, son of Sirach, the reputed author of Ecclesiasticus.

But though that he ne foond no good
  womman,
Yet hath ther founde many another man
Wommen ful trewe, ful goode, and vertuous.
Witnesse on hem that dwelle in Cristes hous:
With martirdom they preved* hire   proved
  constance*.   *1071* constancy
The Romayn geestes* eek maken   stories
  remembrance
Of many a verray* trewe wyf also.   loyal
But sire, be nat wrooth*, al* be it so   angry   although
Though that he seyde he foond no good
  womman;   *1075*
I preye yow, take the sentence* of the man.   meaning
He mente thus, that in sovereyn bontee*   goodness
Nis noon* but God that sit in Trinitee.   isn't any
Ey! For verray God that nys but oon*,   is but one
What make ye so muche of Salomon?   *1080*
What though he made a temple Goddes
  hous?
What though he were riche and glorious?
So made he eek* a temple of false goddis*.   also   see I Kings 7:7-8
How myghte he do a thyng that moore
  forbode* is?   *1084* forbidden
Pardee, as faire as ye his name emplastre*,   plaster over; i.e., whitewash
He was a lecchour and an ydolastre*,   idolator
And in his elde* he verray God forsook,   old age
And if God ne hadde, as seith the book,
Yspared for his fadres* sake, he sholde   father's
Have lost his regne* rather* than he wolde.   kingdom   sooner
I sette right noght of al the vileynye   *1091*
That ye* of wommen write a boterflye*!   i.e., you men   butterfly
I am a womman, nedes moot* I speke,   must
Or elles swelle til myn herte breke.
For sithen* he seyde that we been   since
  jangleresses*,   *1095* chatterboxes
As evere hool* I moote brouke my tresses*,   healthy   I might enjoy my
I shal nat spare for no curteisye   tresses
To speke hym harm that wolde us vileynye."

"Dame," quod this Pluto, "be no longer*   longer
    wrooth.   *1099*
I yeve* it up, but sith I swoor myn ooth   give
That I wolde graunten hym his sighte ageyn,
My word shal stonde, I warne yow certeyn.
I am a kyng; it sit* me noght to lye."   befits
"And I," quod she, "a queene of fairye.
Hir answere shal she have, I undertake*.   guarantee
Lat us namoore wordes heerof make;   *1106*
For sothe*, I wol no lenger* yow   in truth   no longer
    contrarie*."   oppose
    Now lat us turne agayn to Januarie
That in the gardyn with his faire May
Syngeth ful murier* than the papejay*,   *1110*   more merrily   parrot
"Yow love I best and shal and oother noon."
So longe aboute the aleyes* is he goon*   alleys   gone
Til he was come* agayns* thilke* pyrie*   had come   opposite
                           that same   pear-tree
Where as this Damyan sitteth ful myrie
An heigh* among the fresshe leves grene.   aloft
This fresshe May that is so bright and
    sheene*   *1116*   fair
Gan for to syke* and seyde, "Allas, my syde!   sigh
Now sire," quod she, "for aught that may
    bityde*,   happen
I moste han* of the peres* that I see,   must have   pears
Or I moot dye, so soore longeth me*   *1120*   I long
To eten of the smale peres grene.
Help for hir love that is of hevene queene!
I telle yow wel, a womman in my plit*   condition
May han to fruyt so greet an appetit
That she may dyen but she of it have."   *1125*
    "Allas," quod he, "that I ne had heer a
    knave*   servant
That koude clymbe! Allas, allas!" quod he,
"That I am blynd!" "Ye, sire, no fors*," quod   no matter
    she,
"But wolde ye vouchesauf*, for Goddes sake,   grant
The pyrie* inwith* youre armes for to take,   pear-tree   within
For wel I woot* that ye mystruste me,   *1131*   know

Thanne sholde I clymbe wel ynogh*," quod   enough
   she,
"So I my foot myghte sette upon youre bak."
"Certes*," quod he, "ther on shal be no lak,   certainly
Mighte I yow helpen with myn herte blood."
He stoupeth doun, and on his bak she stood,
And caughte hire by a twiste*, and up she   branch
   gooth.   *1137*
Ladyes, I prey yow that ye be nat wrooth*;   angry
I kan nat glose*; I am a rude man*.   i.e., beat around the bush
And sodeynly anon* this Damyan   *1140*   at once   rough fellow
Gan pullen up the smok and in he throng*   thrust
And whan that Pluto saugh* this grete   saw
   wrong,
To Januarie he gaf* agayn his sighte,   gave
And made hym se as wel as evere he myghte.
And whan that he hadde caught his sighte
   agayn,   *1145*
Ne was ther nevere man of thyng so fayn*,   glad
But on his wyf his thoght was everemo.
Up to the tree he caste hise eyen two,
And saugh that Damyan his wyf had
   dressed*   *1149*   prepared
In swich manere it may nat been expressed
But if* I wolde speke uncurteisly*.   unless   unmannerly
And up he yaf* a roryng and a cry   gave
As dooth the mooder* whan the child shal   mother
   dye:
"Out, helpe, allas, harrow*!" he gan to crye.   help
"O stronge* lady stoore*, what dostow*?"   bold   audacious   what are
   And she answerde, "Sire, what eyleth*   ails   you doing
   yow?   *1156*
Have pacience and reson in youre mynde.
I have yow holpe* on bothe youre eyen   helped
   blynde,
Up peril of my soule*, I shal nat lyen*,   I'll stake my soul   lie
As me was taught to heele with* youre eyen,   heal
Was no thyng bet* to make yow to see *1161*   better
Than strugle with a man up on a tree.

God woot* I dide it in ful good entente*."   knows   intention

"Strugle?" quod he, "Ye, algate* in it wente!   at any rate

God yeve* yow bothe on shames deth to   grant
   dyen!   *1165*

He swyved* thee! I saugh* it with myn eyen,   had intercourse with   saw

And elles be I hanged by the hals*!"   neck

   "Thanne is," quod she, "me medicyne fals,

For certeinly, if that ye myghte se,

Ye wolde nat han seyn* thise wordes unto   said
   me.   *1170*

Ye han som glymsyng* and no parfit*   imperfect sight   perfect
   sighte."

"I se," quod he, "as wel as evere I myghte,

Thonked be God, with bothe myne eyen two,

And by my trouthe, me thoughte* he dide   it seemed to me
   thee so!"

   "Ye maze, maze*, goode sire," quod she,   are confused

"This thank have I, for I have maad yow
   see.   *1176*

Allas," quod she, "that evere I was so
   kynde!"

"Now dame," quod he, "lat al passe out of
   mynde.

Com doun, my lief*, and if I have myssayd*,   darling   said amiss

God helpe me so, as I am yvele apayd*. *1180*   displeased

But by my fader soule, I wende* han seyn*   thought to   seen

How that this Damyan hadde by thee leyn*   lain

And that thy smok hadde leyn upon his
   brest."

   "Ye sire," quod she, "ye may wene as yow
   lest*.   it pleases you

But sire, a man that waketh out of his
   sleepe,   *1185*

He may nat sodeynly wel taken keepe*   be aware

Upon a thyng, ne* seen* it parfitly*   nor   see   perfectly

Til that he be adawed* verraily*.   recovered   truly

Right so a man that longe hath blynd ybe

Ne may nat sodeynly so wel yse*   *1190*   see

First whan his sighte is newe come ageyn

As he that hath a day or two yseyn*.   seen
Til that youre sighte ysatled* be a while,   settled
Ther may ful many a sighte yow bigile*.   mislead
Beth war*, I prey yow, for by hevene kyng,   take care
Ful many a man weneth* to seen a thyng,   thinks
And it is al another than it semeth.   *1197*
He that mysconceyveth*, he mysdemeth*."   misapprehends misjudges
And with that word she leepe* doun fro the   leapt
    tree.
This Januarie, who is glad but he?   *1200*
He kisseth hire and clippeth* hire ful ofte   embraces
And on hire wombe* he stroketh hire ful   stomach
    softe,
And to his palays hoom he hath hire lad*.   led
Now goode men, I pray yow, be glad.   *1204*
    Thus endeth heere my tale of Januarie;
God blesse us and his mooder Seinte Marie!

    "Ey, Goddes mercy!" seyde oure Hoost
        tho*;   then
"Now swich a wyf I pray God kepe me fro!
Lo, whiche* sleightes* and subtiltees   what tricks
In wommen been! For ay as bisy as bees
Been they us sely* men for to deceyve. *1211*   hapless
And from a sooth* evere wol they weyve*;   truth swerve
By this Marchauntes tale it preveth* weel.   proves
But doutelees, as trewe as any steel,   *1214*
I have a wyf though that she poure* be,   poor
But of hir tong a labbyng* shrewe* is she,   blabbing scold
And yet she hath an heep of vices mo*   more
Therof no fors*; lat alle swiche* thynges go.   never mind about it   such
But wyte ye what* – in conseil* be it   do you know what   in secret
    seyd –   *1219*
Me reweth soore* I am unto hire teyd*,   I regret greatly   tied
For and* I sholde rekenen every vice   if
Which that she hath, ywis* I were to nyce*.   certainly   too foolish
And cause why*? It sholde reported be   the reason why
And toold to hire of* somme of this   by
    meynee*,   company

Of whom it nedeth nat for to declare,   *1225*
Syn wommen konnen* outen swich   know how to
   chaffare*.[33]   set out such wares
And eek* my wit suffiseth nat therto   also
To tellen al, wherfore my tale is do*."   finished

---

33 Since in line 1226 the Host uses an expression identical with that of the Wife of Bath in her Prologue, line 521, there is little doubt that the Wife is intended.

INTRODUCTION TO THE
FRANKLIN'S TALE

Like the Merchant's Tale, the Franklin's Tale revolves around
the love triangle composed of a husband, a wife, and a squire
who is suitor to the wife, and also like the Merchant's Tale it
employs the motif of the garden, but the resemblance ends there.
The Franklin, a rural landowner of some substance with a lean-
ing towards the ideals of chivalry, does not share the Merchant's
cynical bourgeois attitude to marriage. In fact, for the Franklin
the pendulum swings in the opposite direction, and if he has a
fault, it is an excessively romantic attitude to the relationship
between the sexes. At least, such are the reflections prompted by
a consideration of the tale he tells.

In his tale the Franklin attempts to reconcile two attitudes
towards the relationship between the sexes current in his time.
One attitude was the belief in male domination, which regarded
the woman as a mere chattel of the male with no legal rights of
her own. In this view she was simply a piece of property to be
disposed of by those under whose control she found herself as
they saw fit. She had no say in the choice of a husband and even
when widowed she was still considered a valuable pawn in the
game of amassing family estates. It is this conception of woman's
role that the Wife of Bath reacts against so strongly. On the
other hand was the view of woman summed up under the title
"Courtly Love", discussed at length in the General Introduction.[1]
In this view woman was elevated to a position of eminence far
above that of the mere male. Love between the sexes was regarded as an ennobling force that could exist only outside of marriage, because in marriage the traditional role of the male was to
be the dominant partner. Also, the male was deemed the inferior
of the woman both socially and spiritually, and whatever worth

1 See above, p. xv.

existed in his character came as a result of his love for his lady. It was in these terms that the aristocracy of Chaucer's day liked to imagine themselves, and anyone with any pretensions to gentility sympathized with this point of view about the relationship between the sexes. The Franklin shared these sentiments, and in his tale of the knight Arveragus, the wife Dorigen, and the squire Aurelius, he presents us with a courtship resulting in a marriage that is permeated with these views. But the Franklin, like most Englishmen of his time to judge by the attitude expressed in the literature, wants to preserve the proprieties conferred by marriage as well as the romantic notions about the relationship between the sexes as embodied in the sentiments of Courtly Love. Thus in his tale the knight Arveragus is required to serve the lady as suitor for a long time before she is won, and when she finally consents to marriage she does not dwindle into a wife, to use Congreve's phrase, but remains the courtly lady with a will and an independence of her own. As her husband, the knight Arveragus becomes "Servant in love, and lord in mariage", and the Franklin therefore skilfully combines in the marriage of Arveragus and Dorigen the two attitudes towards the relationship between the sexes that we have been discussing.

Some readers have regarded this reconciliation of two opposing views by the Franklin as the solution to the question concerning which partner should dominate in marriage raised by the Wife of Bath. In the Franklin's solution neither party dominates in the marriage relationship, and each has equal rights. It is true that there is something engaging in the "humble, wys acord" between Arveragus and his wife Dorigen which many readers find attractive. This reaction to the Franklin's view is also supported by modern marriage manuals that constantly cast the husband in the role of suitor to his wife's affections, and by the modern trend to equality of the sexes which insists on the independence of woman. But if the Franklin's solution to the marriage debate results in what might be called the ideal marriage, it is difficult to explain why the ideal marriage of this couple runs into the jeopardy it does. For the hapless Dorigen, while her husband is abroad winning fame as a knight, makes what the medieval romance tradition called a "rash vow" or promise to the love-stricken Aurelius, and she later discovers to her dismay that to keep her reputation as a faithful woman she must consent to adultery with this clever squire. In her moment of crisis the aloof and independent wife sees suicide as the only remedy for her hopeless situation, and she spends a few days recalling all the famous heroines of the past who have preferred death to dishonour. Though she desired the liberty of a Courtly Love mistress from Arveragus before she would consent to marriage, she here exhibits a pitiful incapacity for exercising the responsibilities of that liberty. She is incapable of taking any action on her own at this point. Her unconscious delaying tactic keeps her alive until her husband returns home. When he learns the circumstances, he, in his role of "lord in mariage", orders Dorigen to fulfil her promise to Aurelius. Thus Arveragus, in his moment of crisis, unused to authority, makes a decision which is in effect a negation of his marriage. The crisis in this marriage is only resolved by a force which is exterior to the two marriage partners themselves.

It was mentioned earlier that the garden motif of the Merchant's Tale plays a role in this tale also. Taking the two tales in conjunction with one another we see that the garden motif performs an interesting function. In the Merchant's Tale the garden is the scene of old January's lustful play with his wife, and it is not surprising to find Priapus, with whose name extreme lechery is associated, mentioned in conjunction with January's garden. Nor is it surprising to find that what January considered a paradise or Garden of Eden had a completely different meaning for May, and her impression of hell is reinforced by the appearance of Pluto, the god of the underworld, in that garden also. In the Franklin's Tale, however, we notice that though Dorigen is supposed to keep her assignation with Aurelius in a garden, the two never reach their destination. Thus the paradisal and the hellish connotations that the garden possessed in the Merchant's Tale, though invoked in the Franklin's Tale, are never brought to fruition since the couple never enter the garden. The imagery of spring and winter is used in an interesting way also. Aurelius woos Dorigen in a spring-time garden, and though she rebuffs his proposal, the very fact that she relents to the point of agreeing to his demand should he fulfil what she believes to be an impossible request suggests some kind of unconscious vernal acquiescence on her part. But the occasion when she must live up to her prom- ise to accept him as her lover occurs in winter, and she experi- ences a cold sobering realization of the implications of her prom- ise.

The happy ending of the Franklin's Tale resolves itself with a question, thereby linking the story to a common medieval device called the *demande d'amour*. Though this "question of love" is usually associated with an answer concerning the suitability of two or three contestants for a lady's hand, each contestant pos- sessing a virtue of his own in contrast to the individual virtues of the others, the Franklin skilfully adapts the device to his own purpose in his tale. The reader is thus subtly diverted from a con- sideration of the moral implications of the tale to the solution of what is, after all, merely a riddle, a riddle, moreover, to which there is no hard and fast answer. If we choose to regard the Franklin's Tale as the conclusion of the debate on marriage in the *Canterbury Tales* as a whole, a riddle is an appropriate answer to the question of who should dominate in marriage, husband or wife.

The Franklin's Tale

Thise olde, gentil* Britons* in hir dayes   *noble*   Bretons
Of divers* aventures maden layes,   *different*
Rymeyed* in hir firste* Briton tonge,   *rhymed*   *original*
Whiche layes with hir instrumentz they songe,
Or elles redden* hem for hir plesance,   5   *read*
And oon* of hem have I in remembrance,   *one*
Which I shal seyn with good wyl as I kan.
But sires, by cause I am a burel* man,   *unlearned*
At my bigynnyng first I yow biseche,
Have me excused of my rude speche.   10
I lerned nevere rethorik*, certeyn;   *rhetoric*
Thyng that I speke, it moot* be bare and   *must*
   pleyn.
I sleepe nevere on the mount of Pernaso*,   *Parnassus*
Ne lerned Marcus Tullius Scithero*.[1]   *Cicero*
Colours* ne knowe I none, with outen   *i.e., rhetorical embellishments*
   drede*,   15   *doubt*
But swiche* colours as growen in the mede*,   *such*   *meadow*
Or ellis swiche as men dye or peynte*.   *paint*
Colours of rethoryk been to queynte*;   *strange*
My spirit feeleth noght of swich mateere.
But if yow list*, my tale shul ye heere.   20   *it pleases you*

In Armorik*, that called is Britayne*,   *Armorica*   *Brittany*
Ther was a knyght that loved and dide his
   payne*   *exerted himself*
To serve a lady in his beste wise,
And many a labour, many a gret emprise*,   *deed of chivalric prowess*
He for his lady wroghte* er she were wonne,   *performed*

1 Cicero (106-43 B.C.), Roman orator famous for eloquence.

For she was oon the faireste under sonne, *26*
And eek* therto, comen of so heigh kynrede*   also   lineage
That wel unnethes* dorste* this knyght for   scarcely at all   dared
   drede
Telle hire his wo, his peyne, and his distresse.
But atte laste*, she for his worthynesse,   *30*   at last
And namely, for his meke obeysance*,   attention
Hath swich a pitee caught of his penance*,   distress
That pryvely* she fil of his acord*   secretly   agreed
To take hym for hir housbonde and hir lord,
Of swich lordshipe as men han* over hir   have
   wyves.   *35*
And for to lede the moore in blisse hir lyves,
Of his free wyl he swoor* hire as a knyght   swore
That nevere in al his lyf he, day ne nyght,
Ne sholde upon hym take no maistrie*   sovereignty
Agayn hir wyl, ne kithe* hire jalousie,   *40*   show
But hire obeye and folwe hir wyl in al,
As any lovere to his lady shal,
Save that the name of soveraynetee,
That wolde he have, for shame of his degree*.   out of respect for his position
   She thanked hym, and with ful greet
   humblesse   *45*
She seyde, "Sire, sith* of youre gentillesse*   since   nobility of nature
Ye profre me to have so large* a reyne*,   free   rein
Ne wolde nevere God* bitwixe us tweyne,   may God never allow
As in my gilt were* outher* werre* or stryf.   that through my fault were   either   war
Sire, I wol be youre humble, trewe wyf.   *50*
Have heer my trouthe til that myn herte
   breste*."   burst
Thus been they bothe in quiete and in reste.
For o* thyng, sires, saufly* dar I seye,   one   safely
That freendes everych oother* moot* obeye*   each other   must   yield to
If they wol longe holden compaignye.   *55*
Love wol nat been constreyned by maistrye.
Whan maistrie comth, the god of love anon*   straightway
Beteth his wynges, and farewel, he is gon!
Love is a thyng as any spirit free.
Wommen of kynde* desiren libertee,   *60*   by nature

And nat to been constreyned as a thral*;   slave
And so doon men, if I sooth* seyen shal.   truth
Looke who* that is moost pacient in love,   whoever
He is at his avantage al above*.   in a favourable position
Pacience is an heigh vertu, certeyn,   65
For it venquysseth*, as thise clerkes seyn,[2]   overcomes
Thynges that rigour sholde nevere atteyne*.   attempt
For every word men may nat chide or
    pleyne*;   complain
Lerneth to suffre, or elles, so moot* I goon,   may
Ye shul it lerne, wher so* ye wolde or noon.   whether
For in this world, certeyn, ther no wight* is   person
That he ne dooth or seith som tyme amys. 72
Ire, siknesse, or constellacion*,   influence of the stars
Wyn, wo, or chaungynge of complexion*   change in health
Causeth ful ofte to doon amys or speken.   75
On every wrong a man may nat be wreken*.   avenged
After the tyme moste be temperance*   moderation
To every wight that kan on* governance*.   has skill in   self-control
And therfore hath this wise, worthy knyght
To lyve in ese* suffrance* hire bihight*,   80   happily   forebearance   promised
And she to hym ful wisly gan to swere
That nevere sholde ther be defaute in here*.   her
    Heere may men seen an humble, wys
        acord*;   agreement
Thus hath she take hir servant and hir lord.
Servant in love, and lord in mariage;   85
Thanne was he bothe in lordshipe and
    servage*.   servitude
Servage? Nay, but in lordshipe above,
Sith* he hath bothe his lady and his love.   since
His lady, certes*, and his wyf also,   certainly
The which* that lawe of love acordeth to*.   who   agrees to
And whan he was in this prosperitee,   91
Hoom with his wyf he gooth to his contree,

2 The "Clerk of Oxenford" had told the story of Griselda's incredible patience in the face of unbelievable adversity.

Nat fer fro Pedmark*³ ther* his dwellyng was, · Penmarch, Brittany   where

Where as he lyveth in blisse and in solas*. · comfort

Who koude telle but he hadde wedded be
The joye, the ese, and the prosperitee   *96*
That is bitwixe an housbonde and his wyf!⁴
A yeer and moore lasted this blisful lyf,
Til that the knyght of which I speke thus,
That of Kayrrud was, cleped* Arveragus, · called
Shoop* hym to goon and dwelle a yeer or · prepared
   tweyne   *101*
In Engelond that cleped was eek* Briteyne*, · also   Britain
To seke in armes worshipe* and honour; · reputation
For al his lust* he sette in swich* labour, · pleasure   such
And dwelled ther two yeer, the book seith
   thus.   *105*
Now wol I stynten* of this Arveragus, · cease
And speken I wol of Dorigene his wyf,
That loveth hire housbonde as hire hertes lyf.
For his absence wepeth she and siketh*, · sighs
As doon thise noble wyves whan hem liketh*. · it pleases them
She moorneth, waketh, wayleth, fasteth,
   pleyneth*;   *111* · complains
Desir of his presence hire so distreyneth* · distresses
That al this wyde world she set at noght.
Hire freendes, whiche that knewe hir hevy
   thoght,
Conforten hire in al that ever they may;   *115*
They prechen hire, they telle hire nyght and
   day
That causelees she sleeth* hir self, allas. · slays
And every confort possible in this cas
They doon to hire with al hire bisynesse*, · solicitude

---

3 This place name, and "Kayrrud" later in line 100, and the personal
   names Arveragus and Dorigen are Breton or Celtic in origin, a fact suggesting that Chaucer's source for this story was Breton in origin.

4 These three lines (95-7) are an echo of some of the very ironical remarks
   on marriage in the Merchant's Tale, especially lines 47-8.

Al for to make hire leve hire hevynesse. *120*
By proces*, as ye knowen everichoon*,   in time   every one
Men may so longe graven* in a stoon   carve
Til som figure ther inne emprented be.
So longe han* they conforted hire til she   have
Receyved hath by hope and by reson   *125*
The emprentyng of hire consolacion,
Thurgh which hir grete sorwe gan aswage*;   lessen
She may nat alwey duren* in swich rage*.   remain   such sorrow
And eek* Arveragus in al this care   *129*   also
Hath sent hire lettres hoom of his welfare,
And that he wol com hastily agayn,
Or elles hadde this sorwe hir herte slayn.
Hire freendes sawe hir sorwe gan to slake*,   diminish
And preyde hire on knees, for Goddes sake,
To come and romen hire in compaignye *135*
Away to dryve hire derke fantasye*,   gloomy thoughts
And finally she graunted that requeste,
For wel she saugh* that it was for the beste.   saw
Now stood hire castel faste by the see,   *139*
And often with hire freendes walketh shee
Hire to disporte* upon the bank an heigh*,   to amuse herself   on high
Wher as she many a ship and barge seigh*   saw
Seillynge hir cours where as hem liste* go.   it pleased them to
But thanne was that a parcel of hire wo,
For to hir self ful ofte "Allas!" seith she, *145*
"Is ther no ship of so manye as I se
Wol bryngen hom my lord? Thanne were
   myn herte
Al warisshed* of his bittre peynes smerte*."   cured   smarting
   Another tyme ther wolde she sitte and
   thynke,   *149*
And caste hir eyen dounward fro the brynke,
But whan she saugh* the grisly rokkes blake, saw
For verray feere so wolde hir herte quake
That on hire feet she myghte hire noght
   sustene*.   maintain
Thanne wolde she sitte adoun upon the
   grene,

And pitously in to the see biholde,   *155*
And seyn right thus with sorweful sikes*   sighs
   colde:
   "Eterne God, that thurgh thy purveiaunce*   providence
Ledest the world by certein governaunce,
In ydel*, as men seyn, ye no thyng make.   in vain
But, Lord, thise grisly, feendly* rokkes blake,   devilish
That semen rather a foul confusion   *161*
Of werk than any fair creacion
Of swich a parfit*, wys God and a stable,   perfect
Why han ye wroght this werk unresonable?
For by this werk, south, north, ne west, ne
   eest,   *165*
Ther nys* yfostred* man, ne bryd*, ne beest. is not nourished bird
It dooth no good, to my wit*, but anoyeth*. in my opinion causes harm
Se ye nat, Lord, how mankynde it
   destroyeth?
An hundred thousand bodyes of mankynde
Han rokkes slayn, al be they nat in mynde,
Which mankynde is so fair part of thy werk
That thou it madest lyk to thyn owene
   merk*.   *172* likeness
Thanne semed it ye hadde greet chiertee*   affection
Toward mankynde, but how thanne may it
   bee
That ye swiche meenes make it to destroyen,
Whiche meenes do no good, but evere
   anoyen*?   *176* cause harm
I woot* wel clerkes* wol seyn, as hem leste*, know scholars it pleases
                        them
By argumentz that al is for the beste,
Though I ne kan the causes nat yknowe*, know
But thilke* God that made wynd to blowe that
As kepe* my lord, this my conclusion;   *181* preserve
To clerkes lete* I al disputison*,   leave dispute
But wolde God that alle thise rokkes blake
Were sonken in to helle for his sake!
Thise rokkes sleen myn herte for the feere."
Thus wolde she seyn with many a pitous
   teere.   *186*

Hire freendes saw that it was no disport*   amusement
To romen by the see, but disconfort,
And shopen* for to pleyen somwher elles.   contrived
They leden hire by ryveres and by welles,
And eek* in othere places delitables*.   *191*   also   delightful
They dauncen and they pleyen at ches* and   chess
   tables*.   backgammon
So, on a day, right on the morwe tyde*,   morning
Unto a gardyn that was ther bisyde,
In which that they hadde maad hir
   ordinance*   *195*   arrangement
Of vitaille* and of oother purveiance*,   food   provision
They goon and pleye hem* al the longe day.   amuse themselves
And this was on the sixte* morwe* of May,   sixth   morning
Which May hadde peynted with his softe
   shoures*   showers
This gardyn ful of leves and of floures*. *200*   flowers
And craft* of mannes hand so curiously*   skill   ingeniously
Arrayed* hadde this gardyn, trewely,   adorned
That nevere was ther gardyn of swich prys*   value
But if it were the verray paradys*.   Paradise itself
The odour of floures and the fresshe sighte
Wolde han* maked any herte lighte   *206*   have
That evere was born, but if* to* greet   unless   too
   siknesse,
Or to greet sorwe helde it in distresse,
So ful it was of beautee with plesance.
At after dyner gonne they to daunce   *210*
And synge also, save Dorigen allone,
Which made alwey hir compleint* and hir   lamentation
   moone*   moan
For she ne saugh* hym on the daunce go *213*   saw
That was hir housbonde, and hir love also.
But nathelees*, she moste* a tyme abyde,   nevertheless   had to
And with good hope lete hir sorwe slyde.
   Upon this daunce, amonges othere men,
Daunced a squier biforn Dorigen,
That fressher was and jolyer of array*, *219*   dress
As to my doom*, than is the monthe of May.   in my judgment

He syngeth, daunceth, passynge any man
That is or was, sith* that the world bigan.   since
Ther-with he was, if men sholde hym
   discryve*,   describe
Oon* of the beste farynge* man on lyve,   one   handsomest
Yong, strong, right vertuous, and riche and
   wys,   225
And wel biloved, and holden in greet prys*.   estimation
And shortly, if the sothe* I tellen shal,   truth
Unwityng of* this Dorigen at al   unknown to
This lusty squier, servant to Venus,
Which that ycleped* was Aurelius,   230   called
Hadde loved hire best of any creature
Two yeer and moore, as was his aventure*,   lot
But nevere dorste* he tellen hire his   dared
   grevance*.   suffering
With outen coppe* he drank al his penance.   i.e., without satisfaction
He was despeyred*; no thyng dorste he seye,   in despair
Save in his songes somwhat wolde he wreye*   disclose
His wo, as in a general compleynyng.   237
He seyde he lovede and was biloved no
   thyng*.   not at all
Of swich matere made he manye layes,
Songes, compleintes, roundels, virelayes,[5]
How that he dorste nat his sorwe telle,   241
But langwissheth as a furye dooth in helle.
And dye he moste*, he seyde, as dide Ekko*   had to   Echo
For Narcisus,[6] that dorste nat telle hir wo.
In oother maner than ye heere me seye   245
Ne dorste he nat to hire his wo biwreye*,   disclose
Save that, paraventure*, som tyme at   perhaps
   daunces
Ther* yong folk kepen hir observaunces*,   where   customs
It may wel be he looked on hir face

5 These are the technical names of short lyric poems, forms which Chaucer
  himself used. See pp. 2-3.

6 The nymph Echo in Greek mythology died of her love for the proud
  Narcissus; Ovid, *Metamorphoses*, iii, 342 ff.

In swich a wise* as man that asketh grace, manner
But no thyng wiste* she of his entente*. *251* knew intention
Nathelees*, it happed er they thennes wente nevertheless
By cause that he was hire neighebour
And was a man of worshipe* and honour, reputation
And hadde yknowen hym of tyme yoore*, a long time
They fille in speche*, and forthe moore and- began talking
 moore   *256*
Unto his purpos drough* Aurelius.   drew
And whan he saugh* his tyme, he seyde thus: saw
 "Madame," quod he, "by God that this
 world made,
So that I wiste* it myghte youre herte knew
 glade*,   *260* gladden
I wolde that day that youre Arveragus
Went over the see that I, Aurelius,
Hadde went ther; nevere I sholde have come
 agayn.
For wel I woot*, my servyce is in vayn. *264* know
My gerdon* is but brestyng* of myn herte. reward breaking
Madame, reweth* upon my peynes smerte, have pity
For with a word ye may me sleen* or save. kill
Heere at youre feet God wolde* that I were would to God
 grave*!   buried
I ne have as now* no leyser* moore to seye; just now leisure
Have mercy, sweete, or ye wol do me deye."
 She gan to looke upon Aurelius; *271*
"Is this youre wyl," quod she, "and sey ye
 thus?
Nevere erst*," quod she, "ne wiste* I what ye before knew
 mente.
But now, Aurelie, I knowe youre entente*. purpose
By thilke* God that yaf* me soule and lyf, that gave
Ne shal I nevere been untrewe wyf *276*
In word ne werk, as fer as I have wit.
I wol been his to whom that I am knyt.
Taak this for fynal answere as of me."
But after that, in pleye* thus seyde she: *280* jest
"Aurelie," quod she, "by heighe God above.

Yet wolde I graunte yow to been youre love,
Syn* I yow se so pitously complayne.   *283*   since
Looke what* day that endelong* Britayne*   whatever   all along   Brittany
Ye remoeve* alle the rokkes, stoon by stoon,   remove
That they ne lette* shipe ne boot to goon.   hinder
I seye, whan ye han maad the coost so clene
Of rokkes that ther nys no* stoon ysene*,   is no   seen
Than wol I love yow best of any man.
Have heer my trouthe* in al that evere I   pledge
     kan."   *290*
     "Is ther noon oother grace in yow?" quod
     he.
"No, by that Lord," quod she, "that maked
     me.
For wel I woot* that it shal nevere bityde*.   know   happen
Lat swiche* folies out of youre herte slyde.   such
What deyntee* sholde a man han in his lyf   delight
For to go love another mannes wyf,   *296*
That hath hir body whan so that hym
     liketh*?"   it pleases him
     Aurelius ful ofte soore* siketh*.   sorely   sighs
Wo was Aurelie whan that he this herde,   *299*
And with a sorweful herte he thus answerde:
"Madame," quod he, "this were an inpossible.
Thanne moot* I dye of sodeyn deth   must
     horrible."
And with that word he turned hym anon*.   at once
Tho* coome hir othere freendes many oon*,   then   many a one
And in the aleyes* romeden up and doun,   alleys
And no thyng wiste* of this conclusioun*.   knew   outcome
But sodeynly bigonne revel newe   *307*
Til that the brighte sonne* loste his hewe*,   sun   colour
For th'orisonte* hath reft* the sonne his   the horizon   deprived
     lyght –
This is as muche to seye as it was nyght –
And hoom they goon in joye and in solas,
Save oonly wrecche* Aurelius, allas!   *312*   wretched
He to his hous is goon with sorweful herte;
He seeth he may nat fro his deeth asterte*.   escape

Hym semed that he felte his herte colde; *315*
Up to the hevene his handes he gan holde,
And on his knowes* bare he sette hym doun,   knees
And in his ravyng seyde his orisoun*.   prayer
For verray wo out of his wit he breyde*.   started
He nyste* what he spak, but thus he seyde;   knew not
With pitous herte his pleynt* hath he   lament
   bigonne   *321*
Unto the goddes*, and first unto the sonne*.   gods sun
   He seyde, "Apollo, god and governour
Of every plaunte, herbe, tree and flour*,   flower
That yevest* after* thy declynacion⁷   *325*   gives according to
To ech of hem his tyme and his seson,
As thyn herberwe* chaungeth lowe or   lodging
   heighe*,   i.e., low or high on the hori-   **zon**
Lord Phebus, cast thy merciable* eighe*   merciful eye
On wrecche Aurelie which that am but lorn*.   lost
Lo, lord, my lady hath my deeth ysworn*   sworn
Withoute gilt, but* thy benignytee   *331*   unless
Upon my dedly* herte have som pitee.   dying
For wel I woot*, Lord Phebus, if yow lest*,   know it pleases you
Ye may me helpen, save my lady, best.
Now voucheth sauf* that I may yow devyse*   grant describe
How that I may be holpen*, and in what   helped
   wyse*.   *336*   manner
Youre blisful suster, Lucina*⁸ the shene*,   i.e., the moon bright
That of the see is chief goddesse and queene,
Though Neptunus have deitee in the see*,   is god of the sea
Yet emperisse* aboven hym is she;   *340*   empress

---

7 The "declynacion" is the angular distance of the sun from the celestial
   equator. Apollo (line 323) was the Greek god of youth who became
   identified with the sun god; as sun god, he was known as Phoebus (line
   328).

8 Lucina was the name given to Diana (the goddess of the moon) and to
   Juno in their role as goddesses of childbirth. Lucina was equated also
   with Proserpina, who was abducted by Pluto to the underworld. For this
   reason Aurelius refers to the underworld as "hir owene dirke regioun",
   line 366; see also the Merchant's Tale, lines 1015-19.

Ye knowen wel, lord, that right as hir desir
Is to be quyked* and lighted of youre fir,   quickened
For which she folweth yow ful bisily,
Right so the see desireth naturelly
To folwen hire as she that is goddesse,   *345*
Bothe in the see and ryveres moore and
   lesse*.   great and small
Wherfore, Lord Phebus, this is my requeste:
Do this miracle, or do* myn herte breste*,   cause   break
That now next at this opposicion,[9]
Which in the signe shal be of the leon,   *350*
As preieth hire so greet a flood to brynge
That fyve fadme* at the leeste it   fathoms
   oversprynge*   submerge
The hyeste rokke in Armorik Briteyne*,   Armorican Brittany
And lat this flood endure yeres tweyne.
Thanne, certes, to my lady may I seye,   *355*
'Holdeth youre heste*; the rokkes been   promise
   aweye!'
Lord Phebus, dooth this miracle for me;
Preye hire she go no faster cours than ye.
I seye, preyeth youre suster that she go
No faster cours than ye thise yeres two;   *360*
Thanne shal she been evene atte full* alway,   i.e., full moon
And spryng flood laste bothe nyght and day.
And but she vouche sauf in swich manere
To graunte me my sovereyn lady deere,
Prey hire to synken every rok adoun   *365*
In to hir owene dirke* regioun   dark
Under the ground ther* Pluto dwelleth inne,   where
Or nevere mo* shal I my lady wynne.   *368* more
Thy temple in Delphos* wol I barefoot seke.   Delphi

9 Tides reach their highest point when the sun and moon are in conjunction
(i.e., the same zodiacal sign) or in opposition (i.e., in opposite zodiacal
signs). Aurelius asks the sun and moon at their next opposition to produce a tide covering the rocks on the coast of Brittany to a depth of five
fathoms, and to move at the same pace so that they will be in constant
opposition. Thus there will be no fluctuation in the tide and it will last
two years (lines 359-62).

Lord Phebus, se the teeris* on my cheke,   tears
And of my peyne have som compassioun."
And with that word in swowne* he fil   swoon
   adoun*,   fell down
And longe tyme he lay forth in a traunce.
His brother, which that knew of his
   penaunce*,   distress
Up caughte hym and to bedde he hath hym
   broght,   375
Dispeyred in this torment and this thoght.
Let I this woful creature lye;
Chese he*, for me, wheither he wol lyve or   let him choose
   dye.

   Arveragus, with heele* and greet honour,   prosperity
As he that was of chivalrie the flour*,   380   flower
Is comen* hoom, and othere worthy men.   has come
O blisful artow* now, thou Dorigen,   are you
That hast thy lusty* housbonde in thyne   happy
   armes,
The fresshe knyght, the worthy man of
   armes
That loveth thee as his owene hertes lyf. 385
No thyng list hym* to be imaginatyf*,   it pleases him   imagine things
If any wight* had spoke whil he was oute   person
To hire of love; he hadde of it no doute*.   fear
He noght entendeth* to no swich* mateere,   pays attention   such
But daunceth, justeth*, maketh hire good   jousts
   cheere.   390
And thus in joye and blisse I lete hem dwelle,
And of the sike* Aurelius wol I telle.   ailing

   In langour and in torment furyus
Two yeer and moore lay wrecche Aurelyus
Er any foot he myghte on erthe gon,   395
Ne confort in this tyme hadde he noon,
Save of his brother which that was a clerk*;   scholar
He knew of al this wo and al this werk.
For to noon oother creature, certeyn,

Of this matere he dorste* no word seyn*.   dared say
Under his brest he baar it moore secree* *401*   secretly
Than evere dide Pamphilus for Galathee.[10]
His brest was hool* with oute for to sene,   whole
But in his herte ay* was the arwe* kene*.   always arrow sharp
And wel ye knowe that of a sursanure* *405*   wound healed on the surface only
In surgerye is perilous the cure,
But* men myghte touche the arwe or come   unless
   therby*.   get at it
His brother weepe* and wayled pryvely*   wept in secret
Til atte laste* hym fil in remembrance*   finally he remembered
That whiles he was at Orliens* in France,   Orleans
As yonge clerkes* that been lykerous* *411*   scholars desirous
To reden artes that been curious*   occult
Seken in every halke* and every herne*   nook cranny
Particuler sciences* for to lerne,   recondite knowledge
He hym remembred that upon a day   *415*
At Orliens in studie a book he say*   saw
Of magyk natureel which his felawe
That was that tyme a bacheler of lawe,
Al* were he ther to lerne another craft,   although
Hadde prively upon his desk ylaft*,   *420*   left
Which book spak muchel* of the   a great deal
   operacions
Touchynge the eighte and twenty mansions[11]
That longen* to the moone, and swich folye*   belong foolishness
As in oure dayes is nat worth a flye.
For holy chirches feith in oure bileve* *425*   belief
Ne suffreth noon illusion us to greve.
And whan this book was in his
   remembraunce,
Anon*, for joye his herte gan to daunce,   at once
And to hym self he seyde pryvely,
"My brother shal be warisshed* hastily, *430*   cured

10 Pamphilus is the hero of a popular twelfth-century Latin verse love dialogue.

11 The twenty-eight mansions of the moon correspond to the twenty-eight days in the lunar cycle.

For I am siker* that ther be sciences   sure
By which men make diverse apparences*   illusions
Swiche as thise subtile tregetours* pleye.   magicians
For ofte at feestes have I wel herd seye
That tregetours with inne an halle large   *435*
Have maad come in a water and a barge,
And in the halle rowen up and doun.
Somtyme hath semed come a grym leoun*,   fierce lion
And somtyme floures* sprynge as in a   flowers
    mede*;   meadow
Somtyme a vyne and grapes white and rede;
Somtyme a castel al of lym* and stoon,   *441*   lime
And whan hym lyked*, voyded it* anoon*.   it pleased him   made it dis-
                                 appear   immediately
Thus semed it to every mannes sighte.
Now thanne, conclude I thus, that if I
    myghte
At Orliens som oold felawe yfynde   *445*
That hadde thise moones mansions in mynde,
Or oother magyk natureel above,
He sholde wel make my brother han* his   have
    love.   *448*
For with an apparence* a clerk may make   illusion
To mannes sighte that alle the rokkes blake
Of Britaigne* weren yvoyded* everichon*,   Brittany   removed   every one
And shippes by the brynke* comen and gon,   coast
And in swich forme enduren a wowke* or   week
    two.
Thanne were my brother warisshed* of his   cured
    wo;   *454*
Thanne moste she nedes holden hire biheste*,   promise
Or elles he shal shame hire atte leeste."
    What sholde I make a lenger* tale of this?   longer
Un to his brotheres bed he comen is,
And swich confort he yaf* hym for to gon   gave
To Orliens that he up stirte* anon*   *460*   leaped   at once
And on his wey forthward thanne is he fare
In hope for to been lissed* of his care.   relieved
Whan they were come almoost to that citee,
But if it were a two furlong or thre,

A yong clerk* romynge by hym self they
    mette,   465   scholar
Which that in Latyn thriftily* hem grette*,   in proper fashion   greeted
And after that he seyde a wonder* thyng: marvellous
"I knowe," quod he, "the cause of youre
    comyng."
And er they ferther any foote wente,
He tolde hem al that was in hire entente*.   intention
This Briton* clerk hym asked of felawes 471   Breton
The whiche that he hadde knowe in olde
    dawes*   days
And he answerde hym that they dede* were,   dead
For which he weep* ful ofte many a teere.   wept
Doun of his hors Aurelius lighte anon,   475
And with this magicien forth is he gon
Hoom to his hous and maden hem wel at ese.
Hem lakked no vitaille* that myghte hem   food
    plese,
So wel arrayed* hous as ther was oon*   provided a   it was
Aurelius in his lyf saw nevere noon.   480
He shewed hym, er he wente to sopeer,
Forestes, parkes ful of wilde deer.
Ther saugh* he hertes* with hir hornes hye,   saw   harts
The gretteste that evere were seyn with eye;
He saugh of hem an hondred slayn with
    houndes,   485
And somme with arwes* blede of bittre   arrows
    woundes.
He saugh, whan voyded* were thise wilde   made to disappear
    deer,
Thise fauconers* up on a fair ryver,   488   falconers
That with hir haukes* han the heron slayn.   hawks
Tho* saugh he knyghtes justyng* in a playn,   then   jousting
And after this he dide hym swich* plesaunce   such
That he hym shewed his lady on a daunce,
On which hym self he daunced as hym
    thoughte*.   493   it seemed to him
And whan this maister that this magyk
    wroughte

Saugh it was tyme, he clapte his handes two,
And farewel, al oure revel was ago*! . *496* gone
And yet remoeved they nevere out of the
      hous
Whil they saugh al this sighte merveillous,
But in his studie, ther as* hise bookes be,   where
They sitten stille, and no wight* but they   person
      thre.   *500*
      To hym this maister called his squier
And seyde hym thus: "Is redy oure soper?
Almoost an hour it is, I undertake*,   guarantee
Sith* I yow bad oure soper for to make,   since
Whan that thise worthy men wenten with me
In to my studie ther as* my bookes be." *506*   where
"Sire," quod this squier, "whan it liketh
      yow*,   it pleases you
It is al redy, though ye wol right now."
"Go we thanne soupe," quod he; "as for the
      beste;
This amorous folk som tyme moote* han hir   must
      reste."   *510*
At after soper fille they in tretee*,   negotiation
What somme sholde this maistres gerdon* be,   reward
To remoeven alle the rokkes of Britayne*,   Brittany
And eek* from Gerounde* to the mouth of   also Gironde (River)
      Sayne*.   Seine
He made it straunge* and swoor, so God hym   was reluctant
      save,   *515*
Lasse than a thousand pound he wolde nat
      have,
Ne gladly for that somme he wolde nat goon.
Aurelius, with blisful herte, anoon
Answerde thus: "Fy on a thousand pound!
This wyde world which that men seye is
      round   *520*
I wolde it yeve* if I were lord of it.   give
This bargayn is ful dryve*, for we ben knyt*.   fully completed agreed
Ye shal be payed trewely, by my trouthe.
But looketh now for no necligence or slouthe*   tardiness

Ye tarie us heere no lenger* than to morwe."   longer
"Nay," quod this clerk, "have heer my feith
   to borwe*!"   *526*   as pledge
   To bedde is goon Aurelius whan hym
   leste*,   it pleased him
And wel ny al that nyght he hadde his reste.
What for his labour and his hope of blisse
His woful herte of penaunce hadde a lisse*.   alleviation
Upon the morwe, whan that it was day,   *531*
To Britaigne* tooke they the righte way,   Brittany
Aurelius, and this magicien bisyde,
And been descended ther* they wolde abyde.   where
And this was, as thise bookes me remembre,
The colde, frosty seson of Decembre.   *536*

   Phebus wax old and hewed lyk laton*,   copper
That in his hote declynacion[12]
Shoon as the burned* gold with stremes   burnished
   brighte,
But now in Capricorn adoun he lighte,   *540*
Wher as he shoon ful pale, I dar wel seyn.
The bittre frostes with the sleet and reyn
Destroyed hath the grene in every yerd*.   yard
Janus sit by the fyr with double berd,[13]   *544*
And drynketh of the bugle horn* the wyn;   drinking cup made from ox-horn
Biforn hym stant* brawen* of the tusked   stands meat
   swyn,
And "Nowel!" crieth every lusty* man.   happy
Aurelius in al that evere he kan
Dooth to this maister chiere* and reverence,   hospitality
And preyeth hym to doon his diligence   *550*
To bryngen hym out of his peynes smerte,

12 The declination of the sun is its distance from the celestial equator. The "hot declination" occurs when the sun moves towards the Tropic of Cancer, and the sun grows "ful pale" when it moves south of the equator towards the Tropic of Capricorn.

13 Janus, the Roman god of beginnings, was represented with two bearded heads set back to back.

Or with a swerd that he wolde slitte his herte.

This subtil clerk* swich* routhe* hadde of this man   scholar   such   pity

That nyght and day he spedde hym* that he kan*   hastened / as well as he could

To wayten* a tyme of his conclusion*.   *555*   watch for (a propitious conjunction of the stars)   plan

This is to seye, to maken illusion

By swich an apparence* or jogelrye* –   optical illusion   magic

I ne kan no* termes of astrologye –   don't know any

That she and every wight sholde wene* and seye   believe

That of Britaigne* the rokkes were aweye,   Brittany

Or ellis they were sonken under grounde. *561*

So, atte laste*, he hath his tyme yfounde   finally

To maken his japes* and his wrecchednesse   tricks

Of swich a supersticious cursednesse.

Hise table tolletanes[14] forth he brought   *565*

Ful wel corrected, ne ther lakked nought

Neither his collect ne hise expans of yeeris[15]

Ne hise rootes*, ne hise othere geeris*,   data   equipment

As been* his centris and hise argumentz,[16]   such as are

And his proporcionels convenientz   *570*

For hise equacions in every thyng.[17]

And by his eighte speere* in his wirkyng   eighth sphere

He knew ful wel how fer Alnath was shove*   removed

---

14 Astronomical tables prepared in the thirteenth century for the latitude of Toledo, Spain; hence their name. "Corrected" (line 566) may mean either corrected for the more northerly latitude of Brittany, or free of errors.

15 In his *Treatise on the Astrolabe,* Chaucer says "fro 1 to 20 ben *anni expansi* and from 20 to 3000 ben *anni collecti*". Tables of computation appropriate to the short and the long period of time are meant.

16 The "centris" was part of an astrolabe; the "argumentz", a unit in mathematical computation.

17 The "proporcionels convenientz" were mathematical tables for computing the motions of planets during periods of time less than a year; the "equacions" are probably the divisions of the sphere into the astrological "mansions" or houses.

Fro the heed of thilke* fixe* Aries above,   that same   fixed
That in the nynthe speere considered is.[18] 575
Ful subtilly he kalkuled* al this.   calculated
Whan he hadde founde his firste mansion*,   i.e., of the moon
He knew the remenaunt* by proporcion,   the rest
And knew the arisyng of his moone weel,
And in whos face and terme and everydeel*,[19]   completely
And knew ful weel the moones mansion   581
Acordaunt to* his operacion*,   suitable for   work in hand
And knew also hise othere observances*   requirements
For swiche illusions and swiche meschances*   misdeeds
As hethen folk useden in thilke* dayes,   585   those
For which no lenger* maked he delayes,   longer
But thurgh his magik for a wyke* or tweye   week
It semed that alle the rokkes were aweye.
     Aurelius, which that yet despeired is
Wher* he shal han his love or fare amys*,   whether   fail
Awaiteth nyght and day on this myracle.   591
And whan he knew that ther was noon
     obstacle,
That voyded* were thise rokkes everychon*,   disappeared   every one
Doun to his maistres* feet he fil anon*   master's   straightway
And seyde, "I, woful wrecche, Aurelius,   595
Thanke yow, lord, and lady myn Venus,
That me han holpen* fro my cares colde."   helped
And to the temple his wey forth hath he
     holde
Where as he knew he sholde his lady see.

18 Alnath is another name for the bright star Arietis. According to medieval theory, the planets and the stars were located in spheres that revolved around the earth. The stars were located in the eighth sphere,
but the head of Aries, the true equinoctial point, was in the ninth
sphere. The precession of the equinoxes was determined by computing
the distance between Alnath and the head of Aries.

19 "Face" and "terme" are names for the parts into which the signs of the
zodiac were divided. This wealth of erudite astrological terminology
ironically belies the Franklin's statement in line 558, and it indicates also
Chaucer's keen interest in the various branches of learning of his day.

And whan he saugh* his tyme, anon right*
  hee   *600*   saw   right away
With dredful* herte and with ful humble   fearful
  cheere*   demeanour
Salewed* hath his sovereyn lady deere.   greeted

"My righte lady," quod this woful man,
"Whom I moost drede and love as I best kan,
And lothest* were of al this world   most unwilling
  displese,   *605*
Nere it* that I for yow have swich* disese*   were it not such discomfort
That I moste dyen heere at youre foot anon,
Noght wolde I telle how me is wo bigon,
But certes, outher* moste I dye or pleyne*.   either utter laments
Ye sleen me* giltlees for verray peyne.   *610*   slay
But of my deeth thogh that ye have no
  routhe*,   pity
Avyseth yow* er that ye breke your trouthe*.   consider pledge
Repenteth yow, for thilke* God above,   that same
Er ye me sleen by cause that I yow love.
For madame, wel ye woot* what ye han   know
  hight* –   *615*   promised
Nat that I chalange* any thyng of right   claim
Of yow, my sovereyn lady, but youre grace –
But in a gardyn yond at swich a place
Ye woot right wel what ye bihighten* me,   promised
And in myn hand youre trouthe plighten* ye   pledged
To love me best. God woot ye seyde so,   *621*
Al be* that I unworthy am ther to.   although
Madame, I speke it for the honour of yow
Moore than to save myn hertes lyf right now.
I have do so as ye comanded me,   *625*
And if ye vouche sauf*, ye may go see.   grant it
Dooth as yow list*; have youre biheste* in   it pleases you promise
  mynde,
For quyk* or deed right ther ye shal me   alive
  fynde.
In yow lith* al, to do me lyve or deye,   lies
But wel I woot the rokkes been aweye."   *630*

He taketh his leve, and she astonied* stood.   astonished
In al hir face nas* a drope of blood.   was not
She wende* nevere have come in swich* a   thought   such
   trappe.
"Allas," quod she, "that evere this sholde
   happe!
For wende I nevere by possibilitee   *635*
That swich a monstre or merveille myghte be.
It is agayns the proces* of nature."   course
And hoom she goth a sorweful creature.
For verray feere unnethe* may she go.   scarcely
She wepeth, wailleth al a day or two,   *640*
And swowneth* that it routhe was to see.   swoons
But why it was to no wight tolde shee,
For out of towne was goon Arveragus.
But to hir self she spak and seyde thus,
With face pale and with ful sorweful cheere*,   expression
In hire compleynt as ye shal after heere: *646*
"Allas," quod she, "on thee, Fortune, I
   pleyne*,   complain
That unwar* wrapped hast me in thy cheyne,   unexpectedly
For which t'escape woot* I no socour*,   know   help
Save oonly deeth or dishonour.   *650*
Oon* of thise two bihoveth me* to chese*.   one   it is necessary for me   choose
But nathelees*, yet have I levere* to lese*   nevertheless   I would rather   lose
My lyf than of my body have a shame,
Or knowen my selven fals, or lese my name.
And with my deth I may be quyt, ywis*. *655*   certainly
Hath ther nat many a noble wyf er this,
And many a mayde yslayn hir self, allas,
Rather than with hir body doon trespas?
Yis, certes*, thise stories beren witnesse.   certainly
Whan thritty tirauntz ful of cursednesse   *660*
Hadde slayn Phidon in Atthenes* at feste,[20]   Athens

20 The examples of chaste women that follow are taken from St. Jerome's
   "Letter against Jovinian", a work Chaucer had used for a different purpose in the Wife of Bath's Prologue; see note 14 to that work. The
   Thirty Tyrants, at the close of the Peloponnesian War, established a
   reign of terror in Athens until overthrown by Thrasybulus in 403 B.C.

They comanded* his doghtres for t'areste   i.e., ordered their men
And bryngen hem biforn hem in despit*   malice
Al naked to fulfille hir foul delit,
And in hir fadres* blood they made hem   father's
   daunce   *665*
Upon the pavement, God yeve* hem   give
   myschaunce*!   misfortune
For which thise woful maydens ful of drede,
Rather than they wolde lese hir maydenhede,
They prively been stirt* in to a welle   have leaped
And dreynte* hem selven, as the bookes   drowned
   telle.   *670*
They of Mecene*[21] leete enquere and seke   Messene
Of Lacedomye* fifty maydens eke*,   Lacedaemonia   also
On which they wolden doon hir lecherye.
But was ther noon of al that compaignye
That she nas* slayn, and with a good entente*   was not   will
Chees* rather for to dye than assente   *676*   chose
To been oppressed* of hir maydenhede.   ravished
Why sholde I thanne to dye been in drede?
   "Lo, eek, the tiraunt, Aristoclides,   *679*
That loved a mayden heet* Stymphalides*,[22]   called   Stymphalis
Whan that hir fader slayn was on a nyght,
Un to Dianes* temple goth she right   Diana's
And hente* the ymage in hir handes two,   clasped
Fro which ymage wolde she nevere go.   *684*
No wight* ne myghte hir handes of it arace*   person   wrench
Til she was slayn right in the selve* place.   same
Now sith* that maydens hadden swich despit*   since   scorned so
To been defouled with mannes foul delit,
Wel oghte a wyf rather hir selven slee
Than be defouled, as it thynketh me*.   *690*   it seems to me
   "What shal I seyn of Hasdrubales wyf[23]

21 Messene and Sparta (Lacedaemonia) used to exchange virgins for certain religious rites, according to Jerome.
22 Aristoclides, the tyrant of Orchomenos in Arcadia, Greece.
23 Hasdrubal, Carthaginian leader when the city was destroyed by the Romans at the end of the Third Punic War, 146 B.C. Chaucer refers to his wife's suicide again in the Nun's Priest's Tale, lines 556-61.

That at Cartage birafte* hir self hir lyf?   deprived
For whan she saugh* that Romayns wan*   saw won
   the toun,
She took hir children alle and skipte adoun
In to the fyr, and chees* rather to dye   695 chose
Than any Romayn dide hire vileynye.
    "Hath nat Lucresse*[24] yslayn hir self, allas, Lucrece
At Rome whan she oppressed* was   ravished
Of Tarquyn, for hire thoughte it was a shame
To lyven whan she had lost hir name?   700
The sevene maydens of Milesie*[25] also   Miletus
Han slayn hem self for verray drede and wo
Rather than folk of Gawle* hem sholde   i.e., Galatia
   oppresse*.   ravish
Mo* than a thousand stories, as I gesse,   more
Koude I now telle as touchynge this mateere.
Whan Habradate*[26] was slayn, his wyf so Abradates
   deere   706
Hirselven slow*, and leet hir blood to glyde slew
In Habradates woundes depe and wyde,
And seyde, 'My body, at the leeste way*,   at least
Ther shal no wight defoulen, if I may!'   710
What sholde I mo ensamples heer of sayn*, tell
Sith that so manye han hem selven slayn
Wel rather than they wolde defouled be.
I wol conclude that it is bet* for me   better
To sleen my self than been defouled thus.
I wol be trewe un to Arveragus,   716
Or rather sle my self in som manere,
As dide Democionis* doghter[27] deere   Demotion's

24 Lucrece, a virtuous matron of Roman legend who committed suicide after being ravished by Sextus Tarquin.

25 Miletus was captured and sacked by the Galatians in 276 B.C.

26 Abradates, a king of Susa who submitted to Cyrus the Great; on his death his wife Panthea committed suicide.

27 Demotion's daughter committed suicide after the death of her fiancé lest she be compelled to marry another man.

By cause that she wolde nat defouled be.

"O Cedasus*,[28] it is ful greet pitee · *720*   Scedasus
To reden how thy doghtren* deyde, allas,   daughters
That slowe* hem self for swich manere cas!   slew
As greet a pitee was it, or wel moore,
The Theban mayden that for Nichanoore*[29]   Nicanor
Hir selven slow right for swich manere wo.
Another Theban mayden dide right so,   *726*
For* oon of Macidonye* hadde hire   because   a Macedonian
   oppressed*;   ravished
She with hire deeth hir maydenhede
   redressed*.   compensated for
What shal I seyn of Nicerates* wyf,[30]   Niceratus'
That for swich cas birafte* hir self hir lyf?   deprived
How trewe eek* was to Alcebiades[31]   *731*   also
His love, that rather for to dyen chees*   chose
Than for to suffre his body unburyed be.
Lo, which a* wyf was Alceste*!"[32] quod she.   what a Alcestis
"What seith Omer* of goode Penalopee*?[33]   Homer   Penelope
Al Grece knoweth of hire chastitee.   *736*
Pardee*, of Laodomya*[34] is writen thus,   by heaven Laodamia

---

28 The daughters of Scedasus of Boeotia committed suicide after being
   ravished by two youths.

29 Nicanor, who captured Thebes, fell in love with a virgin who killed herself to escape him. The other Theban maiden of line 726 is not named
   by Jerome.

30 The wife of Niceratus, an Athenian, killed herself to escape from the
   Thirty Tyrants.

31 Alcibiades, an Athenian leader during the Peloponnesian War, was killed
   at the instigation of the Spartan general Lysander and the Thirty Tyrants. His mistress buried his dead body in defiance of his enemies.

32 In Greek legend, Alcestis is said to have consented to die herself in
   place of her husband Admetus.

33 In Homer's *Odyssey,* Penelope, the wife of Odysseus, put off the suitors
   for her hand for many years until her husband returned home from his
   wanderings after the Trojan War.

34 Laodamia, after the death of her husband Protesilaus at Troy, begged
   the gods to grant her three hours with him, at the end of which time
   she killed herself.

That whan at Troie* was slayn Protheselaus*,   Troy   Protesilaus
No lenger* wolde she lyve after his day.   longer
The same of noble Porcia*35 telle I may; *740*   Portia
With oute Brutus koude she nat lyve,
To whom she hadde al hool* hir herte yeve*.   completely   given
The parfit* wyfhod of Arthemesie*36   perfect   Artemisia
Honured is thurgh al the Barbarie*.   heathendom
O Teuta,37 queene, thy wyfly chastitee   *745*
To alle wyves may a mirour bee.
The same thyng I seye of Bilyea*,38   Bilia
Of Rodogone*,39 and eek Valeria."40   Rhodogune
Thus pleyned* Dorigene a day or tweye,   lamented
Purposynge evere that she wolde deye. *750*
But nathelees*, upon the thridde* nyght,   nevertheless   third
Hoom cam Arveragus, this worthy knyght,
And asked hire why that she weepe* so soore,   wept
And she gan wepen ever lenger* the moore.   longer
    "Allas," quod she, "that evere I was born!
Thus have I seyd," quod she, "thus have I
   sworn."   *756*
And toold hym al as ye han herd bifore;
It nedeth nat reherce it yow namoore.
This housbonde with glad chiere* in freendly   cheerful manner
   wyse   *759*
Answerde and seyde as I shal yow devyse*:   tell
"Is ther oght elles, Dorigen, but this?"

---

35 Portia, the wife of Brutus, killed herself after the suicide of her husband following his defeat at Philippi, 42 B.C.

36 Artemisia (*c.* 352 B.C.) erected for her husband Mausolus of Caria (Asia Minor) a splendid tomb which was one of the seven wonders of the ancient world.

37 Teuta, a queen of Illyria who fought the Romans, *c.* 228 B.C.

38 Bilia, wife of Gaius Duillius, a Roman general during the Carthaginian War.

39 Rhodogune, daughter of Darius, killed her nurse for suggesting that she remarry.

40 Valeria, wife of the Roman emperor Galerius (d. A.D. 311), who refused to remarry.

"Nay, nay," quod she, "God help me* so as
    wys*;   may God help me
                                             certainly
This is to* muche, and* it were Goddes wille." too   if
"Ye, wyf," quod he, "lat slepen that is stille*. i.e., let sleeping dogs lie
It may be wel, paraventure*, yet to day. *765* perhaps
Ye shul youre trouthe* holden, by my fay*! pledge   faith
For God so wisly* have mercy up on me,   surely
I hadde wel levere* ystiked* for to be   I had much rather   stabbed
For verray love, which that I to yow have,
But if ye sholde* youre trouthe kepe and   should you not
    save.   *770*
Trouthe is the hyeste thyng that men may
    kepe."
But with that word he brast* anon* to wepe, burst out   straightway
And seyde, "I yow forbede, up* peyne of   upon
    deeth,
That nevere whil thee lasten lyf ne breeth
To no wight* telle thou of this aventure. *775* person
As I may best, I wol my wo endure,
Ne make no contenance of hevynesse*,   sorrow
That folk of yow may demen* harm or   suppose
    gesse."   *778*
And forth he cleped* a squier and a mayde.   called
"Gooth forth anon with Dorigen," he sayde,
"And bryngeth hire to swich* a place anon." such
They take hir leve and on hir wey they gon,
But they ne wiste* why she thider* wente;   knew   thither
He nolde* no wight tellen his entente*.   would not   purpose
Paraventure an heepe of yow*, ywis*, *785* many of you   certainly
Wol holden hym a lewed* man in this,   foolish
That he wol putte his wyf in jupartie*.   jeopardy
Herkneth the tale er ye upon hire crie*;   cry out against her
She may have bettre fortune than yow
    semeth*,   it seems to you
And whan that ye han herd the tale, demeth*. decide

    This squier, which that highte* Aurelius, was called
On Dorigen that was so amorus,   *792*
Of aventure* happed hire to meete   by chance

Amydde the toun, right in the quykkest*   busiest
  strete,
As she was bown* to goon the wey forth   ready
  right
Toward the gardyn ther as* she had hight*,   where   promised
And he was to the gardynward also,
For wel he spyed whan she wolde go
Out of hir hous to any maner place.   *799*
But thus they mette of aventure* or grace*,   chance   fortune
And he saleweth* hire with glad entente*,   greets   cheerfully
And asked of hire whiderward* she wente.   where
And she answerde, half as she were mad,
"Unto the gardyn, as myn housbonde bad*,   ordered
My trouthe for to holde, allas, allas!"   *805*
Aurelius gan wondren on this cas*,   matter
And in his herte hadde greet compassion
Of hire, and of hire lamentacion,
And of Arveragus the worthy knyght
That bad hire holden al that she had hight*,   promised
So looth hym was* his wyf sholde breke hir   so reluctant he was
  trouthe.   *811*
And in his herte he caughte of this greet
  routhe*,   pity
Considerynge the beste on every syde,
That for his lust* yet were hym levere*   desire   he would rather
  abyde*   refrain
Than doon so heigh a cherlyssh
  wrecchednesse*,   *815*   so great a boorish misdeed
Agayns franchise* and alle gentillesse*.   generosity   nobility
For which in fewe wordes seyde he thus:
  "Madame, seyeth to youre lord, Arveragus,
That sith* I se his grete gentillesse   *819*   since
To yow, and eek* I se wel youre distresse,   also
That hym were levere han* shame, and that   he would rather have
  were routhe*,   pity
Than ye to me sholde breke thus youre
  trouthe,
I have wel levere* evere to suffre wo   I much prefer
Than I departe the love bitwix yow two.

I yow relesse*, madame, in to youre hond,   release
Quyt every serement* and every bond   *826*   oath
That ye han maad to me as heer biforn
Sith* thilke* tyme which that ye were born.   since that
My trouthe I plighte, I shal yow never
   repreve*   reproach
Of no biheste*, and heere I take my leve *830*   promise
As of the treweste and the beste wyf
That evere yet I knew in al my lyf.
But every wyf be war* of hir biheste;   take care
On Dorigen remembreth atte leeste.
Thus kan a squier doon a gentil dede*   *835*   perform a noble act
As wel as kan a knyght, with outen drede*."   doubt
She thonketh hym upon hir knees al bare,
And hoom unto hir housbonde is she fare*,   she has gone
And tolde hym al as ye han herd me sayd.
And be ye siker*, he was so weel apayd* *840*   you may be certain pleased
That it were inpossible me to wryte.[41]
What sholde I lenger* of this cas endyte?   longer
Arveragus and Dorigene his wyf
In sovereyn blis leden forth hir lyf.
Nevere eft* ne was ther angre* hem bitwene; again trouble
He cherisseth hire as though she were a
   queene,   *846*
And she was to hym trewe for everemoore.
Of thise folk ye get of me namoore.

Aurelius, that his cost hath al forlorn*,   lost
Curseth the tyme that evere he was born.
"Allas," quod he, "allas, that I bihighte* *851*   promised
Of pured* gold a thousand pound of wighte*   refined by weight
Unto this philosophre! How shal I do?
I se namoore but that I am fordo*.   ruined
Myn heritage moot I nedes* selle   *855*   must I
And been a beggere; heere may I nat dwelle*   remain
And shamen al my kynrede* in this place,   relatives

---

41 Chaucer seems to forget that the story is being recited aloud by the
   Franklin.

But* I of hym may gete bettre grace.   *unless*

But nathelees*, I wol of hym assaye*   *nevertheless* *try (to arrange)*

At certeyn dayes yeer by yeer to paye, *860*

And thonke hym of his grete curteisye.

My trouthe* wol I kepe; I wol nat lye."   *pledge*

With herte soore he gooth unto his cofre*   *money-box*

And broghte gold unto this philosophre,

The value of fyve hundred pound, I gesse,

And hym bisecheth of his gentillesse *866*

To graunte hym dayes* of the remenaunt*, *i.e., time to pay the rest*

And seyde, "Maister, I dar wel make avaunt*, *boast*

I failled nevere of my trouthe as yit.

For sikerly*, my dette shal be quyt *870* *certainly*

Towardes yow, how evere that I fare

To goon a-begged* in my kirtel* bare. *go begging tunic*

But wolde ye vouche sauf* upon seuretee* *grant surety*

Two yeer or thre for to respiten* me, *allow an extension to*

Thanne were I wel, for elles moot* I selle *must*

Myn heritage; ther is namoore to telle." *876*

  This philosophre sobrely* answerde *gravely*

And seyde thus whan he thise wordes herde:

"Have I nat holden covenant unto thee?" *879*

"Yes, certes*, wel and trewely," quod he. *certainly*

"Hastow* nat had thy lady as thee liketh*?" *have you pleases you*

"No, no," quod he, and sorwefully he siketh*. *sighs*

"What was the cause? Tel me if thou kan."

Aurelius his tale anon* bigan *at once*

And tolde hym al as ye han herd bifoore; *885*

It nedeth nat to yow reherce it moore.

He seide Arveragus of gentillesse

Hadde levere* dye in sorwe and in distresse *had rather*

Than that his wyf were of hir trouthe fals.

The sorwe of Dorigen he tolde hym als*; *890* *also*

How looth hire was to ben a wikked wyf,

And that she levere had* lost that day hir lyf, *had rather*

And that hir trouthe* she swoor thurgh *pledge*
  innocence.

"She nevere erst* hadde herd speke of
  apparence*;   *before / illusion*
That made me han of hire so greet pitee. *895*
And right as frely* as he sente hire me,   *generously*
As frely sente I hire to hym ageyn.
This is al and som*; ther is namoore to seyn." *this is everything*
  This philosophre answerde, "Leeve*   *dear*
  brother,
Everich* of yow dide gentilly* til* oother. *each nobly towards*
Thou art a squier, and he is a knyght,   *901*
But God forbede, for his blisful myght,
But if a clerk koude doon a gentil dede* *that a scholar could not*
As wel as any of yow; it is no drede*. *doubt perform a noble act*
Sire, I releesse thee thy thousand pound, *905*
As* thou right now were cropen* out of the *as if had crept*
  ground,
Ne nevere er now ne haddest knowen me.
For sire, I wol nat taken a peny of thee
For al my craft*, ne noght for my travaille*. *skill work*
Thou hast ypayed wel for my vitaille*; *910* *food*
It is ynogh*, and farewel, have good day!" *enough*
And took his hors, and forth he goth his way.

  Lordynges*, this question thanne wol I *gentlemen*
  aske now:
Which was the mooste fre* as thynketh *generous*
  yow*? *it seems to you*
Now telleth me er that ye ferther wende*. *travel*
I kan namoore; my tale is at an ende. *916*

INTRODUCTION TO THE
NUN'S PRIEST'S TALE

The Nun's Priest is unlike the other story-tellers on the Canterbury pilgrimage, for his character is not described to us in the General Prologue. Chaucer makes up for this possible oversight, however; the character of the Nun's Priest is amply revealed to us by the tale he tells. In this tale Chaucer seems to have put into practice an important discovery made during his work on certain of the other tales. That discovery was that it is perfectly possible to make the tale perform several functions simultaneously. The first and most obvious of these functions is to relate the plot, but since the plot is really negligible in this tale, the tale is used to carry out other purposes as well. The tale can function as a revelation of the character of the narrator, and in addition it can demonstrate that character's reaction to previous tales and to other pilgrims. In this way the dramatic interplay we have already noted between the different characters can be incorporated into the tale itself rather than remaining an external element confined to the links between the tales.

We assume that the Nun's Priest was the chaplain of a religious house presided over by the Prioress. If this assumption is correct, then some aspects of his character are explained. In the Middle Ages both men and women were encouraged to join religious institutions for what were really non-religious reasons. For example, a rich merchant with several daughters, in the absence of financially and socially eligible suitors, might place one or more of them in a convent. Or the daughters themselves might go through a period of infatuation with the religious life, join a religious order, and then find themselves irrevocably tied to a life for which they had no real calling. Under these circumstances, considering the large percentage of the population of medieval England that was connected with the Church, it is entirely possible that many of the women with whom the Nun's Priest had to deal in his daily duties in both pulpit and confession box were frivolous, vain, foolish, and perhaps· neurotic.[1] Faced with a number of such women under his spiritual care, the Nun's Priest developed a genial anti-feminism that is remarkable for the way in which it is expressed. This anti-feminism seems as strong in its way as the aggressive feminism of the Wife of Bath, but her outspokenness contrasts strongly with the Nun's Priest's subtlety. Where the Wife of Bath is overtly militant, the Nun's Priest is covertly sly. Where the Wife openly expresses her contempt for the majority of the male sex, the Priest conceals his opinions under the semi-transparent cloak of the tale he narrates. Thus we find in the tale many skilful jokes at the expense of women, and when these jokes become incautious, the Nun's Priest, sensing the hostile eyes of the Wife of Bath upon him and perhaps those of the Prioress as well, takes refuge behind the statement that "Thise ben the cokkes wordes, and nat myne". And of course they are not the cock's words at all.

The chief vehicle for humour in the tale is the relationship between the sexes. The beast fable, the genre to which the tale belongs, makes its satiric point by attributing human characteristics to animals. Chauntecler and Pertelote are more memorable as human beings than as barnyard creatures, though even the barnyard side of their nature is brought in with striking effect at appropriate moments.[2] As human beings they are conceived primarily as being in a husband-wife relationship together. The institution of human marriage has always been peculiarly vulnerable to writers interested in the comic, and so we find in this tale the comedy of marriage exploited to the full. In these terms we are presented with a Chauntecler who is obviously, and here literally, a hen-pecked husband, while Pertelote fusses like a chicken over her husband's health and otherwise reveals herself as a dominating wife.

Like the General Prologue, the tale is almost encyclopedic in its range of material. We are treated to a lengthy discussion of the significance of dreams, a topic intensely absorbing to the medieval

1 Further information on this point is afforded by Eileen Power, *Medieval People* (Boston and New York, 1934), pp. 59-84.

2 As at lines 160, 354, 365-71.

audience. The reader should beware of looking on this discussion as a digression from the main purpose of the tale. If Chauntecler's insistence on the significance of dreams is correct, and later events in the story seem to bear him out, then dreams have a bearing on the question of man's free-will in relation to God's foreknowledge. The Nun's Priest manages to work into his tale a succinct résumé of the central issues in this topic which was also very popular in Chaucer's day. On another and more popular level of knowledge, Pertelote displays an intimate acquaintance with the medicinal properties of a wide variety of herbs. Even a subject as scholarly as medieval rhetoric, with its complex devices for enhancing a tale or adding poignancy to a lament, is brought in, like most of the other information dispensed by the Nun's Priest, at an inappropriate moment. The Nun's Priest's massive learning and his genius for the irrelevant or near-relevant digression are both exploited for their contribution to the humour.

But despite his great learning, or perhaps because of it, the Nun's Priest has a keen sense of narrative and a lively talent for the creation of comic action. Few scenes in literature can equal the riotous confusion of the chase of the fox when that cunning animal has carried Chauntecler off from the barnyard. All the homely details of barnyard life, so effectively itemized in this passage, are enhanced by the narrator's fine command of rhetoric. And the mock-heroic elements are brought into full play when this barnyard tragedy is raised to the level of the great tragic events of history and legend.

When we reach the end of the tale we are brought up short by the reminder that the narrator is, after all, a priest. In a sense this rollicking beast epic with its strong overtones of anti-feminism is a kind of moral fable which is concluded with two explicit moral maxims put into the mouths of the fox and the rooster. And in a moment of sobering seriousness, immediately following these maxims, the Nun's Priest refers to St. Paul's admonition that all that is written is written for our instruction, and earnestly enjoins his audience to take the morality of the tale. At this point, despite the humour of the tale, and despite the superficial moral precepts just related, the audience is confronted with the serious undertones of the tale. These undertones would be more apparent to a medieval audience than they are to a modern one, for the

medieval audience would be acquainted with the medieval bestiary and the traditional allegorical interpretations associated with
the various animals. According to these interpretations the fox is
equated with the devil. If the reader carries this identification of
fox and devil over into the tale just concluded, he begins to see
the morality the Nun's Priest is referring to. The garden-like,
carefully enclosed – though not impregnable – paradise of Chauntecler and Pertelote reminds one of that other garden state inhab-
ited by another couple whose happiness was intruded upon by the
devil. Visions of the Fall of Man rise before the reader, and the
tale begins to assume a very serious morality indeed. This serious
note is not deep enough nor sufficiently sustained to destroy the
comic humour of the tale, but it does serve to remind us that the
tale is told by a priest. That priest might enjoy exercising his wit
at the expense of women, but he is after all a priest, and the salvation of souls is his first duty.

The Nun's Priest's Tale

Thanne spak oure Hoost with rude speche and boold,
And seyde unto the Nonnes Preest anon*,   straightway
"Com neer, thou preest! Com hyder, thou Sir John!¹
Telle us swich thyng* as may oure hertes   such a thing
    glade*.   gladden
Be blithe, though thou ryde upon a jade*!   *5*   worn-out horse
What thogh thyn hors be bothe foul* and   ugly
    lene?
If he wol serve thee, rekke nat a bene*!   don't care a bean
Looke that thyn herte be murie* everemo!"   merry
"Yis, sire," quod he, "yis, Hoost, so moot I*   as I may
    go.
But* I be myrye, ywis*, I wol be blamed!"   *10*   unless certainly
And right anon* his tale he hath attamed*,   right away begun
And thus he seyde unto us everichon*,   every one
This sweete preest, this goodly man, Sir John.

A poure wydwe*, somdel* stape* in age,   widow somewhat advanced
Was whilom* dwellyng in a narwe* cotage   once upon a time small
Biside a grove, stondynge in a dale.   *16*
This wydwe, of which I telle yow my tale,
Syn* thilke* day that she was last a wyf,   since that

---

1 A common and often scornful epithet applied to priests.

In pacience ladde a ful symple lyf,
For litel was hire catel* and hire rente*. 20   possessions income
By housbondrie* of swich as God hire sente   careful management
She foond* hire self and eek* hire doghtren*   provided for also daughters
  two.
Thre larges sowes hadde she, and namo*,   no more
Three keen*, and eek a sheep that highte*   cows was called
  Malle*.   24   Molly
Ful sooty was hire bour* and eek hire halle,   sleeping quarters
In which she eet ful many a sklendre* meel.   scanty
Of poynaunt* sauce hir neded* never a   pungent she needed
  deel*;   bit
No deyntee morsel* passed thurgh hir   delicacy
  throte.
Hir diete was acordant* to hir cote*.   suitable cottage
Repleccion* ne made hire nevere sik;   30   over-eating
Attempree* diete was al hir phisik*,   moderate medicine
And exercise, and hertes suffisaunce*.   heart's content
The goute lette* hire nothyng for to daunce,   hindered
N'apoplexie shente* nat hir heed;   injured
No wyn ne drank she, neither whit ne reed.
Hir bord* was served moost with whit and   table
  blak,   36
Milk and broun breed, in which she foond no
  lak;
Seynd* bacon, and somtyme an ey* or   broiled egg
  tweye,
For she was, as it were, a maner deye*.   a kind of dairy-woman
  A yerd she hadde, enclosed al aboute   40
With stikkes, and a drye dych* withoute,   ditch
In which she hadde a cok heet*   named
  Chauntecleer.
In al the land of crowyng nas* his peer;   was not
His voys was murier than the murie orgon
On massedayes that in the chirche gon.   45
Wel sikerer* was his crowyng in his logge*   more certain lodging
Than is a clokke or any abbey orlogge*   clock
By nature he knew eche ascensioun

Of the equynoxial[2] in thilke* toun,   that
For whan degrees fiftene weren ascended, *50*
Thanne crew* he that it myghte nat been   crowed
    amended.
His coomb was redder than the fyn coral,
And batailled* as* it were a castel wal.   crenelated   as if
His byle* was blak, and as the jeet* it shoon; bill jet
Lyk asure were his legges and his toon*;   *55* toes
His nayles whiter than the lylye flour*,   flower
And lyk the burned* gold was his colour.   burnished
This gentil* cok hadde in his governaunce   noble
Sevene hennes for to doon al his plesaunce,
Which were hise sustres* and his   sisters
    paramours*,   *60* mistresses
And wonder* lyk to hym as of colours,   marvellously
Of whiche the faireste hewed on hire throte
Was cleped* faire damoysele Pertelote.   called
Curteys she was, discreet, and debonaire*,   gracious
And compaignable*, and bar hyr self so   sociable
    faire   *65*
Syn* thilke day that she was seven nyght   since
    oold,
That trewely, she hath the herte in hoold*   in possession
Of Chauntecleer, loken in every lith*;   locked in every limb
He loved hire so that wel was hym therwith.
But swich* a joye was it to here hem synge,   such
Whan that the brighte sonne bigan to
    sprynge,   *71*
In sweete accord, "My lief is faren in
    londe*!"   "My beloved has gone away!"
For thilke tyme*, as I have understonde,   at that time

---

2 According to medieval theory, the celestial equator (the "equynoxial")
revolved around the earth every twenty-four hours. Chauntecleer knew by
nature, for the latitude of his town (line 49), when fifteen degrees of this
equator had risen above the horizon; i.e., he knew when each hour passed,
and crowed accordingly. There is some evidence indicating that, in medieval popular belief, the cock crowed every hour, as Chaucer suggests
here.

Beestes and briddes* koude* speke and
   synge.   *birds   knew how to*
And so bifel, that in a dawenynge*,   *75* *at dawn*
As Chauntecleer among hise wyves alle
Sat on his perche that was in the halle*,   *i.e., in the widow's house*
And next hym sat this faire Pertelote,
This Chauntecleer gan gronen in his throte,
As man that in his dreem is drecched soore*.   *sorely troubled*
And whan that Pertelote thus herde hym
   roore,   *81*
She was agast* and seyde, "O herte deere,   *frightened*
What eyleth yow to grone in this manere?
Ye ben a verray sleper*! Fy, for shame!"   *you are a fine sleeper!*
   And he answerde and seyde thus:
   "Madame,   *85*
I prey yow that ye take it nat agrief*.   *unkindly*
By God, I mette* I was in swich meschief*   *dreamed   misfortune*
Right now that yet myn herte is soore
   afright.
Now God," quod he, "my swevene recche
   aright*,   *have my dream turn out*
And kepe my body out of foul prisoun!   *90*   *favourably*
Me mette how that I romed up and doun
Withinne oure yeerd wheer as I saugh* a   *saw*
   beest
Was lyk an hound* and wolde han* maad   *dog   have*
   areest*   *captured*
Upon my body and han had me deed.
His colour was bitwixe yelow and reed,   *95*
And tipped was his tayl and bothe his eeris*   *ears*
With blak, unlyk the remenant* of his   *the rest*
   heeris*.   *fur*
His snowte smal, with glowynge eyen tweye.
Yet of his look for feere almoost I deye*.   *die*
This caused me my gronyng, doutelees."   *100*
   "Avoy*!" quod she, "fy on yow, hertelees*!   *for shame   spiritless*
Allas," quod she, "for by that God above,
Now han ye lost myn herte and al my love!
I kan nat love a coward, by my feith!

For certes*, what so* any womman seith,[3]   certainly   whatever
We alle desiren, if it myghte bee,   106
To han housbondes hardy*, wise, and fre*,   brave   generous
And secree*, and no nygard, ne no fool,   able to keep secrets
Ne hym that is agast of every tool*,   weapon   (especially in love
Ne noon avauntour*, by that God above!   boaster
How dorste* ye seyn, for shame, unto youre   dare
    love   111
That any thyng myghte make yow aferd?
Have ye no mannes herte, and han a berd?
Allas, and konne ye ben agast of swevenys*?   dreams
No thyng, God woot*, but vanytee* in   knows   foolishness
    swevene is.   115
Swevenes engendren of* repleccions*,   result from   surfeits
And ofte of fume* and of compleccions*,   vapours (from over-indulgenc
Whan humours ben to* habundant in a   too   in drink)   constitution
    wight.[4]
Certes, this dreem which that ye han met*   dreamed
    tonyght
Comth of the grete superfluytee   120
Of youre rede colera*, pardee*,   red choler   certainly
Which causeth folk to dreden in hir dremes
Of arwes*, and of fyr with rede lemes*,   arrows   flames
Of rede beestes, that they wol hem byte,
Of contek*, and of whelpes* grete and lyte*,   strife   dogs   great and small

3 Though many editors locate the Nun's Priest's Tale before the so-called
  Marriage Group of tales (the Wife, Clerk, Merchant, Franklin sequence)
  in the *Canterbury Tales* as a whole, this line is an obvious allusion to
  the main point of the Wife of Bath's Tale and presupposes a knowledge
  of that tale.

4 Pertelote says that bad dreams result from over-indulgence ("repleccion",
  line 116) or from illness (lines 117-18). In Chauntecleer's case, the choleric humour has become preponderant (see General Prologue, note 27),
  and it is usual for persons suffering from an excess of choler to have
  dreams in which red predominates (lines 122-4), just as an excess of
  melancholy causes dreams in which black predominates (lines 128-9).
  Pertelote's remedy is to keep Chauntecleer out of the sun (lines 149-50),
  and to prescribe medicines ("digestyves", line 154) which will absorb the
  excess of the choleric and melancholic humours. Then Chauntecleer will
  be ready for the laxatives which will purge him of the cause of his illness.

Right as the humour of malencolie   *126*
Causeth ful many a man in sleepe to crie
For fere of blake beres*, or boles* blake,   bears bulls
Or elles blake develes wol hem take.
Of othere humours koude I telle also   *130*
That werken* many a man in sleep ful wo*,   trouble sorely
But I wol passe as lightly as I kan.
   "Lo, Caton*,⁵ which that was so wys a   Cato
   man,
Seyde he nat thus, 'Ne do no fors of*   pay no attention to
   dremes'?
Now sire," quod she, "whan we fle* fro the   fly
   bemes,   *135*
For Goddes love, as taak* som laxatyf!   take
Up peril of my soule and of my lyf,
I conseille yow the beste, I wol nat lye,
That bothe of colere and of malencolye
Ye purge yow, and for* ye shal nat tarie,   so that
Though in this toun is noon apothecarie, *141*
I shal my self to herbes techen* yow,   guide
That shal been for youre hele* and for youre   cure
   prow*.   advantage
And in oure yeerd tho* herbes shal I fynde,   those
The whiche han* of hire propretee by kynde*   have nature
To purge yow bynethe and eek* above.   *146* also
Foryet* nat this, for Goddes owene love!   forget
Ye ben ful coleryk* of complexion*;   bilious bodily health
Ware* the sonne in his ascension*   beware lest as it rises higher
Ne fynde yow nat repleet* of humours   overly full
   hoote*.   *150* hot
And if it do, I dar wel leye a grote*   groat (fourpence)
That ye shal have a fevere terciane*,   fever recurring every three
Or an agu* that may be youre bane*.   fever destruction days
A day or two ye shul have digestyves*   medicines for absorbing bile
Of wormes, er ye take youre laxatyves   *155*

⁵ Dionysius Cato, supposed author of the *Distichs of Cato*, is meant; see
the Merchant's Tale, note 5.

Of lawriol*, centaure*, and fumetere*,   laureole centaury fumitory
Or elles of ellebor* that groweth there,   hellebore
Of katapuce*, or of gaitrys beryis*,   caper berry gaiter berry
Of herbe yve*⁶ growyng in oure yerd ther   herb ivy
   mery is*.   where it is pleasant
Pekke hem up right as they growe and ete
   hem yn!   *160*
Be myrie, housbonde, for youre fader kyn*!   father's kin
Dredeth no dreem! I kan sey yow
   namoore*!"   no more

  "Madame," quod he, "graunt mercy of*   many thanks for
   youre loore*.   advice
But nathelees*, as touchyng* daun Catoun*,   nevertheless as for Cato
That hath of wysdom swich* a greet renoun*,   such reputation
Though that he bad* no dremes for to drede,   commanded
By God, men may in olde bookes rede   *167*
Of many a man moore of auctorite*   authority
Than evere Caton was, so moot I thee*,   as I may prosper
That al the revers* seyn of this sentence*,   opposite opinion
And han wel founden by experience   *171*
That dremes been significacions
As wel of joye as of tribulacions
That folk enduren in this lif present.
Ther nedeth make of this noon argument.
The verray preeve* sheweth it in dede.   *176* experience
Oon* of the gretteste auctor*⁷ that men rede   one author
Seith thus, that whilom* two felawes wente   once
On pilgrimage in a ful good entente,
And happed so they coomen in a toun   *180*
Wher as* ther was swich congregacioun   where
Of peple, and eek so streit of herbergage*   scanty accomodation
That they ne founde as muche as o* cotage   one

6 All the herbs listed by Pertelote are mentioned as purgatives by various
  medieval and renaissance medical writers.

7 Probably Cicero (106-43 B.C.) and his work the *De Divinatione* are intended.

In which they bothe myghte ylogged* bee.   *lodged*
Wherfore they mosten* of necessitee   *185* *must*
As for that nyght departen* compaignye,   *part*
And ech of hem gooth to his hostelrye
And took his loggyng as it wolde falle.
That oon of hem was logged in a stalle
Fer in a yeerd* with oxen of the plough. *190* *in a distant yard*
That oother man was logged wel ynough
As was his aventure* or his fortune*,   *chance destiny*
That us governeth alle as in commune*.   *in common*
And so bifel, that longe er it were day,
This man mette* in his bed ther as he lay   *dreamed*
How that his felawe gan upon hym calle *196*
And seyde, 'Allas! For in an oxes stalle
This nyght I shal be mordred* ther* I lye!   *murdered where*
Now helpe me, deere brother, or I dye!
In al haste com to me!' he sayde.   *200*
This man out of his sleep for feere abrayde*.   *awoke*
But whan that he was wakened of his sleepe,
He turned hym and took of it no keepe*;   *paid no attention to it*
Hym thoughte* his dreem nas but* a   *it seemed to him was only*
    vanitee*.   *foolishness*
Thus twies* in his slepyng dremed hee,   *205* *twice*
And atte thridde* tyme yet his felawe   *at the third*
Cam as hym thoughte and seide, 'I am now
    slawe*.   *slain*
Bihoold my bloody woundes depe and wyde.
Arys up erly in the morwe tyde*   *morning*
And at the west gate of the toun,' quod he,
'A carte ful of donge* ther shaltow* se,   *211* *dung you will*
In which my body is hid ful prively*.   *very secretly*
Do thilke carte aresten* boldely.   *have that cart stopped*
My gold caused my mordre*, sooth to sayn*.' *murder to tell the truth*
And tolde hym every poynt how he was
    slayn   *215*
With a ful pitous face, pale of hewe.
And truste wel, his dreem he foond ful trewe,
For on the morwe, as soone as it was day,
To his felawes in* he took the way,   *inn*

And whan that he cam to this oxes stalle,
After his felawe he bigan to calle.   221
The hostiler* answerde hym anon*   inn-keeper   at once
And seyde, 'Sire, youre felawe is agon*.   has gone
As soone as day he wente out of the toun.'
   This man gan fallen in suspecioun*, 225   to grow suspicious
Remembrynge on hise dremes that he
   mette*,   dreamed
And forth he gooth – no lenger* wolde he   longer
   lette* –   delay
Unto the west gate of the toun and fond
A dong cart wente as* it were to donge*   as if   manure
   lond,
That was arrayed* in that same wise   230   outfitted
As ye han* herd the dede man devyse*.   have   describe
And with an hardy* herte he gan to crye: bold
'Vengeance and justice of* this felonye!   for
My felawe mordred* is this same nyght,   murdered
And in this carte heere he lith* gapyng*   lies   with mouth open
   upright.   235
I crye out on the ministres*,' quod he,   magistrates
'That sholden kepe and reulen* this citee.   govern
Harrow*! Allas, heere lith my felawe slayn!'   help
What sholde I moore unto this tale sayn?
The peple out sterte* and caste the cart to   rushed out
   grounde,   240
And in the myddel of the dong they founde
The dede man that mordred was al newe.

   "O blisful God, that art so just and trewe!
Lo, how that thou biwreyest* mordre   reveal
   alway*!   always
Mordre wol out, that se we day by day!   245
Mordre is so wlatsom* and abhomynable   loathsome
To God, that is so just and resonable,
That he ne wol nat suffre it heled* be,   concealed
Though it abyde* a yeer or two or thre.   wait
Mordre wol out! This my conclusioun.   250
And right anon*, ministres of that toun   right away

Han hente* the cartere and so soore hym   seized
  pyned*,   tortured
And eek* the hostiler so soore engyned*,   also racked
That they biknewe* hir wikkednesse anon,   confessed
And were an-hanged* by the nekke bon. *255*   hanged
Heere may men seen that dremes been to
  drede*,   to be feared
And certes*, in the same book I rede,   certainly
Right in the nexte chapitre after this,
·I gabbe nat*, so have I joye or blis!   I'm not joking

  "Two men that wolde han passed over see
For certeyn cause into a fer contree,   *261*
If that the wynd ne hadde been contrarie,
That made hem in a citee for to tarie,
That stood ful myrie* upon a haven* syde.   very pleasantly harbou
But on a day, agayn the even tyde*,   *265*   towards evening
The wynd gan chaunge and blew right as hem
  leste*.   pleased them
Jolif* and glad they wente unto hir reste,   happy
And casten* hem ful erly for to saille.   prepared
But herkneth, to that o* man fil a greet   one
  mervaille:
That oon of hem in slepyng as he lay,   *270*
Hym mette* a wonder dreem agayn* the   he dreamed towards
  day.
Hym thoughte* a man stood by his beddes   it seemed to him
  syde
And hym comanded that he sholde abyde*,   wait
And seyde hym thus: 'If thou tomorwe
  wende*,   travel
Thow shalt be dreynt*; my tale is at an   drowned
  ende!'   *275*
He wook* and tolde his felawe what he   awoke
  mette*,   dreamed
And preyde hym his viage to lette*,   delay his trip
As for that day he preyde hym to byde*.   wait
  His felawe that lay by his beddes syde
Gan for to laughe and scorned hym ful faste.

'No dreem,' quod he, 'may so myn herte
    agaste*   281   frighten
That I wol lette* for to do my thynges*.   put off   business
I sette nat a straw by thy dremynges,
For swevenes* ben but vanytees* and japes*.   dreams   foolishness   deceits
Men dreme alday* of owles, or of apes, 285   every day
And of many a maze* therwithal.   delusion
Men dreme of thyng that nevere was, ne
    shal*.   shall be
But sith* I see that thou wolt heere abyde   since
And thus forslewthen* wilfully thy tyde*,   waste   time
God woot*, it reweth me*, and have good
    day!'   290   knows   I'm sorry about it
And thus he took his leve and wente his way.
But er that he hadde half his cours yseyled*,   sailed
Noot I nat why*, ne what myschaunce* it   I don't know why   mishap
    eyled*,   afflicted it
But casuelly* the shippes botme* rente*,   by chance   bottom   ripped ope
And shipe and man under the water wente
In sighte of othere shippes it bisyde   296
That with hem seyled at the same tyde*.   time
And therfore, faire Pertelote so deere,
By swich* ensamples olde maystow* leere*   such   you may   learn
That no man sholde been to* recchelees*   too   heedless
Of dremes, for I sey thee, doutelees*, 301   without doubt
That many a dreem ful soore is for to
    drede*.   to be feared

"Lo, in the lyf of Seint Kenelm[8] I rede,
That was Kenulphus* sone the noble kyng   Kenulph's
Of Mercenrike*, how Kenelm mette* a
    thyng   305   Mercia   dreamed
A lite er* he was mordred on a day.   little before
His mordre in his avysion* he say*;   vision   saw
His norice* hym expowned* every deel*   nurse   explained   completely

8 The seven-year-old Kenelm, son of Kenulph of Mercia, was murdered in
819.

His swevene*, and bad hym for to kepe hym   dream
   weel*   guard himself well
For traison, but he nas but* sevene yeer oold,   was only
And therfore litel tale* hath he toold*   *311*   little attention   paid
Of any dreem, so hooly was his herte.
By God, I hadde levere* than my sherte*   I had rather   i.e., I owned
That ye hadde rad* his legende as have I!   read   my shirt
Dame Pertelote, I sey yow trewely,   *315*
Macrobeus*[9] that writ the avysion*   Macrobius   vision
In Affrike* of the worthy Cipion*,   Africa   Scipio (Africanus)
Affermeth* dremes, and seith that they been   supports the validity of
Warnynge of thynges that men after seen*.   see afterwards
And forthermoore, I pray yow, looketh wel
In the olde testament of Daniel,[10]   *321*
If he heeld dremes any vanitee*.   foolishness
Reed eek* of Joseph,[11] and ther shul ye see   also
Wher dremes be somtyme, I sey nat alle,
Warnynge of thynges that shul after falle*.   occur
Looke of Egipte the kyng, daun Pharao*,   lord Pharaoh
His baker and his butiller* also,   *327*   butler
Wher* they ne felte noon effect in dremes.   whether
Who so* wol seken actes* of sondry remes*   whoever   deeds   different
May rede of dremes many a wonder* thyng.   marvellous   kingdoms
Lo, Cresus*, which that was of Lyde* kyng,[12]   Croesus   Lydia
Mette* he nat that he sat upon a tree,   *332*   dreamed
Which signified he sholde anhanged* bee?   hanged
Lo, heere Andromacha*, Ectores* wyf,   Andromache   Hector's
That day that Ector sholde lese* his lyf,   *335*   lose

9 Macrobius (*fl. c.* A.D. 400) wrote a commentary on the *Somnium Scipionis* of Cicero, which became a source book of information on dreams for the Middle Ages.

10 See Daniel 7 and 8 for two elaborate dream sequences.

11 Joseph (Genesis 40 and 41) while imprisoned in Egypt interpreted correctly the dreams of Pharaoh's baker and butler, and later the dream of Pharaoh himself.

12 Croesus, king of Lydia (*c.* 560-546 B.C.). The story of his dream is related last in the long sequence of dismal tragedies recited by the Monk immediately before the Nun's Priest tells his tale.

She dremed on the same nyght biforn
How that the lyf of Ector sholde be lorn*   lost
If thilke* day he wente into bataille.[13]   that same
She warned hym, but it myghte nat availle;
He wente for to fighte, nathelees*.   340   nevertheless
But he was slayn anon of Achilles –
But thilke tale is al to* longe to telle,   too
And eek* it is ny* day; I may nat dwelle*.   also   nearly   tarry
Shortly I seye, as for conclusion*,   to conclude
That I shal han* of this avision*   345   have   vision
Adversitee, and I seye forthermoor*,   furthermore
That I ne telle of laxatyves no stoor*,   put no faith in
For they ben venymes*, I woot* it weel!   poisons   know
I hem diffye! I love hem never a deel*.   not one bit
    Now lat us speke of myrthe and stynte*   cease
    al this.   350
Madame Pertelote, so have I blis,
Of o* thyng God hath sent me large grace,   one
For whan I se the beautee of youre face –
Ye ben so scarlet reed aboute youre eyen* –   eyes
It maketh al my drede* for to dyen.   355   fear
For also siker* as *In principio*,[14]   as certainly   "In the begin-
                                                                            ning
Mulier est hominis confusio, –   "Woman is the ruin of man-
    Madame, the sentence* of this Latyn is,   meaning   kind
'Womman is mannes joye and al his blis.'
For whan I feele a nyght your softe syde,
Al be it that* I may nat on yow ryde,   361   although
For that* oure perche is maad so narwe*,   because   narrow
    allas,
I am so ful of joye and of solas*,   pleasure
That I diffye* bothe swevene* and dreem."   defy   dream

13 Andromache's dream does not appear in Homer's *Iliad*. It does, how-
    ever, appear in the retelling of the story of the Trojan War by Dares
    Phrygius, whose work exists in a sixth-century Latin manuscript. It and
    other accounts based on it were extremely popular in the Middle Ages.

14 *In principio*, the opening words of the gospel of St. John; see General
    Prologue, note 15.

And with that word he fley* doun fro the   flew
  beem,   · *365*
For it was day, and eek* his hennes alle,   also
And with a "Chuk!" he gan hem for to calle,
For he hadde found a corn lay* in the yerd.   which lay
Real* he was; he was namoore* aferd*.   royal   no longer   afraid
He fethered Pertelote twenty tyme,   *370*
And trad* as ofte er it was pryme*.   trod   prime (9 a.m.)
He looketh as it were a grym* leoun;   fierce
And on his toos* he rometh up and doun.   toes
Hym deigned nat* to sette his foot to   he did not deign
  grounde.   *374*
He chukketh* whan he hath a corn yfounde,   clucks
And to hym rennen* thanne hise wyves alle.   run
Thus roial as a prince is in his halle
Leve I this Chauntecleer in his pasture*,   feeding
And after wol I telle his aventure.
Whan that the monthe in which the world
  bigan   *380*
That highte* March, whan God first maked   is called
  man,[15]
Was compleet, and passed were also
Syn* March bigan thritty* dayes and two,   since   thirty
Bifel* that Chauntecleer in al his pryde,   it happened
Hise sevene wyves walkynge by his syde, *385*
Caste up hise eyen* to the brighte sonne,   eyes
That in the signe of Taurus hadde yronne*   run
Twenty degrees and oon* and somwhat   twenty-one degrees
  moore,
And knew by kynde* and by noon oother   nature
  loore*   learning
That it was pryme, and crew* with blisful   crowed
  stevene*.   *390*   voice
"The sonne," he seyde, "is clomben* up on   has climbed
  hevene

---

15 It was a common medieval belief that the world was created at the
  vernal equinox. The date of Chauntecleer's adventure is May 3, though
  the phrase "syn March bigan" (line 383) obscures the reckoning.

Fourty degrees and oon, and moore, ywis*.[16]   certainly
Madame Pertelote, my worldes blis,
Herkneth* thise blisful briddes*, how they   listen to birds
   synge,
And se the fresshe floures*, how they   flowers
   sprynge;   *395*
Ful is myn herte of revel and solas*!"   merriment
But sodeynly hym fil* a sorweful cas*,   befell event
For evere the latter ende of joye is wo.
God woot* that worldly joye is soone ago*,   knows gone
And if a rethor* koude faire endite*,   *400*   rhetorician compose
He in a cronycle saufly* myghte it write   safely
As for a sovereyn notabilitee*.   most noteworthy observation
Now every wys man, lat hym herkne me:
This storie is al so trewe, I undertake*,   guarantee
As is the booke of Launcelot de Lake[17] *405*
That wommen holde in ful greet reverence.
Now wol I torne agayn to my sentence*.   main theme

  A colfox*, ful of sly iniquitee,   fox with ears and tail tipped with black
That in the grove hadde woned* yeres three,   dwelt
By heigh ymaginacion forncast*   *410*   by divine predestination
The same nyght thurghout the hegges* brast*   hedges broke through
Into the yerd ther* Chauntecleer the faire   where
Was wont and eek* his wyves to repaire*,   also retreat
And in a bed of wortes* stille he lay   herbs
Til it was passed undren* of the day,   *415*   mid-morning
Waitynge his tyme on Chauntecleer to falle,
As gladly doon thise homycides alle

16 The astronomical allusions in this passage (lines 387-92) confirm the date as May 3 (see preceding note). The height of the sun above the horizon at this latitude, a little more than forty-one degrees (line 392), indicates the hour of Chauntecleer's encounter with the fox to be about 9 a.m.

17 Lancelot, the hero of a medieval romance, whose exploits in love and chivalry surpass the bounds of realistic probability.

That in await* liggen* to mordre* men.   ambush lie murder

O false mordrour, lurkynge in thy den!

O newe Scariot*, newe Genylon*![18]   *420*   (Judas) Iscariot Ganelon

False dissimilour*! O Greek Synon*,[19]   deceiver Sinon

That broghtest Troye al outrely* to sorwe!   utterly

O Chauntecleer, acursed be that morwe

That yow into the yerd flaugh* fro the   flew
   bemes!

Thou were ful wel ywarned by thy dremes

That thilke* day was perilous to thee!   *426*   that same

But what that God forwoot* moot* nedes   foreknows must
   bee,

After the opinion of certein clerkis*.   scholars

Witnesse on hym* that any parfit clerk is,   let him be a witness

That in scole is greet altercacion   *430*

In this matere, and greet disputison*,   disputation

And hath ben of an hundred thousand men.

But I ne kan nat bulte* it to the bren*   sift bran

As kan the hooly doctour Augustyn*,   *434*   St. Augustine

Or Boece*, or the Bisshope Bradwardyn,[20]   Boethius

Wheither that Goddes worthy forwityng*   foreknowledge

Streyneth* me nedely* for to doon a   compels by necessity
   thyng –

"Nedely" clepe* I symple necessitee –   call

Or elles if free choys be graunted me

To do that same thyng or do it noght,   *440*

Thogh God forwoot* it er that it was   foreknew
   wroght*,   done

Or if his wityng* streyneth* never a deel*,   knowledge compels not at
                       all

---

18 Ganelon the traitor, who betrays Roland and his rearguard to the Saracens in the *Chanson de Roland*.

19 Sinon persuaded the Trojans to drag the wooden horse, inside of which were hidden Greek soldiers, within the walls of Troy; *Aeneid*, ii, 154 ff.

20 St. Augustine (354-430) and Boethius (*c.* 475-525) discussed the question of the freedom of the human will. The English cleric Bishop Bradwardine (d. 1349) contributed to the literature on the subject.

But by necessitee condicioneel*.²¹   conditional necessity
I wol nat han* to do of swich* mateere!   have   such
My tale is of a cok, as ye may heere,   *445*
That took his conseil* of his wyf with sorwe   advice
To walken in the yerd upon that morwe   dreamed
That he hadde met* that dreem that I yow
  tolde.   fatal
Wommennes conseils ben ful ofte colde*!
Wommannes conseil broghte us first to wo,
And made Adam fro paradys to go   *451*
Ther as* he was ful myrie and wel at ese.   where
But for* I noot* to whom it myghte displese   because   don't know
If I conseil of wommen wolde blame,
Passe over, for I seyde it in my game*.   in jest
Rede auctors* where they trete of swich   authors
  mateere,   *456*
And what they seyn* of wommen ye may   say
  heere.
Thise ben the cokkes wordes, and nat myne.
I kan noon harm of no womman divyne*.   imagine

Faire in the soond* to bathe hire myrily*   sand   pleasantly
Lith* Pertelote and alle hire sustres* by *461* lies   sisters
Agayn* the sonne, and Chauntecleer so free   in
Soong murier than the mermayde in the
  see –
For Phisiologus²² seith sikerly*   certainly
How that they syngen wel and myrily.   *465*
And so bifel that, as he caste his eye
Among the wortes* on a boterflye*,   herbs   butterfly

21 In "conditional necessity", according to Boethius, *Consolation of Phil-osophy*, bk. iv, pr. 6, man is allowed a measure of free choice, but "simple necessity" (line 438) denies this free choice. Chaucer translated this work by Boethius.

22 A Latin collection of animal lore known in Middle English as the *Bestiary*. The fanciful descriptions of birds and beasts are accompanied by a moral interpretation. It is worth noting that the fox in the *Bestiary* is equated with the Devil.

He was war* of this fox that lay ful lowe.   aware
Nothyng ne liste hym* thanne for to crowe,   it pleased him
But cride anon*, "Cok! cok!" and up he   at once
    sterte*   470   leaped
As man that was affrayed in his herte.
For natureelly, a beest desireth flee
Fro his contrarie*, if he may it see,   enemy
Though he nevere erst* hadde seyn* it with   before   seen
    his eye.   474
This Chauntecleer, whan he gan hym espye*,   notice
He wolde han* fled, but that the fox anon   have
Seyde, "Gentil sire, allas, wher wol ye gon?
Be ye affrayed of me that am youre freend?
Now certes*, I were worse than a feend   certainly
If I to yow wolde harm or vileynye.   480
I am nat come youre conseil* for t'espye*.   secrets   to discover
But trewely, the cause of my comynge
Was oonly for to herkne* how that yow   listen to
    synge.
For trewely, ye have as myrie a stevene*   voice
As any aungel hath that is in hevene.   485
Therwith ye han in musyk moore feelynge
Than hadde Boece[23] or any that kan synge.
My lord, youre fader, God his soule blesse,
And eek youre mooder of hire gentillesse,
Han in myn hous ybeen to my greet ese*,   satisfaction
And certes, sire, ful fayn* wolde I yow   gladly
    plese.   491
But for men speke of syngynge, I wol seye,
So mote I brouke* wel myne eyen tweye*,   enjoy (the use of)   two eyes
Save yow, I herde nevere man so synge
As dide youre fader in the morwenynge*.   morning
Certes, it was of herte* al that he song,   496   from his heart
And for to make his voys the moore strong,
He wolde so peyne hym* that with bothe hise   exert himself
    eyen

23 Boethius, in addition to the philosophical work referred to above in note
    21, wrote a treatise on music.

He moste wynke*, so loude wolde he cryen,   i.e., close both his eyes
And stonden on his tiptoon* therwithal, *500*   tip-toes
And strecche forth his nekke long and smal.
And eek* he was of swich* discrecion*   also such acumen
That ther nas* no man in no region   was not
That hym in song or wisedom myghte passe.
I have wel rad* in *Daun Burnel the Asse, 505*   read
Among his vers, how that ther was a cok,
For* a preestes sone yaf* hym a knok   because gave
Upon his leg while he was yong and nyce*,   foolish
He made hym for to lese* his benefice*.²⁴   lose church living
But certeyn, ther nys* no comparison   *510*   is not
Bitwix the wisedom and discrecion
Of youre fader and of his* subtiltee*.   i.e., the cock's cleverness
Now syngeth, sire, for seinte charitee!
Lat se, konne ye youre fader countrefete*?"   imitate
This Chauntecleer hise wynges gan to bete
As man that koude his trayson* nat espie,   treachery
So was he ravysshed* with his flaterie.   *517*   carried away

    Allas, ye lordes, many a fals flatour*   flatterer
Is in youre courtes, and many a losengeour*,   liar
That plesen yow wel moore, by my feith, *520*
Than he that soothfastnesse* unto yow seith.   truth
Redeth Ecclesiaste²⁵ of flaterye;
Beth war*, ye lordes, of hir trecherye!   beware
    This Chauntecleer stood hye upon his toos,
Strecchynge his nekke, and heeld his eyen
    cloos*,   *525*   closed
And gan to crowe loude for the nones*.   occasion
And daun Russell the fox stirte up* atones*,   jumped up at once

24 A Latin satire of the twelfth century by Nigel Wireker; in the anecdote in question, a cock avenges himself on a priest's son who broke the cock's leg, by failing to awaken the priest's son on time for his ordination, thereby causing him to lose his benefice.

25 There is no discussion of flattery in Ecclesiastes; perhaps Proverbs 29:5 is meant, since both these books of the Bible were attributed to Solomon.

And by the gargat* hente* Chauntecleer,   throat   seized
And on his bak toward the wode hym beer*,   bore
For yet ne was ther no man that hym
    sewed*.   530   pursued
    O destynee, that mayst nat ben eschewed*!   avoided
Allas, that Chauntecleer fleigh* fro the   flew
    bemes!
Allas, his wyf ne roghte nat of* dremes!   did not heed
And on a Friday fil al this meschaunce*!   misfortune
    O Venus, that art goddesse of plesaunce*,   pleasure
Syn that* thy servant was this Chauntecleer   since
And in thy servyce dide al his poweer,   537
Moore for delit than world to multiplye*,   increase
Why woldestow* suffre hym on thy day²⁶ to   would you
    dye?
    O Gaufred*, deere maister soverayn,   540   Geoffrey
That whan thy worthy Kyng Richard* was   Richard I of England
    slayn
With shot*, compleynedest* his deeth so   missile   lamented
    soore,
Why ne hadde I now thy sentence* and thy   wisdom
    loore*   learning
The Friday for to chide* as diden ye?²⁷   scold
For on a Friday soothly* slayn was he.   545   truly
Thanne wolde I shewe yow how that I koude
    pleyne*   lament
For Chauntecleres drede* and for his peyne*. fear torment
    Certes, swich cry ne lamentacion
Was nevere of* ladyes maad whan Ylion*   by   Troy
Was wonne, and Pirrus* with his streite*   Pyrrhus   drawn
    swerd*   550   sword

26 Friday, as the French *vendredi* signifies, was sacred to Venus.
27 Geoffrey of Vinsauf was the author of a rhetorical handbook on poetry, the *Nova Poetria.* One of his examples of the use of rhetorical devices is an elaborate lament for Richard I of England who was fatally wounded in the neck by an arrow on a Friday.

Whan he hadde hent* Kyng Priam by the   seized
   berd
And slayn hym, as seith us *Eneydos**,[28]   the *Aeneid*
As maden alle the hennes in the clos*   yard
Whan they hadde seyn* of Chauntecleer the   seen
   sighte.
But sovereynly* dame Pertelote shrighte*   powerfully   shrieked
Ful louder than dide Hasdrubales wyf   556
Whan that hire housbonde hadde lost his lyf
And that the Romayns hadden brend*   burned
   Cartage*;   Carthage
She was so ful of torment and of rage
That wilfully into the fyr she sterte*   560   leaped
And brende* hir selven with a stedefast   burned
   herte.[29]
   O woful hennes, right so* criden ye,   just as
As whan that Nero brende the citee
Of Rome, cryden senatours wyves
For that hir housbondes losten alle hire
   lyves;   565
Withouten gilt* this Nero hath hem slayn.[30]   i.e., on the senators' part
Now wol I turne to my tale agayn.

   The sely* wydwe*, and eek* hire doghtres   hapless   widow   also
   two,
Herden thise hennes crie and maken wo,
And out at dores stirten they anon*   570   at once
And syen* the fox toward the grove gon   saw
And bar upon his bak the cok away,
And cryden, "Out! Harrow*! and weylawey*!   help   alas
Ha! ha! the fox!" And after hym they ran,

28 For the account of Priam's death at the hands of Pyrrhus, son of
   Achilles, see *Aeneid,* ii, 526 ff.

29 Hasdrubal, a Carthaginian leader when the city was destroyed by the
   Romans at the end of the Third Punic War, 146 B.C. The suicide of his
   wife is used for a different purpose in the Franklin's Tale, 691-6.

30 Nero had a reputation for surpassing cruelty in the Middle Ages; it is
   doubtful, however, if his iniquities extended as far as these lines suggest.

And eek with staves many another man. *575*
Ran Colle oure dogge, and Talbot, and
   Gerland,
And Malkyn with a dystaf in hire hand.
Ran cow and calf and eek the verray hogges,
So fered* for berkyng of the dogges, *579*   frightened
And shoutyng of the men and wommen eek.
They ronne* so hem thoughte* hir herte   ran   it seemed to them
   breek*.   would break
They yolleden* as feendes doon in helle.   yelled
The dokes* cryden as* men wolde hem   ducks   as if
   quelle*.   kill
The gees for feere flowen* over the trees.   flew
Out of the hyve cam the swarm of bees, *585*
So hydous* was the noyse! A, benedicitee*!   hideous   by heaven
Certes, he Jakke Straw[31] and his meynee*   gang
Ne made nevere shoutes half so shrille
Whan that they wolden any Flemyng kille
As thilke* day was maad upon the fox. *590*   that
Of bras* they broghten bemes* and of box*,   brass   trumpets   boxwood
Of horn, of boon*, in which they blewe and   bone
   powped*,   tooted
And therwithal they skriked* and they   shrieked
   howped*.   whooped
It semed as that hevene sholde falle.
Now goode men, I pray yow, herkneth alle.

Lo, how Fortune turneth* sodeynly *596*   reverses
The hope and pryde eek* of hir enemy!   also
This cok, that lay upon the foxes bak,
In al his drede unto the fox he spak,
And seyde, "Sire, if that I were as ye, *600*
Yet sholde I seyn*, as wys* God helpe me,   say   as certainly as
'Turneth agayn*, ye proude cherles* alle!   turn back   fellows

---

31 Jack Straw was one of the leaders of the Peasants' Revolt in 1381. The
   rebels took over sections of the city of London, and many Flemish
   weavers who had settled in the city were killed in the riots.

A verray pestilence upon yow falle!

Now am I come unto the wodes syde;

Maugree* youre heed, the cok shal heere   despite
    abyde.   *605*

I wol hym ete, in feith, and that anon!' "

    The fox answerde, "In feith, it shal be
    don!"

And as he spak that word, al sodeynly

This cok brak from his mouth delyverly*,   nimbly

And heighe upon a tree he fleigh* anon. *610*   flew

And whan the fox saugh* that he was gon,   saw

"Allas!" quod he, "o Chauntecleer, allas!

I have to yow," quod he, "ydoon trespas*,   committed an offence

In as muche as I maked yow aferd*,   afraid

Whan I yow hente* and broghte out of the   seized
    yerd.   *615*

But sire, I dide it in no wikke entente*.   evil intention

Com doun, and I shal telle yow what I mente.

I shal seye sooth* to yow, God help me so!"   truth

    "Nay thanne," quod he, "I shrewe* us   curse
    bothe two!

And first I shrewe my self bothe blood and
    bones   *620*

If thou bigile* me any ofter* than ones*!   trick   more often   once

Thou shalt namoore thurgh thy flaterye

Do* me to synge and wynke with myn eye*.   cause   close my eyes

For he that wynketh whan he sholde see,

Al wilfully*, God lat hym nevere thee*!" *625*   by his own will   prosper

    "Nay," quod the fox, "but God yeve* hym   give
    meschaunce*   misfortune

That is so undiscreet of governaunce*   conduct

That jangleth* whan he sholde holde his   chatters
    pees!"

    Lo, swich* it is for to be recchelees*,   such   heedless

And necligent, and truste on flaterye!   *630*

    But ye that holden this tale a folye*   piece of foolishness

As of a fox, or of a cok and hen,

Taketh the moralitee, goode men!

For Seint Paul* seith that al that writen is,   Romans 15:4

To oure doctryne* it is ywrite*, ywis*.   *635*   instruction written certainly
Taketh the fruyt, and lat the chaf be stille.
Now goode God, if that it be thy wille,
As seith my lord*, so make us alle goode men,   i.e., superior in the Church
And brynge us to his heighe blisse! Amen.

INTRODUCTION TO THE
PARDONER'S PROLOGUE AND TALE

The General Prologue presents the Pardoner as an unsavoury character, emasculate, and perhaps in a homosexual relationship with the Summoner. But Chaucer tells us also in the General Prologue that the Pardoner was "a noble ecclesiaste" – a very fine preacher. Despite the misgivings expressed by the other pilgrims in the Prologue to the Pardoner's Tale, despite their fear that he will recite a ribald story, the tale related by the Pardoner justifies the praise of his ability as a preacher in the General Prologue.

The Pardoner's Tale is essentially a sermon illustrated by an exemplum or moral story. The Pardoner has said that he will demonstrate his preaching techniques, and to do so he treats the pilgrims to an exhibition of himself in action. The text of his sermon is "The love of money is the root of all evil." But like most preachers he does not confine himself strictly to his text; instead, he uses the lengthy preamble to the tale proper to castigate sundry other vices prevalent in the world around him: lechery, drunkenness, gluttony, gambling, and swearing. About two hundred lines of the Pardoner's Tale are taken up in this manner. At first glance the passage might seem to be a digression, but the thoughtful reader will realize that these lines serve a twofold purpose. In the first place they reinforce the remark in the General Prologue about the Pardoner's ability as a preacher, and secondly, the vices castigated in these lines are those possessed to an excessive degree by the three scoundrels who are the principal actors in the Pardoner's story. In other words, Chaucer has directed the passage outside of the tale so that it serves as a commentary on the character of the Pardoner. At the same time he has directed it into the tale itself so that it functions as a device to characterize the three tavern-brawlers.

Like the other stories related by the Canterbury pilgrims, the tale related by the Pardoner is not original with Chaucer. It uses a plot that is common in Oriental literature and that is effectively employed by Kipling in "The King's Ankus" in *The Second Jungle Book*. The origin of the story seems to be eastern, though Chaucer knew it only in versions circulating in the West. The details of the story were all probably in existence before Chaucer's retelling by means of the Pardoner, but one of these details is used in a curious and inexplicable way. The identity of the Old Man who directs the three evil revellers to the fatal treasure beneath the tree is not made clear in Chaucer's story. Some scholars have made a connection between this mysterious figure and the legend of the Wandering Jew; others have pointed to classical sources in which occurs the image of an old man, wearied with age, knocking on the earth and begging entry.[1] Whatever his meaning, this chthonic being, somehow excluded from his natural home the earth itself, adds just the right note of mysterious horror to the tale. Kipling's use of the underground cave of treasure in his story produces the same effect.

Like the tale itself, the character of the Pardoner is not original with Chaucer. The Pardoner is a development from a character in the *Romaunt of the Rose*, Fals Semblaunt by name, or Hypocrisy. And a hypocrite the Pardoner is; the candour of his confessions in the prologue to his tale is equalled elsewhere in the *Canterbury Tales* only by the Wife of Bath. It is this very combination of candour and hypocrisy, however, that makes the incident at the end of the tale difficult to interpret. It was remarked earlier that the Pardoner offers to the other pilgrims the spectacle of himself in action as a preacher, and a very effective preacher he is. At the end of his tale, in keeping with his desire to show off all the tricks of his trade, the Pardoner launches into a peroration condemning the sins he had spent so long castigating in the opening lines of his story. He then demonstrates how he calls upon his audience to step forth, receive his pardon, and make an offering to himself. And in a final burst of candour, he confesses that Christ's pardon is best; he will not deceive his audience of fellow pilgrims. But at this point the Pardoner seems to fall a victim to

---

1 See N. S. Bushnell, "The Wandering Jew and the *Pardoner's Tale*", *Studies in Philology* XXVIII (1931), 450-60, and G. L. Kittredge, *American Journal of Philology* IX (1888), 84-5.

the very sin of avarice that provides the text of his sermon. He offers his absolution – at a reduced price, since he is among friends – to the pilgrims who have heard his story. His trick might have worked had he not made the mistake of asking the Host to be the first contributor. The Host, as sharp a character as ever travelled the road to Canterbury, contemptuously and insultingly refuses the request, and the Pardoner retreats into sullen silence. It takes the tact of the Knight to restore harmony.

The Prologue to the Pardoner's Tale

"Thou beel amy*, thou Pardoner," he*   fair friend   i.e., the Host
sayde,

Telle us som myrthe or japes* right anon*."   funny stories   right away

"It shal be doon," quod he*, "by Seint   i.e., the Pardoner
Ronyon!¹

But first," quod he, "heere at this alestake*   alehouse sign

I wol bothe drynke and eten of a cake."   5

    And right anon the gentils* gonne* to   respectable people   began
crye:

"Nay, lat hym telle us of no ribaudrye*!   ribaldry

Telle us som moral thyng that we may leere*   learn

Som wit*, and thanne wol we gladly heere."   wisdom

"I graunte, ywis*," quod he, "but I moot*   certainly   must
thynke   10

Upon som honest thyng while that I drynke.

    "Lordynges," quod he, "in chirches whan I
preche,

I peyne me* to han* an hauteyn speche*,   take trouble   have   lofty style

And rynge it out as round as gooth a belle,

For I kan* al by rote* that I telle.   15   know   by heart

My theme is alwey oon* and evere was: one

Radix malorum est cupiditas.   "The love of money is the root
of [all] evils", I Tim. 6:10

    "First I pronounce* whennes that I   announce
come*,²   i.e., from Rome

And thanne my bulles* shewe I alle and some.   papal bulls

---

1 Perhaps the name of a Scottish saint (cf. the name of Scott's novel *St. Ronan's Well*); perhaps an obscene pun is intended (runnion).

2 See General Prologue, line 669 and note.

Oure lige lordes seel* on my patente*,   20   bishop's seal   licence
That shewe I first my body to warente*,   for my protection
That no man be so boold, ne preest ne clerk,
Me to destourbe of Cristes hooly werk.
And after that thanne telle I forth my tales.
Bulles of popes and of cardynales,   25
Of patriarkes and bisshopes I shewe,
And in Latyn I speke a wordes fewe
To saffron with* my predicacion*,   adorn   preaching
And for to stire hem to devocion.
Thanne shewe I forth my longe cristal
    stones*   30   glass cases
Ycrammed* ful of cloutes* and of bones;   crammed rags
Relikes been they, as wenen* they echoon*.   believe each one
Thanne have I in laton* a sholder boon   (set) in copper alloy
Which that was of an hooly Jewes sheepe.
'Goode men,' I seye, 'taak of my wordes
    keepe*!   35   pay attention to
If that this boon be wasshe* in any welle*,   washed spring
If cow or calf or sheepe or oxe swelle
That any worm hath ete*, or worm*   that has eaten any worm
    ystonge*,   stung   sna
Taak water of that welle and wassh his
    tonge,
And it is hool* anon*, and forthermoor, 40   healthy at once
Of pokkes* and of scabbe and every soor*   pustules sore
Shal every sheepe be hool that of this welle
Drynketh a draughte; taak kepe* eek* what   pay attention to also
    I telle.
If that the goode man that the beestes
    oweth*   owns
Wol every wyke*, er that the cok hym   week
    croweth,   45
Fastynge, drynke of this welle a draughte,
As thilke* hooly Jew[3] oure eldres* taughte,   that same ancestors
His beestes and his stoor* shal multiplie.   stock

---

3 Probably a Jew of the Old Testament, and there may be a reference to
the story of Jacob in Genesis 30:31 ff.

And sire, also it heeleth jalousie,
For though a man be falle in jalous rage, *50*
Lat maken with this water his potage*,   soup
And nevere shal he moore his wyf mystriste*,   mistrust
Though he the soothe* of hir defaute*   truth   offence
  wiste*,   knew
Al* hadde she taken preestes two or thre.   although
Heere is a miteyn* eek that ye may se; *55*   glove
He that his hand wol putte in this mitayn,
He shal have multipliyng of his grayn
Whan he hath sowen, be it whete or otes*,   oats
So that he offre pens* or elles grotes*.   pence   groats (fourpence)
Goode men and wommen, o* thynge I warne   one
  yow: *60*
If any wight* be in this chirche now   person
That hath doon synne horrible that he
Dar nat for shame of it yshryven* be,   confessed
Or any womman, be she yong or old,
That hath ymaked* hir housbonde   made
  cokewold*,   *65*   cuckold
Swich* folk shal have no power ne no grace   such
To offren to my relikes in this place.
And who so* fyndeth hym out of swich   whoever
  fame*,   ill repute
They wol come up and offre on Goddes
  name,
And I assoille* hem by the auctoritee   *70*   absolve
Which that by bulle ygraunted* was to me.   granted
  By this gaude* have I wonne yeer by   trick
  yeer
An hundred mark* sith* I was pardoner.   unit of currency (13s.4d.)
I stonde lyk a clerk in my pulpet,   since
And whan the lewed* peple is doun yset*, *75*   ignorant   have sat down
I preche so as ye han* herd bifoore,   have
And telle an hundred false japes* moore.   stories
Thanne peyne I* me to strecche forth the   exert myself
  nekke,
And est and west upon the peple I bekke*,   nod
As dooth a dowve* sittynge on a berne*. *80*   dove   barn

Myne handes and my tonge goon so yerne*   eagerly
That it is joye to se my bisynesse.
Of avarice and of swich* cursednesse   such
Is al my prechyng, for to make hem free*   generous
To yeven* hir pens, and namely* unto   give   especially
    me.   *85*
For myn entente is nat but for to wynne*,   gain móney
And no thyng for correccion of synne.
I rekke* nevere whan they been beryed*,   care   buried
Though that hir soules goon a blakeberyed*.   go wandering astray
For certes, many a predicacion*   *90*   sermon
Comth ofte tyme of yvel entencion;
Som for plesance of folk and flaterye,
To been avaunced by ypocrisye*,   hypocrisy
And som for veyne glorie, and som for hate.
For whan I dar noon oother weyes debate*,   argue
Thanne wol I stynge hym* with my tonge   i.e., any opponent
    smerte   *96*
In prechyng, so that he shal nat asterte*   escape
To been* defamed falsly, if that he   from being
Hath trespased to* my bretheren* or to me.   offended   fellow-pardoners
For though I telle noght his propre name, *100*
Men shal wel knowe that it is the same
By signes and by othere circumstances.
Thus quyte* I folk that doon us displesances;   pay back
Thus spitte I out my venym under hewe   *104*
Of hoolynesse, to semen hooly and trewe.
    But shortly myn entente* I wol devyse*:   purpose   explain
I preche of no thyng but for coveityse;
Therfore my theme is yet and evere was,
*Radix malorum est cupiditas**.   "The love of money is the root
                               of [all] evils."
Thus kan I preche agayn that same vice   *110*
Which that I use, and that is avarice.
But though my self be gilty in that synne,
Yet kan I maken oother folk to twynne*   depart
From avarice, and soore to repente.
But that is nat my principal entente;   *115*
I preche no thyng but for coveitise.
Of this mateere it oghte ynogh suffise.

Thanne telle I hem ensamples many oon*   many a one
Of olde stories, longe tyme agoon,
For lewed* peple loven tales olde;   *120*   unlearned
Swiche thynges kan they wel reporte and
    holde.
What, trowe ye*, the whiles I may preche   do you think
And wynne gold and silver for* I teche*,   because   i.e., teach poverty
That I wol lyve in poverte wilfully*?   voluntarily
Nay, nay! I thoghte it nevere, trewely!   *125*
For I wol preche and begge in sondry landes;
I wol nat do no labour with myne handes,
Ne make baskettes and lyve thereby,⁴
By cause I wol nat beggen ydelly*.   in vain
I wol noon of the apostles countrefete*.   *130*   imitate
I wol have moneie, wolle, chese, and whete,
Al* were it yeven* of the pouereste* page,   although   given   poorest
Or of the pouereste wydwe* in a village,   widow
Al* sholde hir children sterve* for famyne.   even if   die
Nay, I wol drynke licour of the vyne   *135*
And have a joly wenche in every toun;
But herkneth, lordynges, in conclusioun:
Youre likyng* is that I shal telle a tale.   desire
Now have I dronke a draughte of corny ale*,   malt-ale
By God, I hope I shal yow telle a thyng   *140*
That shal by reson been at youre likyng;
For though my self be a ful vicious man,
A moral tale yet I yow telle kan,
Which I am wont to preche for to wynne.
Now hoold youre pees; my tale I wol
    bigynne."   *145*

---

4 The Pardoner, judging by the mention of the apostles in line 130, is confusing St. Paul with the third- and fourth-century Paul the Hermit, who was said to be a basket-maker.

The Pardoner's Tale

In Flaundres whilom* was a compaignye once
Of yonge folk that haunteden folye,
As riot, hasard*, stywes*, and tavernes, gambling brothels
Where as with harpes, lutes, and gyternes*, stringed instruments
They daunce and pleyen at dees* bothe day dice
    and nyght, *5*
And eten also, and drynken over hir myght*, more than they can hold
Thurgh which they doon the devel sacrifise
Withinne that develes temple* in cursed wise i.e., the tavern
By superfluytee abhomynable. *9*
Hir othes been so grete and so dampnable
That it is grisly* for to heere hem swere. horrifying
Oure blissed lordes body they totere*. rend (by swearing by different parts of Christ's body)
Hem thoughte* that Jewes rente hym noght it seemed to them
    ynough,
And ech of hem at otheres synne lough*. *14* laughed
And right anon* thanne comen tombesteres*, right away female acrobats
Fetys* and smale, and yonge frutesteres*, shapely female fruit-sellers
Syngeres with harpes, baudes*, wafereres*, harlots cake-sellers
Whiche been the verray develes officeres
To kyndle and blowe the fyr of lecherye
That is annexed unto* glotonye. *20* joined to
The Hooly Writ* take I to my witnesse see Ephesians 5:18
That luxurie* is in wyn and dronkenesse. lechery

Lo, how that dronken Looth* unkyndely* Lot, see Genesis 19:30 ff. unnaturally
Lay by hise doghtres two unwityngly*, without knowing it
So dronke he was he nyste* what he did not know
    wroghte*. *25* did
Herodes*, who so* wel the stories soghte*, Herod whoever should seek
Whan he of wyn was repleet* at his feeste, full

Right at his owene table he yaf* the heeste*　gave　command
To sleen the Baptist John ful giltelees*.　(who was) guiltless
　Senec*[1] seith a good word, doutelees.　30 Seneca　(Matthew 14:1ff.)
He seith he kan no difference fynde
Bitwix a man that is out of his mynde
And a man which that is dronkelewe*,　drunken
But that woodnesse*, fallen* in a shrewe*,　madness occurring in evil
Persevereth lenger* than dooth dronkenesse.　longer　person
O glotonye, ful of cursednesse!　36
O cause first of oure confusion*!　ruin
O original of oure dampnacion,
Til Crist hadde boght us with his blood
　agayn!
Lo, how deere*, shortly for to sayn,　40 dearly
Aboght* was thilke* cursed vileynye*!　paid for　that　sin
Corrupt was al this world for glotonye!
　Adam oure fader, and his wyf also,
Fro Paradys to labour and to wo
Were dryven for* that vice, it is no drede*.　because of　doubt
For whil that Adam fasted, as I rede*,[2]　46 read
He was in Paradys, and whan that he
Eet* of the fruyt deffended* on the tree,　ate forbidden
Anon* he was out cast to wo and peyne.　straightway
O glotonye, on thee wel oghte us pleyne*!　complain
O, wiste a man* how manye maladyes　51 if man knew
Folwen* of excesse and of glotonyes,　follow
He wolde been the moore mesurable*　moderate
Of his diete, sittynge at his table.
Allas, the shorte throte*, the tendre mouth,　i.e., the brief pleasure of
Maketh that est and west and north and　　swallowing
　south,　56
In erthe, in eir, in water man to swynke*　labour
To gete a gloton deyntee* mete and drynke!　luxurious

1 Seneca (d. A.D. 65), Roman dramatist and Stoic philosopher.
2 The Pardoner read this about Adam in St. Jerome's "Letter against Jovinian".

Of this matiere, o Paul*, wel kanstow* trete: St. Paul   can you
"Mete* unto wombe*, and wombe eek* unto   food   belly   also
   mete   60
Shal God destroyen bothe," as Paulus seith*.   I Corinthians 6:13
Allas, a foul thyng is it, by my feith,
To seye this word, and fouler is the dede,
Whan man so drynketh of the white and
   rede*,   i.e., white and red wine
That of his throte he maketh his pryvee, 65
Thurgh thilke* cursed superfluitee!   that same
   The apostle* wepyng seith ful pitously   St. Paul, Philippians 3:18-19
"Ther walken manye of whiche yow toold
   have I –
I seye it now wepyng with pitous voys –
Ther been enemys of Cristes croys*   70 cross
Of whiche the ende is deeth; wombe is hir
   god!"
O wombe, o bely, o stynkyng cod*   bag
Fulfilled of donge and of corrupcioun,
At either ende of thee foul is the soun*!   sound
How greet labour and cost is thee to fynde*! provide for
Thise cookes, how they stampe* and streyne pound
   and grynde   76
And turnen substaunce into accident[3]
To fulfillen al thy likerous* talent*!   gluttonous   appetite
Out of the harde bones knokke they
The mary*, for they caste noght awey   80 marrow
That may go thurgh the golet* softe and   gullet
   swoote*.   sweet
Of spicerie, of leef and bark and roote
Shal been his sauce ymaked by delit,
To make hym yet a newer appetit.
But certes*, he that haunteth* swiche*   certainly   practises   such
   delices*   85 delights
Is deed whil that he lyveth in tho* vices.   those

---

3 "Substance" and "accident" are technical terms derived from Scholastic
   philosophy; the meaning is that the cooks change the raw food from its
   real nature to something more attractive to the palate.

A lecherous thyng is wyn, and dronkenesse
Is ful of stryvyng and of wrecchednesse.
O dronke man, disfigured is thy face!
Sour is thy breeth, foul artow* to embrace,   are you
And thurgh thy dronke nose semeth the
   soun*   91   sound
As though thou seydest ay*, "Sampsoun!   always
   Sampsoun!"
And yet, God woot*, Sampsoun drank nevere   knows
   no wyn!
Thou fallest as it were a styked* swyn*.   stuck   pig
Thy tonge is lost, and al thyn honeste cure*,   care for decency
For dronkenesse is verray sepulture*   96   the very burial
Of mannes wit and his discrecion.
In whom that drynke hath dominacion,
He kan no conseil* kepe; it is no drede*.   secret   doubt
Now kepe yow fro the white and fro the
   rede,   100
And namely fro* the white wyn of Lepe*   especially from   town near
That is to selle in Fysshstrete or in Chepe.[4]   Cadiz, Spain
This wyn of Spaigne crepeth subtilly
In othere wynes growynge faste by,
Of which ther ryseth swich fumositee*   105   vapour
That whan a man hath dronken draughtes
   thre,
And weneth* that he be at hoom in Chepe,   thinks
He is in Spaigne, right at the toun of Lepe,
Nat at the Rochele*, ne at Burdeux* toun,[5]   La Rochelle   Bordeaux
And thanne wol he seye, "Sampsoun!
   Sampsoun!"   110
   But herkneth, lordes, o* word, I yow   one
   preye,
That alle the sovereyn* actes, dar I seye,   notable

4 Fish Street, where Chaucer's father lived, and Cheapside, noted for its
  taverns.

5 The cheaper Spanish wines were mixed with the more expensive Bordeaux
  wines by unscrupulous vintners, as lines 103-4 suggest. The wines of Lepe
  were strong.

Of victories in the olde testament,
Thurgh verray God that is omnipotent,
Were doon in abstinence and in preyere. *115*
Looketh the Bible, and ther ye may it leere*.   learn
   Looke Attilla, the grete conquerour,
Deyde in his sleepe with shame and
   dishonour,
Bledynge ay* at his nose in dronkenesse.⁶   continually
A capitayn sholde lyve in sobrenesse.   *120*
And over al this, avyseth yow* right wel   consider
What was comaunded unto Lamwel*   Lemuel
Nat Samuel, but Lamwel seye I –
Redeth the Bible and fynde it expresly*   explicitly
Of wyn yevyng* to hem that han* justise.⁷   giving   have (responsibility
                                                                                                for
Namoore of this, for it may wel suffise. *126*

   And now I have spoken of glotonye,
Now wol I yow deffenden* hasardrye*.   forbid   gambling
Hasard is verray mooder* of lesynges*,   mother   lies
And of deceite and cursed forswerynges*,   false oaths
Blasphemyng of Crist, manslaughtre, and
   wast* also   *131*   waste
Of catel* and of tyme, and forthermo*   property   furthermore
It is repreeve* and contrarie of honour   reproof
For to ben holde a commune hasardour*,   gambler
And ever the hyer he is of estaat*,   *135*   rank
The moore is he holden desolaat*.   abandoned
If that a prynce useth hasardrye
In alle goveranance and policye,
He is, as by commune opinion,
Yholde* the lasse* in reputacion.   *140*   held   less
   Stilbon⁸ that was a wys embassadour
Was sent to Corynthe in ful greet honour

---

6 Attila, leader of the Huns, died in A.D. 453.

7 As in Proverbs 31:4-5.

8 The story is from the twelfth-century John of Salisbury's *Polycraticus*, where, however, the name is Chiton, not Chaucer's Stilbon.

Fro Lacidomye* to maken hir alliaunce.   Lacedaemonia
And whan he cam, hym happed* par ·   it befell him
    chaunce,
That alle the gretteste that were of that lond
Pleyynge atte hasard* he hem fond*;   *146*   dice   found
For which, as soone as it myghte be,
He stal hym hoom* agayn to his contree,   stole home
And seyde, "Ther wol I nat lese* my name,   lose
Ne I wol nat take on me so greet defame*   disgrace
Yow for to allie unto none hasardours.   *151*
Sendeth othere wise embassadours,
For by my trouthe, me were levere* dye   I would rather
Than I yow sholde to hasardours allye.
For ye that been so glorious in honours   *155*
Shul nat allyen yow with hasardours,
As by my wyl, ne as by my tretee."
This wise philosophre, thus seyde hee.

    Looke eek* that the kyng Demetrius,[9]   also
The Kyng of Parthes*, as the book seith us,   Parthians
Sente him a paire of dees* of gold in scorn,   dice
For he hadde used hasard ther-biforn*, *162*   previously
For which he heeld his glorie or his renoun*   reputation
At no value or reputacioun.
Lordes may fynden oother maner pley *165*
Honeste ynough to dryve the day awey.

    Now wol I speke of othes false and grete
A word or two, as olde bookes trete.
Gret sweryng is a thyng abhominable,
And fals sweryng is yet moore reprevable*.   deserving of reproof
The heighe God forbad sweryng at al;   *171*
Witnesse on Mathew*; but in special   Matthew 5:34
Of sweryng seith the hooly Jeremye*:   Jeremiah 4:2
"Thou shalt swere sooth* thyne othes and nat   truthfully
    lye,
And swere in doom* and eek in   judgment
    rightwisnesse*."   *175*   righteousness

9 Another story from the *Polycraticus*.

But ydel sweryng* is a cursednesse*.   *taking the Lord's name in vain *wickedne[ss]
Bihoold and se that in the firste table
Of heighe Goddes heestes* honurable   *(Ten) Commandments
Hou that the seconde heeste[10] of hym is this:
"Take nat my name in ydel* or amys." *180*   *in vain
Lo, rather* he forbedeth swich* sweryng   *sooner (in the order of the Ten Commandments) *su[ch]
Than homycide or any cursed thyng.
I seye that, as by ordre, thus it stondeth;
This knoweth* that* hise heestes   *i.e., he knows *who
   understondeth,   *184*
How that the seconde heeste of God is that.
And forther over*, I wol thee telle al plat*   *furthermore *flatly
That vengeance shal nat parten* from his   *depart
   hous
That of his othes is to* outrageous.   *too
"By Goddes precious herte," and "By his
   nayles,"
And "By the blood of Crist that is in
   Hayles,[11]   *190*
Sevene is my chaunce*, and thyn is cynk*   *i.e., in a dice game *five
   and treye*!"   *three
"By Goddes armes, if thou falsly pleye,
This daggere shal thurghout thyn herte
   go!" –
This fruyt cometh of the bicched bones*   *cursed dice
   two:
Forsweryng, ire, falsnesse, homycide. *195*
Now, for the love of Crist that for us dyde*,   *died
Lete* youre othes bothe grete and smale.   *forsake
But sires, now wol I telle forth my tale.

Thise riotours thre of whiche I telle,
Longe erst er* prime* rong* of any belle,   *long before *9 a.m. *rang

10 For Protestants, this is the third commandment. Roman Catholics and
   Lutherans combine the first two commandments and divide the tenth
   into two.

11 The abbey at Hailes in Gloucestershire possessed what it claimed was a
   phial of Christ's blood.

Were set hem in a taverne to drynke,   *201*
And as they sat, they herde a belle clynke
Biforn a cors* was caried to his grave.   corpse
That oon* of hem gan callen to his knave,   one
"Go bet*," quod he, "and axe* redily   *205*   quickly ask
What cors is this that passeth heer forby,
And looke that thou reporte his name weel."
    "Sire," quod this boy, "it nedeth
        neveradeel*.   it is not at all necessary
It was me toold er ye cam heer two houres.
He was, pardee*, an olde felawe of youres,   by heaven
And sodeynly he was yslayn tonyght,   *211*
Fordronke* as he sat on his bench upright.   very drunk
Ther cam a privee* theef men clepeth*   stealthy call
    deeth,
That in this contree al the peple sleeth*,   *214*   slays
And with his spere he smoot his herte atwo*,   in two
And wente his wey withouten wordes mo*.   more
He hath a thousand slayn this pestilence*,   during this plague
And maister, er ye come in his presence,
Me thynketh* that it were necessarie   it seems to me
For to be war* of swich* an adversarie.   *220*   be on guard such
Beth redy for to meete hym everemoore.
Thus taughte me my dame; I sey namoore."
"By Seinte Marie!" seyde this taverner,
"The child seith sooth*, for he hath slayn   truth
    this yeer
Henne* over a mile withinne a greet village   hence
Bothe man and womman, child and hyne*   labourer
    and page.   *226*
I trowe* his habitacion be there.   believe
To been avysed* greet wysdom it were   prepared
Er that he dide a man a dishonour."
    "Ye, Goddes armes!" quod this riotour,
"Is it swich peril with hym for to meete?   *231*
I shal hym seke by wey and eek* by strete,   also
I make avow to Goddes digne* bones!   worthy
Herkneth, felawes; we thre been al ones*.   one
Lat ech of us holde up his hand til* oother,   to (the)

And ech of us bicomen otheres brother, *236*
And we wol sleen this false traytour, deeth.
He shal be slayn which that so manye
  sleeth*,   slays
By Goddes dignitee, er it be nyght!"
  Togidres* han* thise thre hir trouthes*   together have pledges
  plight   *240*
To lyve and dyen ech of hem for oother,
As though he were his owene yborn brother,
And up they stirte* and dronken in this   jumped
  rage*,   passion
And forth they goon towardes that village
Of which the taverner hadde spoke biforn.
And many a grisly* ooth thanne han they   horrible
  sworn,   *246*
And Cristes blessed body they to-rente* –   tore to pieces
Deeth shal be deed, if that they may hym
  hente*.   seize
  Whan they han goon nat fully half a mile,
Right* as they wolde han troden* over a   just stepped
  stile,   *250*
An oold man and a poure* with hem mette.   poor
This olde man ful mekely hem grette*,   greeted
And seyde thus: "Now, lordes, God yow
  see*!"   may God preserve you
  The proudeste of thise riotours three
Answerde agayn, "What, carl*, with sory   fellow
  grace*!   *255*   curse you
Why artow* al forwrapped* save thy face?   are you covered up
Why lyvestow* so longe in so greet age?"   do you live
  This olde man gan looke in his visage
And seyde thus: "For I ne kan nat fynde
A man, though that I walked in to Ynde*,   India
Neither in citee nor in no village,   *261*
That wolde chaunge his youthe for myn age;
And therfore moot* I han myn age stille,   must
As longe tyme as it is Goddes wille.
Ne deeth, allas, ne wol nat han my lyf!   *265*
Thus walke I lyk a restelees kaityf*,   wretch

And on the ground, which is my moodres*   mother's
    gate,
I knokke with my staf bothe erly and late,
And seye, 'Leeve* mooder, leet* me in!   dear let
Lo, how I vanysshe, flessh and blood and
    skyn!   270
Allas, whan shul my bones been at reste!
Mooder, with yow wolde I chaunge my
    cheste*,   clothes chest
That in my chambre longe tyme hath be,
Ye, for an heyre clowte* to wrappe me.'   rag made of hair (for burial
But yet to me she wol nat do that grace, 275   cloth)
For which ful pale and welked* is my face.   withered
But sires, to yow it is no curteisye
To speken to an old man vileynye,
But* he trespasse in word or elles in dede.   unless
In Hooly Writ* ye may your self wel rede: Leviticus 19:32
'Agayns an oold man, hoor* upon his heed,   hoar
Ye sholde arise.' Wherfore I yeve* yow   give
    reed*:   282 advice
Ne dooth unto an oold man noon harm now,
Namoore than that ye wolde men did
    to yow
In age, if that ye so longe abyde.   285
And God be with yow where* ye go or ryde!   wherever
I moote go thider* as I have to go."   thither
    "Nay, olde cherl! By God, thou shalt nat
    so!"
Seyde this oother hasardour anon*.   straightway
"Thou partest nat so lightly, by Seint John!
Thou spak right now of thilke* traytour   that same
    deeth,   291
That in this contree alle oure freendes
    sleeth*.   slays
Have heer my trouthe, as thou art his espye*, spy
Telle where he is, or thou shalt it abye*,   pay for it
By God, and by the hooly sacrement!   295
For soothly, thou art oon of his assent*   one who agrees with him
To sleen us yonge folk, thou false theef!"

"Now sires," quod he, "if that ye be so
  leef*   *desirous*
To fynde deeth, turne up this croked wey,
For in that grove I lafte hym, by my fey*,   *faith*
Under a tree, and there he wole abyde.   *301*
Noght for youre boost he wole hym no
  thyng hyde.
Se ye that ook*? Right there ye shal hym   *oak*
  fynde.
God save yow that boghte agayn mankynde,
And yow amende." Thus seyde this olde
  man.   *305*
And everich* of thise riotours ran   *each*
Til he cam to that tree, and there they
  founde
Of floryns* fyne of gold ycoyned* rounde   *florins (coin)*   *coined*
Wel ny* an eighte busshels, as hem   *very nearly*
  thoughte*.   *309*   *it seemed to them*
No lenger* thanne after deeth they soughte,   *longer*
But ech of hem so glad was of that sighte,
For that the floryns been so faire and
  brighte,
That doun they sette hem by this precious
  hoord.
The worste of hem, he spak the firste word:
  "Bretheren," quod he, "taak kepe* what I   *pay attention to*
  seye.   *315*
My wit is greet, though that I bourde* and   *joke*
  pleye.
This tresor hath fortune unto us yeven*,   *given*
In myrthe and jolifee oure lyf to lyven,
And lightly as it comth, so wol we spende.
Ey, Goddes precious dignitee! Who wende*   *would have believed*
Today that we sholde han so fair a grace?
But myghte this gold be caried fro this
  place   *322*
Hoom to myn hous, or elles unto youres –
For wel ye woot* that al this gold is oures –   *know*
Thanne were we in heigh felicitee.   *325*

But trewely, by daye it may nat bee.
Men wolde seyn that we were theves stronge,
And for oure owene tresor doon us honge*.   have us hanged
This tresor moste ycaried be by nyghte,
As wisely and as slyly as it myghte.   *330*
Wherfore I rede* that cut* among us alle   advise lots
Be drawe*, and lat se wher the cut wol falle.   be drawn
And he that hath the cut, with herte blithe
Shal renne* to towne, and that ful swithe*,   run quickly
And brynge us breed and wyn ful prively*,   secretly
And two of us shal kepen* subtilly   *336* guard
This tresor wel, and if he wol nat tarie,
Whan it is nyght we wol this tresor carie
By oon assent* where as us thynketh* best."   common agreement it seems
That oon* of hem the cut broghte in his   one   to us
   fest*,   *340* fist
And bad hym drawe, and looke where it wol
   falle.
And it fil on the yongeste of hem alle,
And forth toward the toun he wente anon*.   straightway
And al so soone as that he was gon,
That oon spak thus unto that oother: *345*
"Thow knowest wel thou art my sworn
   brother;
Thy profit wol I telle thee anon.
Thou woost* wel that oure felawe is agon,   know
And heere is gold, and that ful greet plentee,
That shal departed* been among us thre. *350* divided
But nathelees*, if I kan shape* it so   nevertheless arrange
That it departed were among us two,
Hadde I nat doon a freendes torn to thee?"
   That oother answerde, "I noot* hou that   don't know
   may be.
He woot* how that the gold is with us   knows
   tweye.   *355*
What shal we doon? What shal we to hym
   seye?"
   "Shal it be conseil*?" seyde the first   secret
   shrewe*.   villain

"And I shal tellen in a wordes fewe
What we shal doon and bryngen it wel
  aboute."
  "I graunte," quod that oother, "out of
  doute,   360
That by my trouthe I shal thee nat
  biwreye*."   betray
  "Now," quod the firste, "thou woost wel
  we be tweye,
And two of us shul strenger* be than oon.   stronger
Looke whan that he is set, that right anoon* right away
Arys as though thou woldest with hym
  pleye,   365
And I shal ryve* hym thurgh the sydes tweye stab
Whil that thou strogelest with hym as in
  game.
And with thy daggere looke thou do the
  same,
And thanne shal al this gold departed* be,   divided
My deere freend, bitwixen me and thee. 370
Thanne may we bothe oure lustes* all   desires
  fulfille,
And pleye at dees* right at oure owene   dice
  wille."
And thus acorded* been thise shrewes tweye agreed
To sleen the thridde as ye han herd me seye.
  This yongeste which that wente unto the
  toun,   375
Ful ofte in herte he rolleth up and doun
The beautee of thise floryns newe and
  brighte.
"O Lord," quod he, "if so were* that I   if it were so
  myghte
Have al this tresor to my self allone,
Ther is no man that lyveth under the trone* throne
Of God that sholde lyve so murye as I!" 381
And atte laste* the feend oure enemy   at last
Putte in his thought that he sholde poyson
  beye*   buy

With which he myghte sleen hise felawes
    tweye,
For why* the feend foond hym in swich*   ecause   such
    lyvynge   *385*
That he hadde leve* hym to sorwe brynge.   leave
For this was outrely* his fulle entente*:   completely   purpose
To sleen hem bothe and nevere to repente.
And forth he gooth, no lenger* wolde he   longer
    tarie,
Into the toun unto apothecarie   *390*
And preyde hym that he hym wolde selle
Som poyson that he myghte his rattes quelle*,   kill
And eek* ther was a polcat* in his hawe*   also   weasel   hedge
That, as he seyde, his capons hadde yslawe*,   slain
And fayn* he wolde wreke hym*, if he   gladly   have revenge
    myghte,   *395*
On vermyn* that destroyed hym by nyghte.   animal pests
    The pothecarie answerde, "And thou shalt
    have
A thyng that, al so* God my soule save,   as
In al this world ther is no creature
That eten or dronken hath of this confiture*,   preparation
Noght but the montance* of a corn* of   amount   grain
    whete,   *401*
That he ne shal his lif anon forlete*.   give up
Ye, sterve* he shal, and that in lasse while*   die   less time
Than thou wolt goon a paas* nat but a mile,   at a walk
This poyson is so strong and violent."   *405*
    This cursed man hath in his hond yhent*   taken
This poyson in a box, and sith* he ran   afterwards
Into the nexte strete unto a man
And borwed hym large botels thre,
And in the two his poyson poured he.   *410*
The thridde* he kepte clene for his owene   third
    drynke,
For al the nyght he shoope hym* for to   planned
    swynke*   labour
In cariynge of the gold out of that place.
And whan this riotour, with sory grace*,   a curse upon him

Hadde filled with wyn his grete botels thre,
To hise felawes agayn repaireth* he.   *416* returns
   What nedeth it to sermone of it moore?
For right as they hadde cast his deeth
   bifoore,
Right so they han* hym slayn, and that anon. have
And whan that this was doon, thus spak that
   oon*:   *420* one
"Now lat us sitte and drynke and make us
   merie,
And afterward we wol his body berie."
And with that word it happed hym par cas* by chance
To take the botel ther* the poyson was, where
And drank, and yaf* his felawe drynke also, gave
For which anon they storven* bothe two. died
   But certes*, I suppose that Avycen*[12] *427* certainly Avicenna
Wroot nevere in no canon, ne in no fen* section
Mo* wonder* signes of empoisonyng more marvellous
Than hadde thise wrecches two er hir
   endyng.   *430*
Thus ended been thise homycides two,
And eek the false empoysonere also.
   O cursed synne of alle cursednesse!
O traytours homycide! O wikkednesse!
O glotonye, luxurie*, and hasardrye*!   *435* lechery gambling
Thou blasphemour of Crist with vileynye
And othes grete of usage* and of pride! habit
Allas mankynde, how may it bitide
That to thy creatour, which that the* thee
   wroghte,
And with his precious herte-blood thee
   boghte,   *440*
Thou art so fals and so unkynde*, allas? unnatural
   Now goode men, God foryeve* yow youre forgive
   trespas,
And ware yow* fro* the synne of avarice. beware of

12 See General Prologue, line 432 and note.

Myn hooly pardon may yow alle warice*,   cure
So that* ye offre nobles* or sterlynges*, *445* provided that gold coins
Or elles silver broches, spoones, rynges.   silver coins
Boweth youre heed under this hooly bulle.
Com up, ye wyves, offreth of youre wolle*.   wool
Youre names I entre heer in my rolle anon;
Into the blisse of hevene shul ye gon.   *450*
I yow assoille* by myn heigh power,   absolve
Yow that wol offre as clene* and eek as   pure
   cleer
As ye were born.
          – "And lo, sires, thus I preche.
And Jhesu Crist that is oure soules leche* leech, i.e., healer
So graunte yow his pardon to receyve, *455*
For that is best; I wol yow nat deceyve.

   "But sires, o* word forgat I in my tale.   one
I have relikes and pardon in my male*   bag
As faire as any man in Engelond,
Whiche were me yeven by the popes hond.
If any of yow wole of devocion   *461*
Offren and han myn absolucion,
Com forth anon* and kneleth heere adoun, at once
And mekely receyveth my pardoun.
Or elles taketh pardon as ye wende*, *465* travel
Al newe and fressh at every miles ende,
So that ye offren alwey newe and newe* again and again
Nobles or pens* whiche that be goode and pence
   trewe.
It is an honour to everich* that is heer   everyone
That ye mowe* have a suffisant pardoneer   may
T'assoille yow* in contree as ye ryde, *471* give you absolution
For aventures* whiche that may bityde*. accidents happen
Paraventure* ther may fallen oon or two perhaps
Doun of* his hors and breke his nekke atwo. off
Looke which a* seuretee* is it to yow alle what a security
That I am in youre felaweshipe yfalle, *476*
That may assoille yow bothe moore and
   lasse*   great and small

Whan that the soule shal fro the body passe.

I rede* that oure Hoost heere shal bigynne,   advise

For he is moost envoluped* in synne.   *480*   embroiled

Com forth, Sire Hoost, and offre first anon,

And thou shalt kisse my relikes everychon*,   every one

Ye, for a grote*! Unbokele anon thy purs!"   groat (fourpence)

"Nay, nay!" quod he; "thanne have I
Cristes curs!

Lat be!" quod he; "it shal nat be, so
thee'ch*!   *485*   so may I thrive

Thou woldest make me kisse thyn olde
breech

And swere it were a relyk of a seint,

Though it were with thy fundement*   anus
depeint*!   stained

But by the croys which that Seint Eleyne*   Helena
fond,

I wolde I hadde thy coillons* in myn hond,   testicles

In stide* of relikes or of seintuarie*.   *491*   instead   box of relics

Lat kutte hem of; I wol with thee hem carie.

They shul be shryned in an hogges toord*!"   turd
This Pardoner answerde nat a word;

So wrooth* he was; no word ne wolde he   angry
seye.   *495*

"Now," quod oure Hoost, "I wol no
lenger* pleye   longer

With thee, ne with noon oother angry man."

But right anon the worthy Knyght bigan,

Whan that he saugh* that al the peple   saw
lough*:   laughed

"Namoore of this, for it is right ynough. *500*

Sire Pardoner, be glad and myrie of cheere.

And ye, Sire Hoost, that been to me so deere,

I preye yow that ye kisse the Pardoner.

And Pardoner, I preye thee, drawe thee
neer,   *504*

And as we diden, lat us laughe and pleye."

Anon they kiste and ryden forth hir weye.

Chaucer's Retraction

HERE TAKETH THE MAKERE OF THIS BOOKE HIS LEVE.

Now preye I to hem alle that herkne* this
litel tretys or rede, that if ther be any thyng
in it that liketh* hem, that ther-of they thanken oure Lord Jhesu Crist, of whom proce-
deth al wit* and al goodnesse. And if ther   *5*
be any thyng that displese hem, I preye hem
also that they arrette* it to the defaute of
myn unkonnynge* and nat to my wyl, that
wolde ful fayn* have seyd bettre if I had
hadde konnynge*, for oure boke* seith,   *10*
"Al that is writen, is writen for oure doc-
trine*," and that is myn entente.

Wherfore I biseke yow mekely for the
mercy of God that ye preye for me, that
Crist have mercy on me and foryeve* me   *15*
my giltes*, and namely of my translacions
and enditynges* of worldly vanitees*, the
whiche I revoke in my retraccions; as is the
book of Troilus, the book also of Fame, the
book of the xxv Ladies, the book of the   *20*
Duchesse, the book of Seint Valentynes day
of the parlement of briddes*, the tales of
Caunterbury – thilke* that sownen* in to
synne, the book of the Leon, and many another book if they were in my remembrance,
and many a song and many a leccherous   *26*
lay, that Crist for his grete mercy foryeve me
the synne.

But of the translacion of Boece de conso-
lacione and othere bookes of legendes of   *30*

listen to

pleases

understanding

ascribe
stupidity
gladly
ability i.e., the Holy Bible

Romans 15:4

forgive
sins
compositions foolishnesses

birds
those conduce

seintes and omelies* and moralitee and devo- homilies
cion, that thanke I oure lord Jhesu Crist and
his blisful mooder and alle the seintes of
hevene, bisekynge hem that they from hennes
forth unto my lyves ende sende me grace *35*
to biwayle* my giltes and to studie the sal- be sorry for
vacion of my soule and graunte me grace of
verray penitence, confession, and satisfaccion
to doon in this present lyf, thurgh the be-
nigne grace of hym that is kyng of kynges *40*
and preest over alle preestes, that boghte us
with the precious blood of his herte, so that
I may been oon* of hem at the day of doome one
that shulle be saved.

Heere is ended the book of the tales of
Caunterbury compiled by Geffrey Chaucer,
of whos soule Jhesu Crist have mercy. Amen.